DEBATING DEMOCRACY

DEBATING DEMOCRACY
Native American Legacy of Freedom

BRUCE E. JOHANSEN

with chapters by
Donald A. Grinde, Jr.
and
Barbara A. Mann

Foreword by
Vine Deloria, Jr.

CLEAR LIGHT PUBLISHERS
Santa Fe, New Mexico

Dedication

To Lovell Thompson, who published Forgotten Founders;
To Vine Deloria, Jr., who directed Forgotten Founders *to Lovell
Thompson; and to everyone else who has taken part in the debate
regarding Native American roots of democracy.*

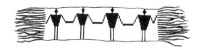

Copyright © 1998 Bruce E. Johansen, Donald A. Grinde Jr., and Barbara A. Mann.

Clear Light Publishers, 823 Don Diego, Santa Fe, N.M. 87501
WEB: www.clearlightbooks.com

First Edition
10 9 8 7 6 5 4 3 2 1

Library of Congress Cataloging-in-Publication Data

Johansen, Bruce E. (Bruce Elliott), 1950–
    Debating democracy : Native American legacy of freedom / Bruce E. Johansen;
with chapters by Donald A. Grinde, Jr., and Barbara A. Mann.
        p. cm.
    ISBN 0-940666-79-0 (paper)
    1. Iroquois Indians—Politics and government. 2. United States—Civilization—
Indian influences. 3. United States—Politics and government—To 1775. 4. United
States—Historiography. I. Title.
E99.I7J626 1996   96-4052
973—dc20   CIP

Printed in Canada
Typographical Layout/Production: V. S. Elliott

Contents

Foreword

D ebating Democracy recounts one of the most intense and exciting topics of the twentieth century—the struggle of the Six Nations Iroquois Confederacy and a small group of hardy scholars to present an alternative understanding of the formative ideas of the Constitutional Fathers in which, most properly, the Iroquois are finally credited with a powerful voice in creating the American government. Scholars had traditionally mentioned in passing that the colonies were admonished by Benjamin Franklin to take a careful look at the manner in which the Six Nations had established their government, stating that it would not do for civilized people such as themselves to lag behind these citizens of the forests.

Historians did nothing with the idea and Iroquoian studies had been dominated by a select group of scholars who had maintained a vise-like grip on everything Iroquois for several generations. Although self-appointed and incestuous to a fault, these scholars deeply believed that they understood EVERYTHING about the Six Nations, going so far as to claim that some ceremonies were introduced by themselves when the traditional people had forgotten them. If the Marines faced a formidable task in landing on Tarawa or the Army had its hands full at Anzio and the Bulge, in assaulting the Iroquoian establishment, Bruce Johansen and Donald Grinde, Jr. would face equally grim fortifications.

Donald A. Grinde, Jr. had published the first extensive exploration of Iroquois influence on the Constitution in 1977 as part of his book, *The Iroquois and the Founding of the American Nation*. Later Bruce Johansen contacted me about a possible publisher for his first venture, since he was getting fiercely negative responses from the presses that were calling on establishment anthropologists to review his manuscript. I recommended he submit the work to Lovell Thompson of Gambit Books, a small press in Boston. Gambit published *Forgotten Founders* in 1982, and within a few months the battle was joined.

The Iroquois old-boys network exploded into an incandescent rage with venomous attacks on Johansen's and Grinde's books, on the authors, and on anyone hardy enough to argue that the thesis should be given a reading on its merits. Popular media became involved after various scholars made statements to the press, and conservative columnists who knew nothing of the argument or the books launched a campaign of ridicule and vilification equalling in intemperance Joe McCarthy's worst tantrums. People seemed to lose their minds over the idea. Whenever the Iroquois "influence theory" was mentioned, the audience would be treated to an establishment tirade that had no evidence to support it and consisted mostly of attacking the status of Johansen and Grinde as scholars. The code phrase was "no reputable scholar" agreed with them—"reputable" scholars of course being the disciples of anthropologists Elizabeth Tooker, William Fenton, William Starna, *et al*.

Johansen and Grinde held their ground, making it plain that the opposition was coming from anthropologists who had not studied any of the relevant historical documents. In effect it was comparable to biologists raging against new ideas in architecture on the grounds that they had been taught differently in art appreciation courses while undergrads.

The establishment never was able to identify any European or Asian tradition in which the idea of maintaining the sovereignty of independent political entities co-existed with constructing a strong central government. Although Iroquois governmental procedures were of course not adopted intact, there was no model of governmental structure for American statesmen except the Six Nations' constitution.

Since none of the Iroquoian establishment figures had much knowledge of political science or theories of government, they kept wrongfully giving John Locke full credit for inspiring our Constitution. A quick survey of the *Federalist Papers* shows that Montesquieu had enormous influence in constitutional thought because of his thesis that geographical expansion doomed national states to become ineffective and eventually perish. The Founding Fathers were concerned over the possibility that the new nation, like the ancient empire of Rome, could simply expand beyond its ability to administer national institutions. There is no question that the Six Nations had solved this problem. The best adaptation the Americans could make became our current arrangement between states and the federal government, but it has not worked nearly as well as the Six Nations' procedures, which also recognized clans as an important element in holding the national fabric together.

This book gives an exciting step-by-step recounting of the great struggle to get a fair hearing from the academic establishment. The authors are more than fair in their characterizations of their opponents, who spared no expense in blackballing them wherever and whenever they could. That such energy could have been expended in trying to outlaw an idea is testimony of the most damning kind that academia considers itself a church and feels that its doctrines, even those without evidence to support them, must be held with fanatical zeal lest heretics enter the temple. This book should be read by everyone who dares to think new thoughts—it may well be your story.

VINE DELORIA, JR.

Acknowledgments

Many thanks to Ray Fadden, John Kahionhes Fadden, Donald A. Grinde, Jr., José Barreiro, Shelly Price-Jones, Sally Roesch-Wagner, Steve Witala, Scott Calbeck, Barbara Mann, and Bruce A. Burton for providing information from their files. Many thanks also to the incredible bibliographic sleuths of the University of Nebraska at Omaha Interlibrary Loan Office. Thanks also are due my wife, Patricia Keiffer, for tolerating my work habits, and to editor Sara Held and publishers Harmon Houghton and Marcia Keegan, for taking this book to press.

BRUCE E. JOHANSEN

Introduction

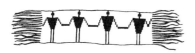

BRUCE E. JOHANSEN

When I began looking for a dissertation topic at the University of Washington two decades ago, I was seeking a subject that would sustain me intellectually, as well as one that would engage an audience and rattle a few cages. The idea that the Haudenosaunee (Iroquois) helped shape the origins of democracy in America came as a surprise to me then. The idea made sense to me only after I began to outline the historical circumstances that caused this synthesis of ideas. I realized, for example, the influence of the Iroquois Confederacy in eighteenth-century diplomacy, which created a need for English colonists to observe their political system. By 1744, Benjamin Franklin was setting into type the admonitions of Canassatego, the Onondaga sachem (chief) and Tadadaho (speaker) of the Iroquois Confederacy, that the English colonists should unite on a federal model like that of the Iroquois:

> Our wise forefathers established union and amity between the Five Nations. This has made us formidable. This has given us great weight and authority with our neighboring nations. We are a powerful Confederacy, and by your observing the same methods our wise forefathers have taken you will acquire much strength and power; therefore, whatever befalls you, do not fall out with one another.[1]

A contemporary observer provided this word-portrait of Canassatego at Lancaster: "a tall, well-made man," with "a very full chest and brawny limbs, a manly countenance, with a good-natured smile. He was about sixty years of age, very active, strong, and had a surprising liveliness in his speech." Dressed in a scarlet camblet coat and a fine, gold-laced hat, Canassatego is described by observers of the Iroquois Council as possessing an awesome presence which turned heads whenever he walked into a room.

Incident by incident, a very interesting sequence of historical events and relationships began to unfold before me. Franklin, once he had set Canassatego's words in type, evolved from printer to diplomat. His first assignments as a statesman took him to the Iroquois in the early 1750s, just as he was assembling plans for his first attempt at colonial union in the Albany Plan of 1754. He observed in the Iroquois, a federal republic governed by local and national councils, which selected its leaders by clan-based consensus. The Iroquois Grand Council at Onondaga operated like the one-house legislature that Franklin would advocate his entire life, with a strict traditional protocol. I learned to my surprise just how tightly woven the Iroquois had become into colonial statecraft. Delegates were summoned to the Albany Congress with Iroquois figures of speech. They arrived to "brighten the chain," to sit under the Tree of Peace, just as, when tea-dumping patriots in Boston needed a disguise, they symbolically dressed as Mohawks—members of one of the nations making up the Iroquois Confederacy.

Iroquois leaders were invited to Philadelphia to observe debates over the Declaration of Independence during the spring of 1775. The fact that they were official guests was indicated by their lodgings. The visiting Iroquois bedded down on the second floor of the Pennsylvania Statehouse, later called Independence Hall, directly above the chamber in which the debates were taking place. In that chamber, on June 11, 1776, the Iroquois delegation gave John Hancock an Iroquois name, "Karanduawn," meaning "Great Tree."

I had an inkling when I began it that an account of how the Iroquois helped shape some of the founders' conceptions of democracy would ruffle a few feathers, in large part because our history was largely bereft of these ideas. I had no idea, however, of the wild ride on which I was about to embark. I learned very quickly that the idea elicited two very different responses from my professorial advisors: absolute denial and raging curiosity. The Iroquois influence thesis also sparked debates in many fields, from American history and Native American studies to anthropology and sociology, political science, and law.

The idea that American Indians had a role to play in the intellectual founding of the United States also encountered the same sort of starkly different reactions in the popular press, especially after it was sucked into the maw of heated debates over multiculturalism in education and "political correctness." The same two reactions—absolute denial and consuming curiosity—surfaced time and again in so many venues that by the early 1990s I began a bibliography to keep track of them.[2] By early 1998, the number of public reactions to the idea was approaching nine hundred items. Paging through my collection still brings a sense of awe and wonder at their variety and vehement nature, both in support and opposition. For example, the idea has been called "fiction" (by George Will) and "idiocy" (by Patrick

Buchanan) spread by "Visigoths in tweed" (by Dinesh D'Souza). I am sure that Rush Limbaugh means nothing personal when he says, with the bombast so typical of his commentary, that my intellectual life's work is "worse than historical revisionism. It's more than the distortion of facts. It's the elimination of facts."

I am forever amazed (and sometimes amused) at the degree to which a desire to keep things as they are can distort reality. In Robert H. Bork's *Slouching toward Gomorrah: Modern Liberalism and American Decline*, for example, I cease to be a mild-mannered middle-aged professor of principally Norwegian extraction who has spent fifteen years at a Midwestern university teaching students how to write newspaper stories and essays on Black Elk. Suddenly, I become one of Bork's crew of politically motivated assassins of Western civilization's most cherished canons, an advocate of the demon multiculturalism. "We have already seen this in feminist and Afrocentric studies," writes Bork, "but it is everywhere. In New York State it is official educational doctrine that the United States Constitution was heavily influenced by the political arrangements of the Iroquois Confederacy." In the Book of Bork research cannot possibly exist on such a silly subject as how the Iroquois Confederacy helped shape democracy. He writes, with an air of apparent authority: "The official promulgation of this idea was not due to any research that disclosed its truth."

Bork's absolute denial that a valid debate exists on the subject is but one of many examples of the subject's ability to rub raw nerves and to bring into focus larger issues related to the nature of truth in history, as well as contemporary debates over multiculturalism, racism, Eurocentrism, and power relationships in higher education.

As the debate over the "influence theory," as it is called, became more combative, we often found our adversaries responding to their caricatures of our assertions, rather than to anything resembling the historical facts of the case itself. If this debate had centered exclusively on historical fact and interpretation, the size of the body of literature on the subject alone would at least have made it an acceptable subject of scholarly discussion and debate. The weight of the evidence convinced many people that the subject was at least arguable.

This is a book about the evolution of an idea and, by extension, about the evolution of all ideas, and how history is made in academia and the popular media. We have been called the authors of "new history" and initiators of a paradigm shift in ways of thinking about Native Americans and their political cultures. We also have been called academic fakirs, weavers of cloth without thread.

At first, the search centered on precedents in the Iroquois Great Law of Peace for the federal model outlined in Benjamin Franklin's Albany Plan of 1754 (and later in the Articles of Confederation and Constitution). Later, research broadened to include the Constitutional Convention itself, as well as American attitudes toward liberty and freedom (expressed most concisely in the Declaration of Independence), the founders' attitudes regarding natural rights, and the development of a movement advocating women's suffrage. Over the years, research also expanded back in time to the years of early English colonization, encompassing Native American political ideas taken up by Roger Williams, founder of Providence Plantations (now Rhode Island) as a refugee from Puritan New England. By the late 1890s, several books were in print describing the historical circumstances which dealt the Iroquois into the transatlantic sequence of events that gave birth to modern notions of democracy. This book seeks to describe the debate over these ideas in our time.

The molding of history is usually taken up in rather restricted circles in the intellectual tar pits where academics determine what will be studied, rather than as a subject for a lay audience. In this case, however, the story is ribald enough to assemble a wider audience and to sustain a narrative. It is also a story with a human as well as an ideological dimension involving a group of scholars, informally called "The Coyote Collective," who found each other through explorations of these ideas, whom the reader will meet as the story unfolds. Before the late 1980s, most of us—John Kahionhes Fadden, Donald A. Grinde, Jr., Sally Roesch Wagner, Barbara Mann, and myself—had carried on our scholarly business without knowledge of the others.

Our investigation centered on the Native American influence on ideas that most Americans usually attribute to their founding fathers, related to freedom, federalism, and the role of the state in human affairs. The notion that American Indian political systems have contributed to our present-day notions of these concepts has caused intense controversy. It has been a wonderful story of discovery and surprise.

I have been surprised repeatedly at the size and diversity of audiences attracted by the idea, as well as the tenacity with which people on both sides of the debate have insisted on the veracity of their positions. At the heart of opposition has been a corps of debunkers for whom Fadden coined the name "Trolls," with the idea that they, like the creatures of European mythology, control access to bridges and exact a toll from those who cross. Most of these people call each other "Iroquois experts"; the reader will meet them in the pages that follow.

As a freshly minted doctor of philosophy, I was rather ignorant of the current politics of the issue. After I learned why I was having trouble getting publishers and grants for what I thought was a good idea, I was peeved at them for making my life more difficult than it would have been otherwise. Now, as an older professor, with tenure and an endowed chair, I look back in wonder at the "Iroquois experts" who had worked long and hard to build scholarly reputations in a context they understood, only to have their "subjects" talk back to them. They had staked everything on a belief that seemed immutable to them: that the Iroquois had nothing to do with the evolution of democracy in America. Their absolute denials made excellent press (the media love a sharply delineated contest over a novel subject) and helped to spread the idea. The idea became, I told John Fadden in a woefully inelegant moment, "The shit they couldn't get off their shoes."

The "Trolls" were reacting to, and only very rarely understanding, a paradigm shift in the way that many non-Indian Americans think of Native Americans. The "Vanishing Race" was winning back its languages, some of its land, and a new sense of purpose in the last third of the twentieth century. At the same time, many people who felt their interests threatened were reacting to multiculturalism and "political correctness," at a time when the numbers and influence of non-European Americans were growing in the United States, spurring no small measure of xenophobia. The "influence" idea came to the marketplace of ideas in this context.

As we Coyotes undertook our individual journeys, we were tracing the journeys of other inquiring minds—of the Onondaga Canassatego and the Mohawk Hendrick, of Benjamin Franklin, Thomas Jefferson, Thomas Paine, Elizabeth Cady Stanton, Matilda Joslyn Gage, Karl Marx, Friedrich Engels, Lewis Henry Morgan, and others. All had the experience of walking, in reality or only metaphorically, in the shoes of another people practicing another way of life.

To understand how profoundly societies of American Indians helped shape our ancestors, we must try to place ourselves in their shoes: relatively small groups of immigrants, or sons and daughters of immigrants, on small islands of settlement, surrounded, at least for a time, by more widespread American Indian confederacies with whose members they traded, socialized, and occasionally made war for almost two centuries before the Constitution was ratified. In the middle of the eighteenth century, Boston and Philadelphia, each with about thirty thousand residents, were considered large cities.

Our popular history identifies the impetus of European immigration as a desire for freedom from tyranny and oppression—for political freedom and economic opportunity, two goals that have lain behind every movement for social change in our history. Economic opportunity often came at the expense of the Native peoples at the same time that the immigrants saw, in them, a metaphor for liberty. So, when the colonists needed a symbol to oppose British taxation without representation, it should not be surprising that they dressed up as Mohawks.

All along our journeys, we often were surprised at the complexity of history. Emerging from the archives where we began our searches, we were also surprised at how simplistically all of this was being taken by opponents of our ideas, who seemed instantly to disregard the possibility that the taproots of democracy could grow out of both European and Native American political cultures. We found ourselves accused of overstating our case by opponents who then themselves stretched it to absurdity just to show how ridiculous it was.

No, the founders didn't copy the Iroquois, any more than they copied the Greeks, the Romans, the Magna Carta, or the Swiss cantons. The founders wove an intellectual blanket out of their history, as they knew it, and their perceptions of Native confederacies with which they lived day by day. With a knowledge of Native American societies and symbols, this rushing river of thought becomes easier to understand. There is much more to history than simple conquest: whenever peoples meet, they absorb each others' ideas. As the conquering Romans absorbed Greek culture and political ideas, Europeans in America constructed a cultural amalgam in their new homeland.

As the influence idea spread, the counterattack on it escalated. The debate was taking place at a time when Native peoples across the Americas had been seeking to emerge from a marginalized status in Western academic studies. The debate would not have been so emotional if it were simply a scholarly discussion regarding the role of certain ideas in history. The often shrill pitch of opposition to assertions of a Native American role in the development of democracy indicates that the debate followed intellectual fault lines tracing claims to both truth and power.

One problem with this debate has been the refusal of influence thesis opponents to develop a clearly defined, straightforward argument of their own. Instead, they have often resorted to violating classic (European) principles of argumentation, employing such common strategies of deception as:

1. *Reductio ad absurdum*. In this strategy the attacker trivializes or caricatures the argument without directly replying to it. The idea may be simplified (as with insistence that we wished to prove that the founders "copied" the Constitution from the Iroquois). The idea also has been over-

stated in order to discredit it. This may be the only scholarly debate in recent years in which some participants believed they could close the case merely by calling the assertions of their opponents "the silliest idea I've ever heard."

2. *Appeal to authority.* This debate has featured a remarkable number of appeals to unnamed or assumed authorities. If one reads the criticism without having read the documentary record, one could be led to believe that a coordinated body of scholarly evidence exists that explicitly refutes the influence idea. The scholarly literature refuting the idea by 1996 amounted to one scholarly article by Temple anthropology professor Elisabeth Tooker, in which she relies mainly on sources published by others who have sought to build a mosaic of history regarding the influence thesis; one chapter on James Wilson in the book *Tribes and Tribulations* (1995) by Laurence Hauptman; and the "anti-influence" part of a forum in the summer 1996 edition of *William and Mary Quarterly* by Philip A. Levy and Samuel Payne.

3. *Ad hominem argumentation.* This style of attack ignores the issues at hand and concentrates on the assumed motives and character of those advancing them. In the influence debate, opponents have repeatedly stated that "traditional Iroquois" and their intellectual fellow travelers are advocating an historically baseless idea for public relations purposes, because they are Native American (or have been influenced by Native American "activists") and are therefore incapable of scholarly "objectivity." Having attempted to destroy the personal credibility of the idea's supporters, its opponents may persuade themselves that they do not need actual historical evidence to refute the ideas themselves.

4. *Argument by design.* The attacker constructs a "straw man"—a wild exaggeration of the opponent's argument—which may be easily discredited without troublesome references to the nuances of the issue itself.

5. To this stew of illogic, add *paternalism.* Scholars who sometimes call themselves "friends of the Indian" assert that the influence thesis is nothing but an attempt by the developing field of Native American studies to define Indian culture within the context of the majority culture. They know what's best for Native Americans, who, they say, are foolishly comparing their political culture to that of the emerging United States in an attempt to get some late-twentieth-century respect.

The same abuses of argumentation should be familiar to any observer of our political process, where a preference for bombast over substance has reduced many debates to a mixture of clichés and ad hominem gutterspeak.

As we explored history, trying to do our work with "clean eyes," we found ourselves identifying with other people who fought the dominant assumptions of their own times, a trait shared by nearly all of the revolutionary minds we studied. In the 1700s, Jefferson, Franklin, Thomas Paine, and others had their eyes opened to new realities in America. In the 1800s, Gage, Stanton, Marx, Engels, and Lewis Henry Morgan experienced similar intellectual challenges. Each was constrained by his or her own times and circumstances. Jefferson held slaves. Franklin speculated in Indian lands. Marx and Engels envisioned an economic model without ecological analysis. Morgan, who is generally regarded as the founder of American anthropology, developed a cultural arrogance that led him to characterize the Iroquois, from whom he had learned so much, as "barbarians."

Intercultural contact is complex, but generally people take from another culture what they think will be of use in their own, through their own eyes, on their own terms. Thus, Jefferson and Franklin incorporated certain aspects of Native American polities and ignored others, such as the role and influence of women. Stanton and Gage developed that aspect of our composite national character a century later, again with reference to an Iroquois society with which both were familiar.

In our own time, following an explosion of debate over the influence idea in the late 1980s, everyone—from Tom Hayden to Patrick Buchanan— seems to have taken a stand on what has become a very hotly contested issue. These ideas became a horror-story of political correctness to many conservative commentators, while they also played a role in Canadian debates over a new constitution. We found Iroquois ideas of democracy being applied to contemporary problems by a wide range of thinking people, from historians, to lawyers and judges, to political scientists, artists, musicians, and engineers.

I have never lost my sense of profound surprise at how readily the influence thesis incited so many incredulous reactions, especially vehement denial among many people who know very little of the historical context— and even some, such as Arthur Schlesinger, Jr., who do. The issue is clearly more than a tempest in an academic teapot. For those who are attached to the notion that our intellectual history is exclusively European—and that European culture is superior to that of the rest of the world, the introduction of Native America into this discourse poses some fundamental problems of historical interpretation and even—or especially—self-definition concerning who we believe ourselves to be as Americans.

In academia, the mechanisms of denial are at once subtle and insidious. Some scholars with established academic influence have sought to maintain their ideological control by denying the influence of Native Americans' political intellect. What follows here is a story of suppression, manipulation, and distortion of information by the usual means, such as denial of access to journals of academic discourse and grant funds. Such denial directly limits the opportunities of non-European scholars as well as non-"Western" ideas, not to mention our ability to fashion a complete, credible history.

These tactics have parallels in public debate, with information management, spin control, and the concurrent massage of the press to limit discussion to what Noam Chomsky calls an agenda of "permissible debate." What makes the story really interesting is the fact that the idea has been gradually accepted as historically valid despite these attempts at manipulation, distortion, and suppression. In some cases, the heat and bitterness of the Trolls' denials have actually helped spread these ideas. If one can find irony in the fact that American Indian thought is salted into the most fundamental aspects of the United States' official ideology, one may also find sweet irony in the fact that this point is being worked into our history during a "conservative revolution."

Many of these critics have quoted Arthur Schlesinger, Jr.'s *Disuniting of America* (1992), a short polemic turned out quickly by a liberal historian whom conservative reviewers embraced fervently. Schlesinger took issue with "history for self-esteem," or "feel-good history," by which, he said, self-interested minority groups seek to express their points of view in school curricula. This point of view was not invented by Schlesinger. Several conservative commentators had used it before him.

In its most extreme form, this political correctness horror story is sometimes held responsible for just about every uncivilized evil to befall Europe since the barbarians took down the Roman Empire. Dead White European Males (DWEMs) roll in their graves at the sound of the influence issue, according to some commentators.

In *Forbes* magazine, Dinesh D'Souza, a research fellow at the American Enterprise Institute, targeted "a new barbarism—dogmatic, intolerant, and oppressive" that he asserted had "descended on America's institutions of higher learning . . . a neo-Marxist ideology promoted in the name of multiculturalism." An example of such thinking, wrote D'Souza, was the idea "that the Iroquois Indians in America had a representative democracy which served as a model for the American system."

The core of the Iroquois ethnohistorical establishment has been opposed to the idea, in opposition to traditional Haudenosaunee leaders such as Oren Lyons. Elisabeth Tooker and other opponents of the idea have been joined in pointed debate on this issue by Native American scholars such as Vine Deloria, Jr. and Ward Churchill, as well as history professor Wilbur Jacobs.

The influence thesis has been taken up in some unusual places, from the magazine *Sassy*, which is intended mainly for teen-aged girls, to the stage act of singer Buffy Sainte-Marie, who has been engaged in efforts to educate Native American young people. Oneida singer Joanne Shenandoah mentioned the idea as she opened the three-day 1994 Woodstock music festival, a reprise of the event of 1969, with a Haudenosaunee delegation before about 250,000 people. The issue also made a brief splash in the intellectual waters on which the U.S. Navy floats. During the fall of 1995, a few months before he killed himself, Chief of Naval Operations Jeremy Boorda issued a memo to all commands recommending observation of Native American democratic traditions.

Native American democratic traditions have played a role in Canada's contemporary debate over what form of federalism will serve its peoples best in the future. In a speech on June 12, 1992, Joe Clark, President of the Privy Council and minister responsible for constitutional affairs, said that Native Canadians have the right and responsibility to govern themselves, and cited the Iroquois example. A 1993 report by Canada's Royal Commission on Aboriginal Peoples argues that the Canadian confederation has come to resemble the Iroquois League more over time, moving gradually from exclusive reliance on its British origins.

American Indian (especially Iroquois) democratic precedents have been used in the United States to support political decentralization as a way to break down the "special-interest state" by Tom Hayden, a founder of Students for a Democratic Society in the 1960s and a California state senator in the 1990s. Hayden called for a decentralization on "a Jeffersonian, or Quaker, or Iroquois" model in an economy based in an ecosystem balanced for generations to come. On the other hand, Martin W. Lewis debunked the Iroquois' example as a model for decentralization in his *Green Delusions: An Environmentalist Critique of Radical Environmentalism* (1992), arguing that participatory democracy may not eliminate social repression.

Iroquois precedents for democracy were permeating school curricula across the United States by the 1990s. Literature published by the second National School Celebration stressed America's patriotic heritage for several million elementary school children, taking a decidedly multicultural tack.

James W. Loewen spent a year at the Smithsonian surveying the twelve leading high school history textbooks, and concluded that none of them made history interesting. He set out to do that in *Lies My Teacher Told Me*

(1995). One of the themes that Loewen described is the influence of the Iroquois' system of government on the framers of the Constitution. Loewen devotes a chapter to portrayals of Indians in high school texts, calling them "the most lied-about subset of our population."

Despite the jarring nature of some of the debate over the issue, the idea that Native American confederacies are an important early form of democracy has become established in general discourse. History is made in many ways, by many people; the spread of the idea that Native American confederacies (especially the Haudenosaunee Confederacy) helped shape the intellectual development of democracy in the United States and Europe is an example of how our notions of history have been changing with the infusion of multicultural voices. It is fascinating to watch the change in all its forms—and the debate over the issue in all its cacophonous variety. With the metaphor of a journey in mind, we invite the reader to travel, with us, along the trail of discovery that helped to make history of an idea.

NOTES

1. Carl Van Doren and Julian Boyd, *Indian Treaties Printed by Benjamin Franklin* (Philadelphia: Pennsylvania Historical Society, 1938), 75.

2. See, for example, Bruce E. Johansen, *Native American Political Systems and the Evolution of Democracy: An Annotated Bibliography* (Westport, Conn.: Greenwood Press, 1996).

1.

"What the Hell Is This?"

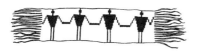

Bruce E. Johansen

We Indians laid the foundation of freedom and equality long before any
Europeans came and took it up, but they do not give us credit . . .

Lakota author Charles Eastman,

in a speech from *American Indian Magazine* 1919[1]

"What the hell is this?" was the response of Vernon Carstensen, a member of my Ph.D. committee at the University of Washington, when I suggested to him in 1978 that I might be doing my dissertation describing how Benjamin Franklin's and Thomas Jefferson's political ideologies were shaped by American Indian ideas of democracy. Crusty, irascible Vernon Carstensen, professor of the "history of the westward movement," expressed what most of the other professors who advised me were feeling. They asked me: Where did you get the notion that American Indian political systems, particularly the Great Law of the Iroquois, played a major role in shaping the early European-American notions of liberty and federalism as the United States was being formed?

The idea had been surprising news to me. I considered myself a decently educated person, and to my knowledge, democracy had been produced by white men in powdered wigs. The first suggestion of it had come to me from Sally Fixico, a Native American student at Evergreen State College, in 1975, while I was working at the *Seattle Times,* researching a series of articles on Native peoples of Washington State. Fixico showed me a paper she had written describing how the Great Law of the Iroquois helped shape the evolution of the United States.

I expressed my surprise in print for the first time in 1976. I had convinced the city desk that the bicentennial of the Declaration of Independence ought to be marked in the *Times* by a series on Native Americans, because no one of European descent had lived in what is now Washington State in 1776. As part of that series, I wrote a sidebar, headlined "Bicentennial? It Isn't Their Birthday Party," which mentioned similarities between Franklin's Albany Plan of Union (1754) and the Iroquois political system.[2]

Two years later, as a Ph.D. student in search of a dissertation topic, I heard the same assertion from John Crazy Bear, a footloose Seneca who was living near the University of Washington campus, making silver jewelry that he sold at the Pike Street Market, where I first met him. Crazy Bear was not the kind of guy most orthodox anthropologists would regard as a "reliable" informant. He was a former alcoholic who had substituted copious marijuana smoking for booze. He had an eighth-grade education and had acquired the name "Crazy Bear" while on a camping trip, after he saw someone or something that (or whom) he took to be a Sasquatch (or "crazy bear"). Crazy Bear had a sparkle in his eye which revealed an intelligence that standardized tests could not have measured. He was sure—absolutely sure—that everyone in his family had told him that the Iroquois Great Law of Peace played an important role in the establishment of the United States.

When I had asked Sally Fixico how she came by her information, she said: "My grandmother told me." When I told her that was not the kind of source I could use for a newspaper story, she said, "You're the investigative reporter. You find them."

At that time, I had no idea that Iroquois elders had approached a young Native American scholar, Donald A. Grinde, Jr., in Buffalo, New York, with the same idea that Sally Fixico and Crazy Bear had presented to me in Seattle. Grinde published the first extensive exploration of the idea in 1977 as part of his book, *The Iroquois and the Founding of the American Nation*.[3] I found Grinde's book as I explored the idea in my Ph.D. dissertation, completed in 1979 at the University of Washington. The dissertation was revised and published as a book in 1982, under the title *Forgotten Founders: Benjamin Franklin, the Iroquois and the Rationale for the American Revolution*.[4]

Grinde and I followed each other through the printed record for almost a decade before we met at Cornell University in 1987. Shortly after that, we joined as coauthors in a common effort when the subject of "Iroquois influence," as it came to be called, became an object of intense debate.

After two decades of research, we believe that enough historical evidence exists to assert responsibly that the ideas contained in the American Indian societies bordering the thirteen original British colonies played a substantial role (along with English and other European precedents), in forging attitudes concerning basic liberties that helped shape our basic political character and our subsequent history. In a world still in ferment over the same ideas of liberty, it is high time to give credit to American precedents that preceded the revolution begun in 1776.

Both Grinde and I had hopes of making the subject a matter of scholarly and popular debate, but twenty years ago we hardly suspected the vehemence with which our dream would come true. For that, we can thank the debate over multicultural history, and renewed interest in the early history of the United States, due in part to the Constitution's bicentennial and the quincentenary of Columbus' first landing, as well as the end of the second millennium on the Christian calendar—all of which coincided with a new wave of American Indian intellectual self-assertion.

For enlivening the debate we also can thank the phalanx of "Iroquois experts" whom John Kahionhes Fadden christened "The Trolls," because, like the imaginary European beings of yore, they controlled access—in this case, to the realm of acceptable scholarly debate. Within a few years of publishing our first books on the subject, Don and I found ourselves in the midst of an often passionate, bare-knuckle debate over the origins of concepts that Americans prize most highly.

Initially, our ideas were met with scorn in academia. Only one of the five people on my Ph.D. examining committee had heard even rumors of American Indian democracy's effect on the new United States before I suggested the topic in 1977.[5] Vernon Carstensen asked me how I planned to research the topic: "Sit around a council fire and smoke the peace pipe?" Not too many footnotes would curl out of the fire, he inferred. He and the rest were steeped in the Western academic tradition that trusted only paper—"documentary sources." I planned, therefore, not to rely on the oral history of the Iroquois, but to test it by a thorough examination of the papers of Franklin and Jefferson and as many other primary and secondary sources describing them as I could find. Grinde also used archival research, combined with detailed knowledge of Native American governmental structures and cultural history.

In the University of Washington History Department, "the history of the West" was largely taught as the chronicle of the colonial westward movement across the United States, of nation building. Likewise, most of our intellectual history was considered to have begun with the Puritans and moved westward. Because I was taking my doctorate in communications with a history minor, I proposed to call it a case study in the communication of ideas between cultures, a Ph.D-caliber mouthful.

I did not know it at the time, but the same idea was occurring to other non-Indians. My files now contain a short newspaper clipping, dated August 14, 1975, reporting that U.S. Congressman William F. Walsh read into *The Congressional Record* an essay by Nancy Duffy of WHEN-TV, whose "delightful brief essay . . . acknowledges [that] Benjamin Franklin and Thomas Jefferson . . . recognized a form of democracy among the Iroquois, 'whose Five Nation League of Peace precipitated our own Constitution.'" As I assembled a history of the idea, I continued to be surprised at the number of shorthand references to it in older publications. One of the most unexpected was a piece in *Forbes* magazine, by James Cook, which said: "The six Iroquois nations were among the most politically sophisticated peoples in the world, forming the famed Iroquois Confederation . . . that provided a model in its system of checks and balances for the U.S. Constitution."[6] This was published in 1981.

President John F. Kennedy may have heard the idea in prep school or college; he wrote the following in a preface to a 1960 paperback edition of William Brandon's *American Heritage Book of Indians*: "The League of the Iroquois inspired Benjamin Franklin to copy it in planning the federation of States."[7]

I had no inkling at this time that the idea of American Indian political influence had been common among Native Americans for many decades. It was not until I began writing this book, in 1995, that I crossed paths with the following quotation from the Lakota author Charles Eastman, in a speech he gave in 1919. The quotation raises two interesting points other than the antiquity of the idea that Native American political beliefs helped shape the United States: first, the speaker is from the Plains, not the Northeast. How did he learn of the influence idea? Secondly, Eastman is speaking at the nadir of American Indian populations in the Americas, the so-called "era of the vanishing race."

> We Indians laid the foundation of freedom and equality long before any Europeans came and took it up, but they do not give us credit. . . . We were [of] that character, that original American character. . . . We must keep our heads and our hearts together, [and] keep our old characteristics that we have contributed to this country—those contributions which have been put into the Constitution of the United States itself.[8]

"An Appeal for Justice" (1948), by Indians of the St. Regis Reservation, Hogansburg, New York, observes that, among many contributions of Native Americans to Euro-American culture, "[We] showed them the workings, the operation of a great democracy, the Iroquois Confederacy, a system unknown

in Europe or Asia." The statement says that many Indians fought for democracy in World War II, and argues against termination of treaties.[9]

Tehanetorens (Ray Fadden), a teacher of many younger Mohawks and
founder of the Six Nations Indian Museum at Onchiota, New York, began
exploring the idea of Iroquois influence on democracy in the 1940s. During
the 1990s, he watched ideas of Iroquois democracy spread around the world
in ways that he had foreseen a half-century earlier. In 1995, Mohawk artist
and teacher John Kahionhes Fadden was assembling an anthology of his
father's writings when he sent me a booklet titled *The History of the Oneida
Nation*. The booklet was not dated, but probably published about 1950. I
read with awe as Ray Fadden outlined some of the same sources that had
spurred me to write a dissertation on the subject of Iroquois democracy and
its influence a quarter century later, including Felix Cohen's 1952 essay in
The American Scholar. John told me that Cohen had owned a cabin at Buck
Pond, within walking distance of Onchiota, before he died of cancer in 1953.
Cohen and Ray Fadden were close friends, and without a doubt they discussed "influence" four decades before it became a subject of popular debate.

In a 1952 *American Scholar* article titled "Americanizing the White
Man," which would play an important role in my own early research, Cohen
wrote:

> . . . *it is out of a rich Indian democratic tradition that the distinctive political
> ideals of American life emerged. Universal suffrage for women as well as for
> men, the pattern of states within a state that we call federalism, the habit
> of treating chiefs as servants of the people instead of their masters, the
> insistence that the community must respect the diversity of men and the
> diversity of their dreams—all these things were part of the American way of
> life before Columbus landed.*[10]

Cohen is best known for his landmark text on American Indian law, first
published in 1942. Regarding American Indians' ability to govern themselves, he wrote:

> *Indeed, it may be said that the constitutional history of the Indian tribes covers
> a longer period and a wider range of variation than the constitutional history
> of the colonies, the states, and the United States. It was some time before the
> immigrant Columbus reached these shores, according to eminent historians,
> that the first federal Constitution on the American Continent was drafted, the
> Gayaneshagowa, or the Great Binding Law of the Five (later six) Nations
> (Iroquois). It was in this constitution that Americans first established the*

democratic principles of initiative, recall, referendum, and equal suffrage. In this constitution, also, were set forth the ideal[s] of the responsibility of governmental officials to the electorate, and the obligation of the present generation to future generations . . .[11]

Ray Fadden wrote that the time would come "when the institutions, polity, eloquence, and achievements of this remarkable people [the Iroquois] will be themes of study for our youth in schools and colleges."[12] In the 1990s, then in his eighties, Ray Fadden was watching his prophetic statement come true.

In *The Patriot Chiefs* (1958), Alvin Josephy wrote:

So unique a native organization, resting on high-minded principles of republicanism and democracy, eventually quickened the interest of many colonial leaders, including Benjamin Franklin, but the gap between the two races was too wide and dangerous in the eighteenth century to permit the study of the Iroquois system or its origins. . . .[13]

Throughout the eighteenth century, the republican and democratic principles that lay at the heart of the Five Nations' system of self-government had been included among the studies of the philosophers of Europe and America who were seeking a more just and humane way for men to be governed."[14]

Josephy later wrote that "it would be impossible to trace more than an indirect influence of the Iroquois League . . . on the United States government as it was constituted in 1789," but said that certain practices, such as congressional conference committees, resemble the debating procedures of the Iroquois Grand Council.[15]

Still other writers had taken up the issue.[16] Paul A. W. Wallace, professor of English at the University of Pennsylvania and author of *White Roots of Peace*, made references to the idea. Wallace compares the structure of the Iroquois League to that of the United Nations, which was being chartered at the time *White Roots of Peace* was published. In the introduction to that book, Wallace writes that the "United Nations of the Iroquois . . . provided a model for, and an incentive to, the transformation of the thirteen colonies into the United States of America."[17]

In a paper published in the *Bulletin of the New York State Archaeology Society*, which was read to the World Geophysical Year Science Forum, March 2, 1955, William N. Fenton wrote:

The Six Nations of the Iroquois were very much in the minds of colonial politicians, several of whom had their first lessons in diplomacy at the fire of Indian councils. The old men of the Longhouse, as they styled their confederacy, on several occasions suggested their league as a model for the thirteen colonies.[18]

Thirty years after Fenton's essay was published, opponents of the influence idea would sometimes be called "Fentonites" because many of them had studied under him in the anthropology department at the State University of New York at Albany. Fenton himself, however, has no other published commentary on the issue.

Well into the 1990s, I was finding old references to this idea that were new to me. For example, I walked out of our campus library in Omaha one late-fall day with the news that the Oakland, California Unified School District had published a classroom guide detailing Iroquois contributions to democracy in 1972.[19]

In 1974, a year before my own curiosity was roused by Sally Fixico, Virgil Vogel had raised the influence theory in his documentary history of the American Indian:

Montaigne, Rousseau, and Jefferson paid tribute to the Indian capacity to organize human affairs in a libertarian manner. The Iroquois developed a system of confederated government which, according to Benjamin Franklin, served as an example for his Albany Plan of Union, and eventually for the Articles of Confederation. Felix Cohen has lashed the assumption that our democracy was born in Greece.[20]

In 1981, also unknown to me at the time, a brief account was published in *Akwesasne Notes* describing how, at a conference in Montreal, "during a heated public conference debate with an Indian delegation, a Marxist member rose and asked the chief to quit the religious rituals before the meeting and proceed to more serious business." Akwesasne Mohawk traditional subchief Tom Porter rose from the audience and told the European-bred Marxist how deeply his Iroquois ancestors had influenced not only Benjamin Franklin and Thomas Jefferson, but Karl Marx and Friedrich Engels as well. "Therefore, sire, you understand that it's not Marx's great grandson who will come and dictate the way to manage our business," said Porter. The brief item indicates that "The accuser sat back on his chair quietly and remained silent."[21]

In 1978 I began to explore the subject of Iroquois influence on the thought of Franklin and Jefferson for a Ph.D. dissertation. To counter my professors' assumptions that it was not a researchable idea, I started an annotated bibliography of sources. I got up to four hundred sources before William E. Ames, my Ph.D. advisor, agreed that the subject was researchable. The publication of Grinde's book confirmed to me that my own study was feasible.

Wonderfully ignorant of the politics of the situation, I wrote to Elisabeth Tooker, in Albany, telling her that I had been looking into the subject. I asked her, "Do you know of any good sources?" She wrote me that the subject was not worth research. From her perspective, the case was closed. I was discouraged until a friend, Choctaw filmmaker Phil Lucas, gave me a citation for Cohen's 1952 essay "Americanizing the White Man" (in *The American Scholar*), in which the idea of Native influences on our democratic traditions was so elegantly stated that I could not resist the quest for the footnotes Cohen did not provide.

Lucas and I were intellectual partners in this quest from the beginning. At the time, Lucas was working on the University of Washington campus at the Public Broadcasting System station KCTS, assembling his series "Images of Indians," which explored ways in which Native Americans had been portrayed in Hollywood movies. Lucas read drafts of my dissertation as I prepared them and, in the spring of 1982, when *Forgotten Founders* was going to print, he played a key role in producing *Night of the First Americans*, a stage play, at Washington, D.C.'s Kennedy Center.

Night of the First Americans was a privately funded benefit performance organized to provide scholarships for Native American college students. Its cast included Will Sampson, Jonathan Winters, Lorne Greene, Paul Ortega, Vincent Price, Ironeyes Cody, Doc Tate, Martin Sheen, Dennis Weaver, Loretta Lynn, Dick Cavett, Will Rogers, Jr., Hoyt Axton, Sammy Davis, Jr., and Wayne Newton. It was a gala affair, with about 2,800 people in attendance, some of whom paid as much as $1,000 each for tickets. Vice-President George Bush sat in the president's box, behind his usual vapid smile, and the newspapers in Washington, D.C. reflected on the interstice between American Indians and tinseltown. Script segments on treaty violations in the Black Hills and the 1973 occupation of Wounded Knee were axed because the Reagan administration objected to them; actors David Soul and Max Gail lost their lines.

Despite behind-the-scenes politics, *Night of the First Americans* was a rollicking evening. A piece in the "Style" section of *The Washington Post* observed that "at the end, it was almost impossible to bring the curtain down.

The whole cast, on stage for their final bows, kept on dancing; they didn't want to stop and nobody in the audience seemed eager to leave."[22]

When the lights finally faded on stage, there were no proceeds. Organizers had told the press they would clear $200,000, but the event lost $300,000.[23]

The script of *Night of the First Americans* included a long segment describing Native American influence on American political institutions and ideas, some of it borrowed from galley proofs of *Forgotten Founders:*

MARTIN SHEEN: . . . *If you look in your children's history books, you'll be reminded of the fact that during that time many of the settlers had been conditioned by a European class structure in which the rights of man, to the extent that they existed, were derived from the monarch. . . . And most Europeans assumed that was the only way it could be . . .*

. . . For countless generations before Columbus' arrival, many Indian nations had functioned within a structure in which the power remained in the hands of the governed . . .

The beauty of the Indian structure was in its simplicity. . . . It was, in fact, so simple that most people didn't even notice it existed.

But there were some who noticed it. And among those was Benjamin Franklin.

Franklin was a brilliant man whose genius lay in his ability to put to practical use whatever he perceived in life . . . like his use of the printing press for pamphleteering . . . his adaptation of the principles of electricity to the lightening rod . . . and his recognition of the efficiency within the structure of something called the Iroquois Confederacy.

Light change is now complete. We see projection of Iroquois Longhouse. Lights up on Dennis [Weaver].

DENNIS WEAVER: *The Iroquois Confederacy was a league of, first five, and later six Indian nations who were once bitter enemies but who now lived in peace.*

Franklin was fascinated by the bond between the People of the Longhouse (as they were called), a bond which was actually an early form of American federalism.

The purpose of the Confederacy was to protect the participating nations from outside aggression and to prevent centralized authority from within. In fact, the only absolute authority was consensus. So successful was this league in its operation that there had been peace among the Iroquois for over five hundred years.

Franklin, realizing the strength of this kind of structure and the importance it could have in the colonists' stand against the Crown, minced no words in communicating his feelings about it. . . . "It would be a strange thing," said Franklin, "if Six Nations of ignorant savages should be capable of forming a scheme for such an union, and be able to execute it in such a manner, as that it has subsisted [for] ages, and appears indissoluble, and yet a like Union should be impracticable for ten or a dozen English colonies."

WILL SAMPSON: *As for the "ignorant savages," they knew the power of their Confederacy, and actually urged the colonists to adopt a similar form. . . .*

"Our wise forefathers established union and amity between the Six Nations," said the great Onondaga Chief Canassatego. "We are a powerful Confederacy and by your observing the same methods our forefathers have taken, you will acquire much strength and power; therefore, whatever befalls you, do not fall out with one another . . . "

Franklin would fight to get the federalism that he observed among the Six Nations adopted as a structure of the new nation that would become the United States of America.

MARTIN SHEEN: *But there were other founding fathers who would be attracted by the Iroquois as well. . . . Within three years of his arrival in America, Thomas Paine was sitting around a council fire with the Iroquois, learning their language and their culture. What he learned amazed him, for the Iroquois had somehow evolved . . . a form of government that was unheard of even in ancient Greece and Rome. . . . There were no slaves here. . . . No despots. . . . All people were equal. . . . It was true government by the consent of the governed. . . . There were free elections with the additional safeguards of referendum and recall . . . and suffrage for men and women . . .*

Dennis Weaver next picked up the narrative, citing Thomas Jefferson's observation that, among Indians, "Public opinion is in the place of law and restrains morals as powerfully as laws ever did anywhere." . . . In later years, these ideas would serve as inspiration for Jefferson in the writing of one of man's greatest manifestos . . . the Declaration of Independence."

As Phil Lucas factored the influence idea into *The Night of the First Americans,* I was getting my first major published exposure for it in *Four Winds,* a magazine of Native American literature and art published in Austin, Texas. This contact also had come through Lucas, who wrote a piece on his series "Images of Indians" for the magazine.[24]

Forgotten Founders was the hardest to sell of any book I have written, before or since (I have sold thirteen, including this one). It also has been the most successful, and the longest-lived, sixteen years as I write. After my Ph.D. was approved in late 1979, I tried to market it as a book. Trade publishers routinely found it too academic, and from academic publishers I got confused or soundly negative reviews.

Early in my search for a publisher, I thought I had the University of Pennsylvania Press on the line. Editor Warren Slesinger was enthusiastic about the book, and wanted an endorsement from reviewers to take the book to the press's editorial committee. He didn't get it. The first unsigned review said that my idea had been concocted "by radical Indian groups and their sympathizers." I was slighted for things that I did not do, such as include an encyclopedic description of European precedents for democracy. The reviewer said that I had claimed Indian precedent counted for as much as the Founders' European heritage, which I never did. The reviewer said that no other sources had advanced this thesis (he or she had not read Grinde's first book), and contended that I offered no "proof" of the idea. Finally, the reviewer advised Slesinger to get another review from Francis Jennings, director of the Newberry Library's Center for the Study of the American Indian in Chicago. The second review stated flatly that Franklin and Jefferson "clearly projected an image of Graeco-Roman republicanism and democracy, which they had learned in school, onto the local native population."[25]

I tried many other presses, academic and trade. A reviewer for Cornell University Press stated that Franklin and Jefferson had not been important in creating "national institutions," so studying them would not reveal anything about Native precedents. I was advised to cite standard anthropological sources and to study European history.[26] I kept getting similarly worded rejections from a number of university presses. Much later, I realized that the same "experts" were shutting the idea down over and over again. After approaching about thirty publishers, I asked Vine Deloria, Jr. for advice. He provided four possible publishers, and Lovell Thompson's Gambit was among them, despite the fact that Deloria's only communication from Thompson had been a rejection letter.

Thompson, who was then eighty years of age, decided to make mine one of roughly four books he published per year from a small office in Ipswich, Massachusetts. He had worked at Houghton-Mifflin from his graduation from Harvard in about 1920 until 1968, when he faced mandatory retirement. At Houghton-Mifflin, Thompson had worked mainly as head of the trade division. As publisher of Gambit, however, Thompson managed the entire book, from conception, through editing, to distribution and promotion. We sat on his screened porch for many hours, long into the night, editing the manuscript by the light of a hurricane lamp. Between visits, Thompson wrote some of the most erudite letters I have ever read.

Thompson also leaned heavily on his fellow alumni from Harvard for endorsements of the book, and so we entered the publishing fray with a phalanx of liberal historians touting it. Henry Steele Commager gave *Forgotten Founders* a ringing endorsement; John Kenneth Galbraith said that it gave him lots of information and "a worse conscience" because he had not known of the ideas earlier.

Arthur Schlesinger, Jr. wrote to Lovell Thompson from the City University of New York July 14, 1982:

> *I have finally had a chance to read* The Forgotten Founders—*and I am glad you persevered. You may quote me as follows on it:* "The Forgotten Founders *is a tour-de-force of ingenious and elegant scholarship, offering justice at last to the Indian contributions to the American Constitution."*[27]

Schlesinger told Thompson that he hoped galleys of the book had been sent to Richard B. Morris and James McGregor Burns, "who are co-chairmen of a commission set up by the American Historical Association and the American Political Science Association to celebrate the bicentennial of the Constitution. The book should stimulate them to bring the Indians into the act." He also advised sending the book to Deloria and "other Indian publicists." Schlesinger seemed to have given the book's bound galleys a close reading—close enough to correct "John Hobbes" to "Thomas Hobbes" on page 104. Curiously, a decade later, Schlesinger's memory seemed void of this encounter as he vigorously denied the Iroquois role in the development of democracy in his polemic *The Disuniting of America* (1992).

Once it was published in the fall of 1982, *Forgotten Founders* elicited an incredible diversity of reactions, including some impressive reviews in the trade press and some large newspapers. Most academic journals initially ignored the book. At that time, the idea that American Indian political organization helped shape our own seemed to be a frontier outpost of mystery, myth, and rumor, far off their cognitive maps.

Below, I have listed a sampling of the reviews:

"A stimulating and unexpected view of history." —The Atlantic Monthly

"The Indians did indeed give us more than corn."
—*Michael Parfit in* Los Angeles Times Book Review, *December 21, 1982*

"A refreshing and provocative view . . . " —New Age

"A thoughtful venture into an area clearly in need of more research."
—Publishers Weekly

"Johansen . . . has assembled an imposing array of facts to support his findings." —Carl R. Baldwin, St. Louis Post-Dispatch

"Perhaps the greatest hidden secret in all American history . . . "
—Harvey Wasserman, In These Times

"One is never sure just how much is being claimed . . . the sources need to be used more critically to distinguish the mere rhetorical use of the 'noble savage' idea from the actual borrowing and influence that he seems to assert."
—Karen Ordahl Kupperman, Journal of Interdisciplinary History

"Forgotten Founders rests on a misconception, draws on limited research, and is written with small attention to the meaning of the sources it does use."
—Bernard W. Sheehan, Indiana University

"Although this is a book I wish I could praise . . . it reads like the dissertation it once was . . . "
—David Stineback, American Indian Quarterly (Spring, 1989)

I even got a little fan mail from the Daughters of the American Revolution. In 1984, Mrs. Leona S. Postell wrote to me from the DAR's Waukesha, Wisconsin chapter. Mrs. Postell said she had read the review of *Forgotten Founders* in the *Milwaukee Sentinel* a year earlier and had suggested that it become part of the DAR's celebration of Constitution Week the following September. "It was so well liked," she wrote, "that several members asked to borrow the book." Mrs. Postell wrote that she reviewed the book in her annual report to the chairman of the DAR's American Indian Committee. The chairman wrote Postell "a two-page letter in reply, she was so pleased." Mrs. Postell was sure "she's going to include this in her report to the national DAR in Washington, D.C."[28]

In 1986, Amy Wallace described attempts to shape an influence school of thought in the 1930s by William Sidis, known principally as the child genius who, in 1914 at age sixteen, was the youngest person to graduate from Harvard.

Wallace noted that none of the present-day scholars who have explored Native Americans' democratic traditions had heard of Sidis's earlier, unpublished work. I was intrigued by Sidis's account because he got his information from Native American acquaintances (as had I). He also seemed to receive the information with the same sense of discovery that I had felt. Wallace also had read my first book on the subject. "An excellent work," she wrote, "complete with footnotes [that is not true] and an extensive bibliography, is Bruce E. Johansen's *Forgotten Founders*, published in 1982 by Gambit Publishers."[29] Ironically, Sidis's unpublished manuscript was found in Ipswich, Massachusetts, home of Gambit, although neither Lovell Thompson, owner of Gambit, nor I knew of it when *Forgotten Founders* was published there.[30]

Sidis kept secret the fact that he was writing an eight-hundred page history of the United States through the eyes of its original inhabitants. The second half of this unpublished manuscript, which Sidis titled "The Tribes and States," has been lost, but the first half survives. Done without standard scholarly annotation, Sidis's history describes native forms of governance at length, and argues that the natives of New England (in particular the Penacook Confederacy) were more democratic than the Iroquois, whom Sidis describes as oligarchic. He maintains that the Penacooks were more democratic because they had no custom of inherited chieftainship titles which run within family lines, such as those that comprise the Iroquois Grand Council.

Sidis seems to have recorded most of his account from Native American acquaintances in the Boston area, because he spells names very unconventionally. Sidis contends that "Canessetego" (his spelling), the Onondaga chief, set out to shape America's development through Benjamin Franklin. Sidis maintains that the Albany Plan was largely a result of Canassatego's communication with Franklin and was adapted from an Iroquois model.

The Iroquois themselves continued to pass information from one generation to another on the role their confederation had played in the origin of the United States. Alberta Austin described the workings of the Haudenosaunee government in a history of Iroquois families, two volumes compiled by the Seneca Nation Curriculum Development Project during the 1980s, which records the memories of Iroquois elders. Most are Seneca, but all the other nations are represented. One of the accounts is from Leon Shenandoah, the present Tadadaho (speaker) of the Haudenosaunee central council at Onondaga. On the subject of constitutional influence, he said:

> *When the United States copied our form of government in the 1750s, they left out spirituality. This is what I learned as a child. . . . Our religion is within the government and our government is within our religion. It is entwined. If the government goes off to one side . . . the religion will then pull you back in*

line. . . . [One] counteracts the other. . . . But when the United States joined
the 13 colonies and copied our form of government, they held their meetings in
one house, and their church (their beliefs) in another house. . . . It's not
under the same roof like we do.[31]

By the mid-1980s, Lovell Thompson and I were working on a second
book on the influence issue. I managed to publish much of the chapter that
would be titled "Mohawks, Axes and Taxes" in *Exemplar of Liberty* in the
English magazine *History Today*.[32] Lovell's wife Mary died in 1985. A few
months after her death, I called Thompson. We talked for a while, then he
stopped. After a long pause, he said, "I have brain cancer." The phone went
dead, and we never spoke again.

A few months later, in mid-December, 1986, passing through Chicago's
O'Hare airport, I picked up a copy of the *Chicago Tribune*, and found a wire
service obituary of Thompson. In the years since, I have often thought how
much he would have enjoyed watching the debate that *Forgotten Founders*
helped instigate unfold during the next few years. Having rescued that book
from so many slush piles, he would have been very happy watching the
intellectual feathers fly.

NOTES

1. Charles Eastman, *American Indian Magazine*, no. 3 (1919): 145–52.

2. Bruce Johansen, "The Indian's Past May Be His Future," *Seattle Times*, May 9, 1976, A–1, E–1.

3. Donald A. Grinde, *The Iroquois and the Founding of the American Nation* (San Francisco: Indian Historian Press, 1977).

4. Bruce E. Johansen, *Forgotten Founders: Benjamin Franklin, the Iroquois and the Rationale for the American Revolution.* (Ipswich, Mass.: Gambit, 1982).

5. That one professor was Russell Barsh, an ex-officio member of the committee from the College of Business Administration, who had an extensive background (including a law degree) in the legal history of American Indians. The historians knew nothing of it.

6. James Cook, "The American Indian Through Five Centuries," *Forbes*, November 9, 1981, 118. The sixth nation, the Tuscaroras, joined the Confederation about 1710.

7. William Brandon, *The American Heritage Book of Indians* (New York: Dell, 1961).

8. Eastman, *American Indian Magazine*, 145–52.

9. This statement was first published in *The American Indian* 4, no. 3 (1948) and reprinted in Wayne Moquin's 1973 collection *Great Documents in American Indian History.* (New York: Praeger, 1973).

10. Felix Cohen, "Americanizing the White Man," *The American Scholar* 21, no. 2 (Spring 1952): 179–80.

11. Felix Cohen, *Handbook of Federal Indian Law* (Albuquerque: University of New Mexico Press, 1942), 128.

12. Tehanetorens (Ray Fadden), *The History of the Oneida Nation* (Hogansburg, N.Y.: Akwesasne Mohawk Counselor Organization, n.d.), 7. Fadden also stated his case for Iroquois influence in a booklet titled "The Formation of the Ho-de-no-saune or League of the Five Nations" (1948). Fadden wrote: "Their [the Iroquois] handiwork was found to be good, so good that those who know of it cannot help but marvel; so good that its greatest features are found in the government of today's United States. Indians of today, we deserve to feel good about the great men of our history."

13. Alvin Josephy, *The Patriot Chiefs* (New York: Viking, 1958), 9.

14. Josephy, *Patriot Chiefs,* 28.

15. Alvin Josephy, *The Indian Heritage of America* (New York: Bantam, 1969), 33.

16. Later I would find a mimeographed newsletter from 1928 containing a discussion of the idea by William B. Newell. In the newsletter of The Society for the Propagation of Indian Welfare, Newell listed items that "History Books Do Not Tell," among them "THAT the Iroquois Indians had one of the most remarkable political organizations ever formed and upon which the United States government is based." See William B. Newell, ed., *The Six Nations* 2, no. 2 (April 1928): 7.

17. Paul A. W. Wallace, *White Roots of Peace* (Philadelphia: University of Pennsylvania Press, 1946), 3. This book was reprinted in 1980 by the Center for Adirondack Studies, and in 1994 by Clear Light Publishers, Santa Fe, New Mexico. Wallace quotes Franklin's 1751 letter to James Parker, his printing partner, and also notes similarities between the Iroquois Great Law of Peace and the United Nations Charter. In his letter, Wallace cites sources such as Carl Van Doren, Benjamin Franklin, and Lewis Henry Morgan in support of an assertion that the Iroquois League's model helped shape Franklin's Albany Plan of Union but adds that the sources he has in hand contain "no hint . . . of any explicit connection between the Iroquois League and the Constitutional Convention." In 1942, in an essay that was part of *Meet Dr. Franklin,* Julian Boyd said that Franklin "proposed a union of the colonies [at Albany in 1754], and he found his materials in the great confederacy of the Iroquois." See Julian P. Boyd, "Dr. Franklin: Friend of the Indian," in Ray Lokken, ed., *Meet Dr. Franklin* (Philadelphia: Franklin Institute, 1981) 240.

18. William N. Fenton, "The Science of Anthropology and the Iroquois Indians," *Bulletin of the New York State Archaeology Society* no. 6 (March 1956): 10–14.

19. Katie Beals and John J. Carusone, *Native Americans: The Constitution of the Iroquois League* (Oakland, Calif.: Unified School District, 1972). At about the same time, in *Our Indian Heritage*, her collection of profiles of Indian leaders, C. Fayne Porter introduced Hiawatha, who "brought the Iroquois together into an early self-governing league that may have influenced the colonial Continental Congress." The chapter on Hiawatha is titled "Father of Our Constitution?" Beginning with a discussion of the founders, it asks, "What was the genesis of this revolutionary idea?" See also C. Fayne Porter, *Our Indian Heritage: Profiles of Twelve Leaders* (New York: Chilton Books, 1964), ix, 7, 19–21.

20. Virgil Vogel, *This Country Was Ours: A Documentary History of the American Indian* (New York: Harper & Row, 1974), 298. The Swiss writer Elemire Zolla also briefly raised the subject at about the same time as Vogel, in his *The Writer and the Shaman* (1973). Zolla described Edmund Wilson's introduction to the Iroquois, as he researched *Apologies to the Iroquois* (1960): "He discovered that the Constitution of the United States was influenced by the unwritten constitution of the Iroquois Confederation, that Benjamin Franklin had been inspired by it to unify the American colonies." Wilson's interest in the Iroquois was first stirred in the 1950s by the Mohawk land-rights activist Standing Arrow, who told Wilson that Benjamin Franklin "had been influenced by the example of the Iroquois Confederacy in his project for uniting the American colonies. It has always, I found, been the boast of the Iroquois that our written Constitution, with its federal authority balanced against states' rights, was derived from their unwritten one." See Edmund Wilson, *Apologies to the Iroquois* (New York: Farrar, Straus & Cudahy, 1960), 47.

21. "Iroquois Irony," *Akwesasne Notes*, Early Summer, 1981, 28.

22. Joseph McLellan, "'First American' Celebration: Night of Originals," *Washington Post*, March 5, 1982, B–1.

23. Mark Trahant, "Native Perspectives," *Gannett News Service*, March 12, 1992, accessed via LEXIS.

24. *Four Winds*, edited by Charles J. Lohrmann, was a wonderful forum, which used very exacting four-color printing and paper stock thicker than the *National Geographic*. The magazine ran my article as its cover story. Two years later, when I submitted another article, I got a mimeographed notice that said the magazine had been "permanently suspended"—the overhead was just too high.

25. Correspondence, Warren Slesinger to Bruce Johansen, January 3, 1980.

26. Correspondence, Bernard Perry to Bruce Johansen, August 26, 1980.

27. Personal correspondence, Arthur Schlesinger, Jr. to Lovell Thompson, July 14, 1982.

28. Personal correspondence, Mrs. Leona S. Postell to Bruce Johansen.

29. Amy Wallace, *The Prodigy* (New York: E. P. Dutton, 1986), 202. Young Sidis had learned to read English by the age of two, and had typed in English and French

at four. By age five, he had developed a perpetual calendar. By that age, Sidis spoke five languages and could memorize railroad timetables after a single glance. Tutored by his father, a Harvard psychiatry professor, Sidis disposed of elementary school in six months, and high school in a year. At age eight, he was educationally ready for college. The deans of Harvard declined to enroll him until age fourteen for social, not intellectual, reasons.

30. See also Bruce E. Johansen, "William James Sidis' Tribes and States: An Unpublished Exploration of Native American Contributions to Democracy," *Northeast Indian Quarterly* (Spring/Summer 1989): 16–20.

31. Alberta Austin, *Ne'Ho Niyo' De:No': That's What It Was Like* (Lackawanna, N.Y.: Rebco Enterprises, 1986), 177–78.

32. Bruce Johansen, "Mohawks, Axes and Taxes: Images of the American Revolution," *History Today* (London, England), April 1985, 10–18. The "second book" begun under Lovell Thompson's editorship was eventually merged with Donald Grinde's new research to become *Exemplar of Liberty* (1991).

2.

Clio, Clan Mothers, and Collegial Cacophony

Memoirs of My Misspent Youth in Iroquois History

DONALD A. GRINDE, JR.

When I moved to Erie, Pennsylvania in 1971, fresh out of graduate school at the University of Delaware and preparing to teach Native American history at Mercyhurst College, I was acutely conscious that I was moving into Iroquois or Haudenosaunee country. In addition to being an assistant professor of history, I was in charge of the Mercyhurst College Archives, which was dedicated to the local history of northwestern Pennsylvania and western New York. In my trips to Warren, Pennsylvania, I learned of the work of Merle H. Deardorff, Arthur C. Parker (Seneca), and William N. Fenton. I soon became acquainted with the debate over the building of the Kinzua Dam near the Allegany Reservation of the Senecas. By 1966, the dam was dedicated and had flooded the only Indian reservation in Pennsylvania (the Cornplanter Grant) and parts of the Allegany (Seneca) reservation in western New York. Done in the name of flood control for Pennsylvania and western New York, the dam had forced the eviction of numerous Seneca families and flooded their homelands and sacred burial sites.

Because I am an American Indian scholar of Yamasee descent, my students expected me to be able to discuss the Kinzua Dam controversy in an informed fashion. So I had to familiarize myself quickly with the political events, engineering decisions, and Haudenosaunee opposition to the dam, and I met some of the Senecas who had opposed it.

In 1973, I became the director of museum studies and assistant professor of history at the State University of New York, College at Buffalo. My teaching duties there included American Indian history, which was integral to the museum studies program. A part of my job was outreach to Buffalo area history, art, and science museums. It was in this way that I met the director of the Buffalo and Erie County Historical Society, Walter Dunn, who was teaching in the museum studies program. During the 1970s, the Buffalo and Erie County Historical Society was updating its aging exhibits. One of the oldest and most stereotypical of the exhibits was on the Iroquois. Wanting the museum to have good community relations, Walter Dunn contacted Iroquois people in western New York to solicit their input and cooperation in creating new exhibits and programs. He quickly learned that American Indian people strongly resented the displaying of American Indian human remains. This resentment caused a dilemma for Dunn since the museum had for years displayed an Iroquois skeleton in a glass case near the entrance. Museum docents loved to show schoolchildren the remains of the dead Indian. For a couple of generations, Buffalo-area parents remembered the day they had first seen the Indian remains in the museum as children and then fondly took their children to see them as well. Although viewing those American Indian remains had no educational value, they seemed to reassure Buffalonians who might otherwise be uneasy about the nature of European conquest in western New York. Periodically, this uneasiness was quickened by the knowledge that Iroquois people still lived on a half-dozen reservations in western New York. For many people, the dead Indians seemed much better than the living and increasingly vocal Iroquois of the late twentieth century. Certainly, the dead Indians gave no answers except absolute subjugation and posed no embarrassing questions as the living ones did.

At any rate, Dunn decided to hire some Iroquois Indians on his staff and enlisted my help in transforming the museum's exhibits on the Haudenosaunee. He hired Richard (Rick) Hill, a young Tuscarora Indian artist trained at the Chicago Art Institute, to revamp the Iroquois exhibits. Rick contacted me within a few weeks of my arrival in Buffalo. Warily, while sizing me up, Rick told me that he and many other traditional Iroquois people wanted the American Indian human remains in the museum to be reburied in Mother Earth before proceeding with the creation of the new Iroquois exhibits. I told him that I fully understood and sympathized with his views. A decade earlier while I was an undergraduate at Georgia Southern College, I had tried to stop the transporting of bones of the Yamasee people from archaeological excavations on the Sea Islands in Georgia.

With this common bond, Rick Hill began to plan the return of the burials to the earth and to create a meaningful exhibit on the Iroquois with my support. I made the acquaintance of Iroquois leaders in western New York, including Oren Lyons (Onondaga), Corbett Sundown (Seneca), and Beeman Logan (Seneca). Rick Hill and I presented a paper at the Ontario Archaeological Society's 1974 meeting in Toronto arguing for returning American Indian burials to the earth. Although the paper was quite controversial, it was subsequently published in the society's magazine.[1] A year or so later, the province of Ontario passed legislation to improve the protection of Indian burials as a result, in part, of our activities. But there was very little change or interest in such legislation in the United States.

A couple of years later, however, the Buffalo and Erie County Historical Society formally returned its American Indian remains to the Iroquois for reburial, and a new Haudenosaunee exhibit, designed by Rick Hill and other Iroquois advisors was formally opened. Oren Lyons spoke eloquently at the ceremony that returned the burials and opened the museum exhibit. He expressed hope that this was only the beginning of many more burial returns. He praised the Buffalo and Erie County Historical Society for its concern with improving community relations with Iroquois people as well as recognizing the necessity of having contemporary American Indian people participate in the development of new exhibits about their ancestors.

The exhibit aroused controversy within the ranks of academe. It was one of the first exhibits about American Indians that utilized American Indians as advisors and not just "informants." This new way of preparing an exhibit reconfigured the existing power relationships between the dominant Iroquois "experts" (white anthropologists and other academics) and the Iroquois people themselves. I quickly learned that when power and money are involved, the so-called academic "friends of the Indian" become remarkably staunch in the defense of their academic prerogatives and expertise. The academic experts were adamant and vituperative in their attacks on American Indians like Rick Hill and me, whom they viewed as "troublemakers." William N. Fenton perceived Rick Hill as an Indian activist who was "stopping him from gaining grant money" in Iroquois studies.

It became clear that many non-Indian anthropologists viewed the return of American Indian human remains as a threat to their continued hegemony in American Indian studies. Some argued that the return of the human remains threatened the "data base" of physical and archaeological anthropologists. They suggested that American Indian religious concerns about returning burials to Mother Earth were examples of "science" being hampered by the restraints of traditional Native American religions. Personally, I have never been convinced that displaying Native American bones and measuring them away from their context ever served much of a scholarly purpose. Few people would argue that we should, for instance, dig up all Vietnam veterans in our national cemeteries to gain a better knowledge of the dangers of Agent Orange, and even fewer would argue that once the veterans' bones were exhumed and examined, they should be put on shelves in museums so that they would be handy for future research whims. In

essence, appropriating American Indian bones for study is more of a statement about the status of American Indians after conquest and subjugation
than it is about "science." Fortunately, the American Indian Religious
Freedom Act of 1978 has worked to stop such practices.[2]

Other issues concerning Native American rights were brewing at that
time as well. In 1967, George A. Thomas (Onondaga), as Tadodaho (Head
Chief) of the Iroquois Confederacy, called for the return of the New York
State Museum's wampum collection to the Iroquois Confederacy. Thomas
asserted that "The wampum tells of old, old agreements and passes on the
thoughts of our grandfathers. We would like to see them. Our people want to
touch them."[3] I remember how concerned the chiefs at the Tonawanda
Seneca Reservation were about the return of the wampum belts to the
Iroquois Confederacy chiefs, who needed them for their traditional governmental practices. William N. Fenton and others had stopped the return of
these belts to their Indian owners by arguing that they were cultural artifacts
that were "as American as apple pie." It was argued that the Iroquois
wampum belts housed in the New York State Museum belonged to all Americans, not just to the Haudenosaunee people. It was also asserted that the
New York State Museum was a safer, more secure place for the storage of the
wampum belts despite the fact that a fire at the New York State Library had
destroyed some of the wampum belts in the early twentieth century.[4]

In actuality, these arguments simply revolved around power. In the late
nineteenth century at the height of the white racist backlash after the Civil
War, the wampum belts were taken from the Iroquois by anthropologists and
hobbyists in New York who were allegedly concerned with cultural and
material preservation. Anthropologists and American Indian hobbyists
argued that "real" Indians were dying out and the Iroquois Confederacy was
virtually a shadow of itself. In 1898, the Onondaga Council of Chiefs had
agreed to deposit the wampum belts in the New York State Museum, and in
1909, a law was passed that made the State of New York the custodians of the
belts. It was claimed that the new generation of Iroquois were not being
trained to continue age-old traditions into the twentieth century. Hence, the
New York State Museum should take and maintain possession of these important historical artifacts for the benefit of all "Americans." The stereotype
of the "real" Indian as the "vanishing American" is argued in every generation by anthropologists to discredit Indians who do in fact preserve and
transmit traditional knowledge and culture. The argument continues to be
about power rather than cultural preservation and traditional knowledge.
The question is whether Iroquois culture will continue to grow and adapt

over time or whether the dynamic oral traditions will be deadened in written texts and captured in artifacts that non-Indian scholars have dominion over. By the 1960s, anthropologists were arguing that the belts were part of the larger history of New York State and that returning them to the Onondagas would set a dangerous precedent for other groups wishing to reclaim their religious and cultural artifacts.

By the time I arrived in Buffalo in the early 1970s, William N. Fenton and his academic allies had won the first round of this confrontation about the return of the wampum belts. The traditional Iroquois chiefs assured me, however, that they saw the struggle for the wampum belts in a broader context and longer timeline, and also felt confident they would ultimately regain them. During the 1960s, William N. Fenton had been director of the New York State Museum when Nelson A. Rockefeller was governor of New York. Rockefeller had a special interest in American Indians since his father, John D. Rockefeller, Jr., had sent him and his brothers out west to visit American Indian reservations in the 1920s with John Collier. Also, Nelson Rockefeller, like William N. Fenton, was a graduate of Dartmouth College for Indians.

At some point in the late 1960s, it seems that Rockefeller began to be somewhat persuaded by the Iroquois chiefs' arguments that the wampum belts belonged to them. While he was governor, Rockefeller seriously considered constructing a museum at the Onondaga Reservation outside of Syracuse, New York to deposit the disputed wampum belts. The idea was that the wampum belts could be used by the Iroquois chiefs at Confederacy meetings, and they could also be displayed and interpreted at the museum by the Iroquois for the general public when they were not in use. This decision would have empowered the Iroquois not just to regain their wampum belts for traditional use but also to meet with the public in the position of skilled interpreters of these important cultural artifacts. This idea was obviously a threat to the Iroquoianist anthropological establishment's power. Influential scholars like William N. Fenton saw this proposal as a plan that would weaken their hegemony in American Indian studies. In 1971, the New York State Legislature insulted the Iroquois by passing the Pisani bill, which provided for the return of five wampum belts if a museum was constructed on the Onondaga Reservation outside of Syracuse, New York. Since the Onondagas disagreed with these provisions and there was no money to build such a facility, they rejected this token solution.[5] Finally, in 1996 on July 4, seventy four wampum belts were returned to the Iroquois Confederacy.

When Fenton found out about Rockefeller's larger plans for returning the Iroquois wampum belts, he contacted Rockefeller and asked that he not do anything until they met each other at the Dartmouth reunion later that year. After the Dartmouth reunion, Rockefeller apparently decided not go through with his plans to build a museum at Onondaga with state funds and return the Iroquois wampum belts to the traditional chiefs of the Iroquois Confederacy.

The issues of American Indian reburials and the return of the Iroquois wampum belts resonated throughout Indian America during the 1970s. Vine Deloria, Jr. observed that through these issues the Iroquois traditional chiefs "were struggling to reconstruct the League on its traditional basis."[6] I was immersed in these struggles from the start of my academic career, and it was these experiences that prepared me for my active role in the debate over the Iroquois influence on the development of American government.

Since the reburial issue and the return of the wampum were questions that were already present when I arrived in western New York, I initially made common cause with many Iroquois people in these struggles. The controversy over the Iroquois influence on the development of the United States government was to become a significant part of my scholarly life in the next quarter century. I remember the first time I heard the topic mentioned. When a group of older Iroquois women came to my office in the fall of 1973 to discuss Title IV school programs for American Indian children in the Buffalo schools, we talked at length of the need to revise Iroquois historical and cultural presentations to Native American children, since they were heavily laden with notions of conquest, domination, and cultural purity. Clearly, everyone felt that the Native American voice was muted in the school programs for Native children. During this conversation, someone brought up the notion of the Iroquois influence on American government.

My initial reaction was to discount the idea on the basis that the United States Constitution was itself an instrument that played a pivotal role in the conquest and subjugation of all Native American peoples through treaty-making and the unilateral acts of Congress that sought to destroy Native American societies. However, the older women persisted in their arguments about the Iroquois influence on American government, talking of Benjamin Franklin's role and urging me to read an article by Felix Cohen that had advanced the idea. Shortly after this conversation in the fall of 1973, I received a copy of Felix Cohen's article from Ruth John (Seneca).

Meeting with the Iroquois women again, I asked, "Why do you persist in your belief that the Iroquois had an influence on American government?"

After a long pause, one of the old women sitting in my office simply stated: "Because it is true and it was passed down to us by the old people."

Several Iroquois, especially Larry Green (Mohawk), asked me to look into this matter through the white man's documents and write something about it that would be useful in the schools and in the revision of American history textbooks, since I was then one of the few American Indian scholars with a Ph.D. in history. Because I had been taught to take the counsel of my elders seriously, I agreed, with a bit of reticence, to take on the task.

The next year, 1974, Elizabeth Salmieri (Cayuga) came to my office and inquired about using the Lazarus Seneca Claims Papers that were being organized for deposit at the SUNY Buffalo library. At that time, she was the Cayuga tribal historian and also worked for a law firm which was pursuing New York State land claims for the Cayugas. As she and I perused the documents in the Seneca Claims collection, we discussed a wide variety of topics relating to American Indian history. Always supportive of my research, she urged me to pursue my project on the Iroquois influence on American government. I remember her being a very brave woman; she went blind while doing her research and then went in for laser treatments, which restored her sight and enabled her to continue her projects in Cayuga history.

During the mid-1970s, I was active at the Buffalo North American Indian Center. I served in a variety of positions on the Board of Directors with Gloria Simmons (Lumbee), Joe Villagomez (Seneca), Ronald LaFrance (Mohawk), Germaine Mike (Cayuga), Larry Green (Mohawk), Luke Abrams (Seneca), Vivian Logan (Delaware) and others. As a young American Indian professional, I dealt with the Bureau of Indian Affairs, the Office of Native American Programs, the Indian Health Service, and American Indian CETA programs. Although these funding agencies sought to foster self-help programs, they often had a paternalistic bent that blunted their effectiveness. Although economic needs within the Buffalo American Indian community were unique, the larger society always wanted to treat us like every other "minority." This caused untold problems for those of us trying to work for change and empowerment in the urban Native American community.

During this time, I received encouragement from Ron LaFrance, Chairman of the Buffalo North American Indian Center, who was working in the public schools. He also urged me to study the Iroquois influence on American government and write more about Iroquois history. He asserted that there was "a great need for better American Indian and Iroquois curriculum materials in the public schools."

In 1975, I began to teach Native American history one evening a week on the Cattaraugus and Allegany Seneca Indian reservations, in western New York. The Seneca Nation had received a grant through the United

Southeastern Tribes to train more Senecas as teachers, and I was asked to teach American Indian history on Seneca reservations. The program offered evening classes on the reservations and then encouraged students to continue their studies at SUNY Buffalo. My students on the Cattaraugus and Allegany reservations were mostly older women. Still in my late twenties, I was in the odd position of teaching my elders, but my students and I soon struck a bargain. Basically, I would teach my elders about the history of U.S. American Indian policies, and they would teach me about Iroquois history and political theory. In this way, we created a mutually beneficial exchange of ideas and knowledge. Their insights were invaluable in the conduct of my research, and their encouragement was crucial since I was getting little aid and encouragement from established academics.

Initially, I had thought that my research on this topic would be limited, since I was still imbued with the notion that Euro–Americans and Native Americans had lived in two discrete societies on the eastern seaboard from the beginning of contact. My conversations about the topic with other American historians at the time usually ended with a sense of bemusement on their part. It seemed incredible to them that democratic ideas could come from "savages." This was very disturbing to me because even liberal historians sought to marginalize Native American ideas when I brought them up in our conversations. Anthropologists discounted the idea totally. It was accepted as doctrine that few if any non-Indians understood American Indian political structures until the advent of anthropology in America, under the aegis of Lewis Henry Morgan, in the first half of the nineteenth century. I was troubled by the notion that knowledge about Iroquois political structures appeared to be the exclusive realm of the anthropologists and the knowledge of contemporary Iroquois people seemed irrelevant to them.

In the midst of these experiences, I wrote a faculty research grant proposal about the Iroquois influence on American government and submitted it twice (1975 and 1976) to the SUNY Research Foundation. Each time it was rejected out of hand with very little comment. The second rejection was considered unusual since faculty were encouraged to resubmit research proposals after incorporating previous critical comments by scholars reviewing the grant applications. I was not yet aware of the profound opposition to this line of research among the Iroquoianist scholars—I was simply puzzled by the terseness of comments and the lack of encouragement to pursue this line of scholarship. At this time, some Iroquois people encouraged me to attend the annual Iroquois conference near Albany, New York but I decided not to go. I had heard from many Iroquois traditionalists that the white academic Iroquois scholars were very arrogant and anti-Indian in their demeanor.

As the bicentennial of the American Revolution approached in the mid 1970s, federal and state grant money became available for community celebrations of this historic event. William N. Fenton and other academics wanted to develop a program to circulate the Iroquois wampum belts in the New York State Museum within New York State. The idea was to create a traveling exhibit that would display the wampum belts in the major cities of New York State. However, Fenton needed the consent of the Iroquois chiefs, who were unhappy with the state's failure to return the wampum belts.

I attended a meeting at the Buffalo Museum of Science to discuss these matters in the winter of 1975 (Corbett Sundown and Oren Lyons urged me to go since I was an American Indian historian and museologist). Since I had never met William N. Fenton, I resolved to listen to the deliberations between him and many of the Iroquois elders gathered there. Fenton argued that the wampum belts belonged to all New Yorkers and that his bicentennial proposal was for the benefit of everyone. Since Fenton needed the support of the Iroquois community to gain the grant, he argued that this exhibit would promote an awareness of New York State Indians. He also proposed that Iroquois leaders play a crucial role in the development of the exhibit.

Following a long pause after Fenton finished his remarks, Corbett Sundown rose and stated that Fenton had "a lot of gall for even proposing such an exhibit to the Iroquois people." Chief Sundown pointed out that Fenton had stopped the return of the wampum belts to the traditional chiefs several years earlier. Sundown chastised Fenton and stated, "You should not ask for our cooperation regarding the display of the wampum belt collection." Corbett Sundown asserted that cooperating with Fenton on exhibiting the wampum belts would give tacit approval by the Iroquois leadership to the state's refusal to return the wampum belts.

Fenton countered Sundown's remarks by stating that "the return of the wampum belts was an unreasonable request" and that this exhibition would allow the Iroquois people to interpret and gain access to these important cultural treasures. He hinted that this might be the only time that traditional people might be allowed such broad-based access to the belts.

Next, Beeman Logan rose and stated, "There will be no cooperation with you on such a proposal." Fenton noted that there was a lot of money involved in these grants and hinted that Iroquois advisors would gain some cash for their efforts. He did not say that he himself and several other academics stood to gain a great deal from the proposed grant as well.

Upset by such offers, Oren Lyons and several other younger leaders de-nounced the proposal while Fenton attempted to speak privately with some of the Iroquois leaders on the matter. Towards the end of the discussion, I stated: "The wampum belts served little use to history in the New York State Museum. They were, essentially, disembedded from their cultural base and they should be returned to where they could, once again, function as a central part of the political and cultural life of the Haudenosaunee." I pointed out that a fire in the New York State Library about seventy-five years before had destroyed many of the belts, so that even maintaining a secure storage facility could not be cited as their justification for continuing to keep the wampum belts. Shortly after these comments, the meeting ended with the Iroquois people resolved to renew and strengthen their efforts to secure the return of the wampum belts to their possession. Fenton complained that he was losing grant monies and an opportunity to share Iroquois history with the people of New York. Some of Iroquois leaders, as they filed out, stated that Fenton "was arrogant and insensitive"—despite his having been a life-long student of Iroquois ways.

In 1974, I was asked to serve on the Board of Directors of the American Indian Historical Society by Rupert Costo (Cahuilla) and Jeanette Henry Costo (Eastern Cherokee). Shortly afterwards, I was also appointed to the editorial board of the *Indian Historian* (a publication of the American Indian Historical Society). I was pleased to become a part of the American Indian controlled organization that published books through the Indian Historian Press, scholarly articles in the *Indian Historian,* a children's magazine, *The Weewish Tree,* and the national Indian newspaper, *Wassaja.* Under the tute-lage of Jeanette and Rupert Costo, I received an education about the realities of scholarly life for an Indian in the latter part of the twentieth century. From them I learned that although we, as American Indians, were interested in advancing our point of view vis-a-vis American history and Native American culture, the scholarly establishment was sorely threatened by our presence and our agendas. These non-Indian scholars pretended to cloak themselves in "objectivity" and claimed that American Indian scholars were less able to function impartially in American Indian studies.

While learning the realities of my life as a scholar, I remember talking to a Euro–American scholar of American Indian history who pointed out to me that the last thing that a white scholar wanted was to be characterized as "pro-Indian." Grants, fame, fortune, and scholarly credibility would be denied any non-Indian on the basis of such an accusation. He also stated that it was assumed that most American Indian scholars were "pro-Indian" and that this was one of their major problems in the scholarly world. I asked him if such standards were applied to European scholars who studied French history: "Were all white people who studied European history considered "pro-white?" While comprehending the thrust of my argument, the white historian glanced at the ground and muttered something about "double standards" and about how American Indian people would just have to learn to live with such things for now.

After some conversations and words of encouragement from Rupert and Jeanette Costo, I resolved to push ahead with my designs to publish a book on the Iroquois influence on American government. I was buoyed by the knowledge that a significant number of Iroquois historical documents were deposited in the Archives at SUNY Buffalo by the Lazarus law firm (legal counsel in the Seneca Nation Claims Case). I knew that copies of treaties, diaries, and public papers relating to the Iroquois would soon be readily available to me.

By 1975, I also realized that very little funding would be forthcoming for my research, given the predispositions of the scholarly establishment on the topic. I resolved perforce to do the project anyway, knowing full well that it would probably make me a pariah amongst the Iroquoianists. I had come to realize that the most important confrontations are those that have much at stake for all sides concerned.

As I formulated the Iroquois influence project in my mind and completed some preliminary reading, I began to talk about the project with Jeanette Costo at the American Indian Historical Society in San Francisco. Jeanette and Rupert Costo thought that it would be a good publication for the Indian Historian Press. With these assurances, I researched and wrote *The Iroquois and the Founding of the American Nation*. Having no research funds, I relied heavily on the documents in the Seneca Nations Claims Collection at the Archives at SUNY Buffalo. My purpose was to produce a popular trade book that re-examined the role of the Iroquois in the American Revolution. Obviously, a part of the re-examination would be the Iroquois influence on the evolution of American government.

In early 1976, after about eighteen months of research and writing, I sent the manuscript in for revision and publication to the Indian Historian Press. Jeanette and Rupert Costo relayed many useful suggestions by the scholarly reviewers of the manuscript, and they also offered many criticisms of their own. The book came out in the fall of 1977 shortly after I had moved to California to take a position in the History Department at California Polytechnic State University, San Luis Obispo.

My initial impression was that the book fell stillborn from the press. There seemed to be little interest in this topic in mainstream academia. Some American Indian scholars like Vine Deloria, Jr., Ward Churchill, John Mohawk, and Oren Lyons commented favorably, but most non-Indian scholars ignored it. Wilbur R. Jacobs, Professor of History, University of California at Santa Barbara was the only non-Indian scholar that seemed to take the issue of the Iroquois influence on American government seriously, and he gave me encouragement.

Throughout the early 1980s, I continued to have an interest in the Iroquois influence on American government, but I was more actively researching twentieth-century American Indian policy and California Indians. I filed away items that related to the Iroquois topic, and I read Bruce Johansen's *Forgotten Founders*, which dealt with the Iroquois influence on American political traditions. As director of Native American studies at the University of Utah from 1981 to 1984, I had the opportunity to talk with Vine Deloria, Jr. about the Iroquois influence on American government, and he gave me encouragement as well.

But it was not until I received a summer research grant from the Meredith Fund and Americans for Indian Opportunity in 1986 that I began seriously to contemplate writing another book on the Iroquois influence. In my travels to research libraries and archives in the summer of 1986, I became convinced that there was still much that could be done on this controversial topic. Heartened by my preliminary findings in the summer of 1986, the Meredith Fund and Americans for Indian Opportunity extended the grant to enable me to pursue my research for the 1987–1988 academic year.

At every stage of my research, I received aid and encouragement from many people. In the summer of 1987, I visited Ray Fadden (Mohawk) at the Six Nations Museum in Onchiota, New York, and we discussed some of my findings amongst the papers of the founders of the United States. Ray and his son John encouraged me to do more in-depth research. Ray told me that a scholar had come to see him years ago with a story about the New York Sons of Liberty sending wampum belts to the Iroquois in 1766 during the Stamp Act Crisis. The Sons of Liberty asked the Iroquois to intercept British troops coming down the Hudson River from Canada that were to reinforce the occupation of New York City. After the Sons of Liberty corresponded with the Iroquois, they erected a "pine post . . . called . . . the Tree of Liberty" where they conducted their daily exercises (the imagery of the Liberty Tree could easily be derived from the Iroquois Great Tree of Peace, which symbolizes the government of the Iroquois). After the conversation, the man had promised Ray a copy of the document, but he had never returned. Ray asked me if I knew of such a document. I told him that I had not found it, but I would look for it. Oddly enough six months later, I found the documentary evidence about the New York Sons of Liberty sending wampum belts to the Iroquois in the "Journals of Captain John Montresor 1757–1778"[7] and I informed Ray Fadden of my discovery. I often think of that event with fondness and as a novel example of how contemporary oral "traditions" can help in historical research.

While based in Washington, D.C. in 1987–1988 with a research fellowship, I pursued my research in the archives and libraries of major east coast cities. During this time, I met Bruce Johansen at a conference in Philadelphia. We became friends as we discussed the debate over the Iroquois influence on American government. Bruce and I were introduced by Toni Truesdale, a teacher and artist in Philadelphia. Bruce and I were concerned that some people like Elisabeth Tooker were trying to pit his ideas concerning the Iroquois influence on American government against mine.[8] Seeing that this intellectual pursuit would benefit only those who opposed our ideas, Bruce and I resolved to join forces and write a book together.

It was also in Philadelphia that Bruce Johansen and I first encountered Elisabeth Tooker, Professor of Anthropology, Temple University. We were giving papers on the Iroquois influence at the Atwater Kent Museum in early 1988 when Professor Tooker, who was in the audience rose and pounded her fist on a table and emphatically stated, "There is little evidence to support these contentions and no reputable scholar gives such research any credence."

I challenged Tooker's pejorative statement by pointing out that on the eve of the Constitutional Convention, John Adams had asserted that there was a need to conduct "a more accurate investigation of the form of governments of . . . modern Indians"[9] when writing a constitution for the United States. I also stated that Adams asserted that "great philosophers and politicians of the age" were attempting to "set up governments of . . . modern Indians."[10]

Nonplussed, anthropologist Tooker stated before the entire audience: "You historians can quote anything to prove a point."

Prior to our meeting, Professor Tooker, at the urging of Professor James Axtell at the College of William and Mary, had applied for and received a grant from the National Endowment for the Humanities to write an article debunking the idea of the Iroquois influence on American government. The article appeared in *Ethnohistory* in 1988.[11] Although evidently unfamiliar with the documentary evidence surrounding the development of American government, she waded into the fray convinced that her preconceived notions about the debate would prevail. When I asked her if she had "looked at the papers of the fifty-five delegates to the Constitutional Convention,." she said, "I have not examined those documents."

It was a classic case of a theoretical anthropologist being confronted with historical data that interfered with foregone conclusions.

Subsequently, Bruce Johansen, Sally Wagner, Elisabeth Tooker, and I were on a panel discussing the Iroquois influence on American government at an ethnohistory conference in Chicago in 1989. Tooker admitted that there might be something to our arguments but stated that Professor Johansen and I were not qualified "to discern the real nature of the Iroquois influence on American government." Tooker gave no reasons for her statements. Unfortunately, this kind of *ad hominem* argumentation has been a hallmark of Professor Tooker's reasoning for more than a decade.

After this flurry of conference papers, Professor Johansen and I published *Exemplar of Liberty* in 1991, and it was well received in Native American circles. Our purpose was to provide access to the historical evidence and scholarly discussion surrounding this controversy, while putting forward our own interpretations of the extent of Iroquois influence on American government.

Frankly, I believed in 1991 that the American people and the scholarly world were not ready to deal honestly and openly with American Indian ideological influences on American government. My hope was that we would plant a seed that would grow and be nourished by subsequent research and interest on this topic. If Professor Johansen and I have done nothing else, we have challenged the American intellectual community's overweening dependency on European concepts and ideas. Never again will the birth of the United States be the exclusive domain of Europeans and Euro–Americans.

NOTES

1. Donald A. Grinde, Jr. and Richard Hill, "Indian Historians Examine the Prehistory and History of the Iroquois: Problems in Methodology and Records," *Ontario Archaeology* no. 25 (Summer 1975).

2. See Christopher Vecsey, ed., *Handbook of American Indian Religious Freedom* (New York: Crossroad Publications, 1995) for a fuller discussion of the issues.

3. "Wampum Belts Asked: Chief [Thomas] Demands State Return Them," *Syracuse Herald Journal*, March 25, 1967.

4. William N. Fenton, "The New York State Wampum Collection: the Case for the Integrity of Cultural Treasures," *Proceedings of the American Philosophical Society* December 1971 115; and see also William H. Fenton, "Return of Eleven Wampum Belts to the Six Nations Iroquois Confederacy on Grand River, Canada," *Ethnohistory* 36 (Fall 1989): 392–411, for Fenton's token attempt to sidetrack the issue of the return of *all* the wampum belts in the New York State Museum to the Onondagas in New York State.

5. *Syracuse Herald-Journal*, July 2, 1971.

6. Vine Deloria, Jr., *God is Red* (New York: Dell, 1973), 20.

7. "Journals of Captain John Montresor," April 4, 1766, *Collections of the New York Historical Society* (New York, 1888–1949), 2nd Set, XIV, 357, 367–68.

8. See Elisabeth Tooker, "The United States Constitution and the Iroquois League," *Ethnohistory* 35 (Fall 1988): 305–36.

9. Charles F. Adams, ed., *The Works of John Adams* (Boston: Little Brown, 1851), 4, 298.

10. Ibid., 4, 296.

11. See Tooker, ". . . Constitution and the Iroquois League," 305–36.

3.

The Coyotes Form a Collective

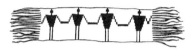

Bruce E. Johansen

The bicentennial of the U.S. Constitution in 1987 heightened interest in its history and origins, both European and American. Combined with increased interest in the history of U.S. minority groups, the emphasis on the Constitution initiated an explosion in citations of work asserting American Indian roots of democracy. In retrospect, the surge of interest in the subject during 1987 now seems timely and natural. In 1986, however, I did not see it coming. Lovell Thompson had just died, and taken Gambit with him. Before he died, Lovell had sold his stock, name, and interest to Bruce Shaw, publisher of Harvard Common Press, which had a reputation for tactful money management, best-selling cookbooks, and titles such as *How to Have a Baby in Boston*. I figured that *Forgotten Founders* had had its day in the sun. At the time, I knew no other publishers that might have been interested in the second book I was preparing on the same subject. I could not have known that I would join with people I had not yet met to establish a new field of scholarly study.

I got an inkling of what was to come one day late in 1986, via a phone call from Bruce Shaw. He had been examining the contract for my book, which he had purchased from Lovell Thompson, and he had noticed that the paperback option had not been exercised. Shaw was calling to tell me that he wanted to exercise it. Shaw wanted to bring the book out under a more general subtitle than *Benjamin Franklin, the Iroquois, and the Rationale for the American Revolution*, which had been used on the hardbound edition. We settled on *How the American Indian Helped Shape Democracy*.

I got another inkling of what was to come early in 1987, with a call from José Barreiro at Cornell. He invited me to speak at the forthcoming conference, "Cultural Encounter: The Iroquois Great Law of Peace and the U.S. Constitution," to be held September 11–12. Barreiro also said that the

56

Cornell American Indian Program's journal, *Northeast Indian Quarterly*, would publish an excerpt from *Forgotten Founders*.[1] Barreiro and the rest of the staff at the Cornell American Indian Program (AIP) were calling together people who had researched the subject, along with traditional Iroquois who had been told that their ancestors had shaped the American intellectual revolution as part of their oral history. For the first time, scholars and Native American traditional people gathered to study the idea.

By the last day of the Cornell conference, some of the participants were calling it "historic." The euphoria was so thick that I cautioned some of them that time has to pass before anything can be called "historic." Time has, and it was. A number of people who had been working on the idea individually came together at these conferences, and began to share information and plan to coauthor articles and books, and to conduct other acts of academic mischief. A random inquiry was becoming an organized pursuit.

Planning for the Cornell conference also spurred the first nationwide burst of publicity regarding the idea that Native American confederacies may have shaped the formative United States; it was this swell of publicity that drew the "Troll" counterattack a year later. In its Sunday, June 28, 1987 edition, the *New York Times* published a piece quoting Oren Lyons in support of the influence thesis. "If Americans are going to celebrate the anniversary of their Constitution, we figure that we had better tell them where the idea came from," said Lyons. John Mohawk was quoted as saying that "what made the colonists American as opposed to English was their experiences with the Indians."

The *Times* article presented an outline of the historical circumstances suggesting an Iroquois role in the evolution of the Constitution. The article jumped the gun on New York State Education Department plans to include this material in its study guides—September 1988 was suggested. The piece also contained a concise description of the founders' thought process by Stephen L. Schechter, executive director of the New York State Bicentennial Commission: "They contemplated examples from Europe, examples from Greco-Roman times, examples from the Bible . . . and they also looked at Native American examples, particularly the Iroquois Confederacy."[2]

This article drew a response from a number of influence opponents that was not published in the *Times*. Submitted to the op-ed page, the statement defined the issue very narrowly, as "the contention . . . that the Constitution of the United States was modelled after the League of the Iroquois." Any such supposition is "at variance with the historical and ethnographic record," the statement continued, as it lectured Indian advocates of the idea, asserting that "this dubious reading of history exhibit[s] a comparable disrespect for the very real and great accomplishments of their ancestors."

Most Iroquois did not appreciate being lectured on how to respect their elders. To be told by a group of white academics that their reading of history abused their own ancestors supremely rankled today's traditional Haude-nosaunee, reminding many of them that, throughout the history of Indian-white contact, some of the most disastrous policies the same ancestors had faced were, in their own times, advanced by self-proclaimed "friends of the Indian." That was how both allotments of land and forced termination of tribes were "sold" to Congress, the first a century ago; the second, six decades after that.[3]

The statement also illustrated its authors' ignorance of the historical record by asking whether the founders knew of the Iroquois Grand Council's basic operating procedures. At about the same time, Donald Grinde was discovering through his reading of John Adams's *Defence of the Constitutions* that the founders carried a description of this system (and many others) to the Constitutional Convention itself, in Adams's book.

The opponents' statement concluded with an embrace of the Anglo-Saxon myth that "members of the Constitutional Convention codified more than a century of Anglo-American tradition and experience." It was signed by James Axtell, William N. Fenton, William T. Hagan, Francis Jennings, and Elisabeth Tooker—all names that proponents of the idea would come to know well in coming months, as the debate was joined in academic meetings, public forums, and publications.

A United Press International dispatch (August 20, 1987) quoted Oren Lyons on Iroquois history and the Great Law's relationship to U.S. funda-mental law. The dispatch also quoted me in support of the influence thesis, with Michael Kammen, Cornell professor of history and constitutional scholar, in opposition, saying that "There is no scholarly evidence to support the claims of the Iroquois Confederacy on the Founders."[4]

The *Cornell Chronicle*, the newspaper of the university's administration, featured side-by-side announcements of two conferences scheduled during September at the university: the American Indian Program's conference on the Great Law of Peace and the Constitution September 11–12, and another conference—titled "Has the Constitution Endured?"—a week later that featured a speech by former senator and secretary of state Edmund S. Muskie (a 1939 graduate of Cornell's Law School).[5] The organizers of the AIP con-ference prepared quickly for the response as roughly four hundred people registered from all over the United States, spilling out of preassigned meeting rooms and lecture halls. The other conference, which was sponsored by Cornell's administration, registered about one hundred.

The AIP conference built a network of scholars, teachers, artists, and traditional Haudenosaunee, all dedicated to challenging ethnocentric notions of American history. In the eyes of some established "experts" on the Iroquois, we may have been "renegades." We had managed to offend the core of established Iroquoian studies, a group of academics whose works I had read as a doctoral student. At Cornell, my eyes were first opened to the full social, political, and academic consequences of the ideas I had begun exploring, on my own, in archival research a decade earlier.

José Barreiro provided an early forum for the influence argument in the *Northeast Indian Quarterly*, which he edited, beginning in the early 1980s. Barreiro would go on to edit the printed proceedings of the September conference at Cornell University.[6] Barreiro completed his Ph.D. in English at Cornell, and his first book, *The Indian Chronicles*, was nominated for the *Los Angeles Times* Book Award.

In the fall 1988 issue of NEIQ, Barreiro described the debate over the "influence thesis," giving it that name for the first time. Summarizing the results of the 1987 Cornell conference on the subject, Barreiro compared the controversy to that aroused by Martin Bernal's *Black Athena*, a book that makes a case that some of Greek culture came from Africa. He concluded: "It would be most valuable now to have proponents and opponents of the influence thesis present their conclusions at a public forum."[7] The face-to-face debate that Barreiro proposed took a few months to develop. In the meantime, the idea that Native American democracies helped to shape the political origins of the United States spread further into popular consciousness.

The same day that the Cornell conference began, at Prospect Park in Brooklyn, oversized puppets and papier-mâché animals were part of the cast of the Bread and Puppet Theater as it performed *The Archetypal Slogan Circus*. The *New York Times* "Weekender Guide" described the circus as:

> part allegory and part comedy . . . includ[ing] puppets representing the Founding Fathers as well as women and landless Americans who were neglected by the Constitution. The 90-minute show was inspired not only by the Constitution, but also by its Iroquois precursor, known as "Kaianerekowa" [The Great Binding Law or Great Law of Peace].[8]

A week later, a gathering of New York City officials and their guests paid tribute to the signing of the Constitution 200 years earlier. A United

Press International dispatch reported: "A hushed audience listened as Chief Leon Shenandoah told them the history of the Six Nations Iroquois Confederacy, whose unwritten 'constitution' served as a guide for the framers of the Constitution."[9]

The *National Geographic* also published a special edition on the Constitution in September 1987, which included an oblique mention of the influence issue. According to scuttlebutt on the academic grapevine, this treatment had been whittled down from a more extensive version after the Trolls intervened. The brief article describes the Iroquois Great Law of Peace, then asks: "Could it be that the U.S. Constitution owes a debt to the Iroquois?"[10] The article briefly described Franklin's view of Native politics.

At about the same time, Jonathan Ferziger reported in a United Press International dispatch dated August 25, 1987, that the New York State Bicentennial Commission was developing a series of "Constitutional Minutes" for television, including one on "the state's first great constitution- maker, the legendary Hiawatha, who brought New York's Indian tribes together in the Iroquois Confederation even before the white man discovered the continent."[11] Also during the summer of 1987, Ganondagan, in central New York State, was dedicated as the state's first Native American State Historic Site. An article in the *New York Times* quoted Seneca scholar John Mohawk, who created the texts for seventy stainless-steel signs at the historic site:

> *The Six Nation Confederacy played a pivotal role not only in Indian affairs but in the thinking of men like Benjamin Franklin and Thomas Jefferson when it came to drafting plans for how the United States was to be governed. And so their legacy had some effect on the Declaration of Independence, the Constitution, and the Bill of Rights, with which we live today.*[12]

The debate began to appear with more frequency in scholarly books about the time of the Cornell conference. For example, in *Toward an American Revolution* (1988), Jerry Fresia brought the Iroquois Great Law of Peace into his discussion of the U.S. Constitution's ideological shortcomings. He wrote:

> *For the Iroquois, the concept of "the people" meant something very different from what the Framers had in mind. Their law and custom provided for the relatively equitable distribution of wealth, universal suffrage, and a confederation of states similar to the one described in the Articles [of Confederation].*[13]

Charles L. Mee, Jr. raised the subject in The Genius of the People (1987): "[John] Rutledge always admired the Iroquois Indians, particularly their legal system, which gave autonomy for their internal affairs, but united them for purposes of war." Mee wrote that Rutledge opened a meeting of the constitutional Committee of Detail by reading from an Iroquois account from 1520, which began "We, the people, to form a union, to establish peace, equity, and order . . ." Mee concluded: "He commended the phrasings to his colleagues—and so, in some part, the preamble to the new constitution was based on the law of the land as it had been on the east coast before the first white settlers arrived."[14]

Reviewing Mee's *The Genius of the People* in the *Los Angeles Times* a week after the Cornell conference, John Denvir, a professor of constitutional law at the University of San Francisco, agreed with Mee that "The majestic 'We the people' which opens the Constitution was most likely copied from an Iroquois document."[15] The *Christian Science Monitor* picked up Mee's assertion in its series "Constitutional Journal," a day-by-day account of the 1787 convention: "John Rutledge is reported to have opened today's session by pulling from his pocket a copy of a Constitution drawn up in 1520 by five Iroquois Indian nations."[16] The use of the term "a copy" was curious here, because significant portions of the Iroquois Great Law of Peace were not committed to European-style writing until the late nineteenth century. A truly comprehensive version was not published in English until the early 1990s.[17]

As Mee's book was being reviewed, John Kahionhes Fadden was interviewed in the *Philadelphia Inquirer* in support of the idea that the Iroquois helped shape American political institutions. The article mentioned Franklin's relationship with the Iroquois, his comments on their government, and Canassatego's 1744 speech at Lancaster.[18]

On October 1, 1987, Sally Smith, coordinator of Project Equal, of the New York City Board of Education, wrote to Fadden, thanking him for illustrations of his which were used in an exhibit on the Iroquois and democracy to be used in schools there. The exhibit was designed to sit on a table in the school library.[19] The project was titled "Forgotten Founders: The Iroquois Confederacy and the Founding of the American Nation." During 1987, Fadden also wrote and illustrated two "Field Workbook Leaflets," "a service of the Young Worker Program . . . of the New York State Historical Association." The leaflets, both titled "Native Americans in New York State: Symbols of the Haudenosaunee," outlined ways in which European colonists adopted some of the symbols and ideas of the Iroquois.

Within months of the Cornell conference, the influence idea was penetrating political discussion on a national level. On December 2, 1987, the U.S. Senate Select Committee on Indian Affairs heard testimony on

Senate Concurrent Resolution 76, "To acknowledge the contribution of the Iroquois Confederacy of Nations to the development of the United States Constitution . . ."

This contribution was noted in order to "reaffirm the continuing government-to-government relationship between Indian tribes and the United States as established in the Constitution." The resolution noted that "The original framers of the Constitution, among them George Washington and Benjamin Franklin, are known to have greatly admired the concepts, principles, and governmental practices of the Six Nations of the Iroquois Confederacy." It resolved to "acknowledge the historical debt which this Republic . . . owes to the Iroquois Confederacy and other Indian nations for the demonstration of enlightened, democratic principles of government . . . "[20]

A States News Service Dispatch by Marybeth Farrell detailed views related to the Senate resolution.[21] The effort was said to have been spearheaded by Oren Lyons with the help of Senators Daniel Inouye and Daniel Evans, who were chair and vice-chair respectively of the Senate Select Committee on Indian Affairs. Reaction to the Senate resolution was immediate. Francis Jennings, director emeritus of the D'Arcy McNickle Center for the History of the American Indian, was reported to have said that the resolution "destroys my faith in the historical literacy of the Senate." The article quoted Donald Grinde in support of influence, and a number of other historians against the idea. Several historians and constitutional scholars gave their "spin" on the resolution in another States News Service dispatch by Farrell, released September 22. "They [the Senate] just swallowed a public-relations effort," James Axtell was reported to have said.[22]

Late in May, 1988, just as the debate over the Senate resolution died away, the influence idea surfaced again after President Reagan told students at Moscow University that the United States had given reservations to American Indians to "humor" them. In the Pacific Northwest, newspaper reporters called Joe de la Cruz, president of the Quinault Nation Council, for a response to President Reagan's opinions. De la Cruz said that Reagan was ignoring the debt that U.S. institutions owe Native precedents:

> The president is like a lot of Americans who do not understand the United States' own Constitution and the reason for the treaties, which are part of the law of the land. That is because American history does not teach the part that the Indians played in the formation of the U.S. Constitution.[23]

Robert W. Venables, a visiting associate professor in Cornell University's American Indian Program, rebutted Reagan's remarks. He concentrated on Reagan's assumption that American Indians are "primitive." "As a label derogating an entire race," wrote Venables, "'primitive' could hardly be applied to the Mayas of Mesoamerica, the builders of the Chaco Canyon complex in New Mexico, or the political democracy of the Iroquois in the Northeast, who recognized women's political and economic rights centuries before Europe and the United States."[24] Without knowing of Venables' response at the time, I also took issue with Reagan's remarks in the *Omaha World-Herald*, asserting that Indian influences are woven into the United States national character, and that Reagan was ignorant of most of them.[25]

A public-service advertisement trumpeting Iroquois influence on democracy appeared during 1988 in *Newsweek* and *People*, and was displayed in *Advertising Age's* "Global Gallery" of advertising. The advertisement was sponsored by American Indian Arts and Amerinda, and created by Drossman, Lehman, Marino Advertising Agency, all of New York City.[26] It featured an Iroquois wampum belt above a headline, "You're Looking at the First Draft of the Constitution," followed by text describing briefly how founders such as Franklin and Jefferson utilized Iroquois concepts. Wampum belts were used as a form of written communication to jog the memory during public events and to seal diplomatic agreements. Traditionally, the Iroquois and other Native Americans did not use wampum as money, a practice that was begun by the Dutch and adopted by the English because the colonies lacked any other readily available form of legal tender. For a time in the seventeenth century, students at Harvard even paid their tuition in wampum.

In an August 1, 1988 *Newsday* business section story, Daniel Kahn described the efforts of Drossman, Lehman, Marino on behalf of Amerinda, including creation of the print advertisement and poster, as well as a public-service video spot on the same theme. The story noted that the agency, which usually accepts only multi-million dollar accounts from corporate clients, did this public service campaign on a budget of $10,000.[27] A brief piece in the business section of the *New York Times* observed: "Although it is still considered a controversial theory in educational circles, the idea that our Founding Fathers were inspired in creating our Constitution by the ancient Iroquois Confederacy is presented as fact in a new public-service advertising campaign . . ."[28]

Late in 1988, news reports described efforts by Gerald F. Heath, an owner of New Day Productions (a film company), who was said to be trying to get

President Reagan to endorse a project "to teach students of all ages about the Iroquois Confederacy of Nation's [sic] influence on the U.S. Constitution."[29] *Forgotten Founders* played no part in this effort, and I never met Mr. Heath. I did meet a half-dozen other independent filmmakers during the middle and late 1980s who were drawn to the subject of influence. All had good intentions, but none of them was able to raise the kind of money necessary to produce a documentary film.

Time and again, filmmakers took the influence idea to the National Endowment for the Humanities, whose officious minions sent their proposals to their "Indian experts," many of whom we knew well by this time as Trolls. The reviews were not signed, but by 1988 we knew who had written them—the same folks spinning the same phrases in blind review after blind review for the academic presses that had rejected *Forgotten Founders* a few years earlier.

To an academic, the strategy of the Trolls was obvious. With channels of publication and diffusion blocked for the influence idea, its advocates not only encountered personal frustration, but professional problems as well. Professors without publications in the appropriate places generally do not get tenure, not to mention citations by other authors. By the late 1980s, some breaks were appearing in this dam of misinformation (such as the Cornell Conference), but access to most scholarly journals, grant funds, and other necessities of academic research remained largely closed. In fact, when I went through tenure review in 1988, two of the eight people voting on my case rejected me on grounds that my work was not appearing in the proper places, although I had published three books by that time.

The most serious attempt at making a film devoted to the idea was mounted by Phil Lucas. In the late 1980s, as the idea was being raised in the context of the constitutional bicentennial, Phil and his associate Michael Korolenko produced an inch-thick application for NEH plus a full hour of video script, along with a request for $400,000 to finish the project. Reviewers for NEH asserted that "no reputable historian, ethnohistorian, or anthropologist believes the contention that the Constitution is in any sense an imitation of the Iroquois League."[30]

The influence idea continued to spread despite the denial of government funding. Millions of schoolchildren were exposed to the idea in late 1988 through *Junior Scholastic*, which carried an article by Ira Peck (with artwork by John Kahionhes Fadden) titled "The People of the Longhouse."[31] The article described Iroquois governance and its effect on the colonists, especially Benjamin Franklin. Ross Garon also contributed a piece on "Native American Contributions to Society" to *Scholastic Update*, a publication aimed at teachers. The Iroquois Confederacy was described briefly, along with its effects on Benjamin Franklin from the Albany Plan to the Constitutional Convention.[32] At about the same time, a third-grade class at Weller Elementary School, Fairbanks, Alaska, under the direction of Mrs. Eleanor Heacock was assembling "The Haudenosaunee (Iroquois), the Colonists and the U.S. Constitution," a class project.

Toni Truesdale, the United Indians of Delaware Valley, and other sponsors organized "We Desire to Sit under the Same Tree of Peace . . . ," a conference in Philadelphia that ran from April 29 through May 2, 1988.[33] This was the first of several events in Philadelphia that provided a forum for the influence thesis. Truesdale had attended the Cornell conference, and it was at her house that Don Grinde and I first came to know each other personally. We met over her kitchen table two years in a row; shortly thereafter, we decided to collaborate on the book that became *Exemplar of Liberty*. As two scholars plying the same general turf, we had to decide whether we should cooperate or compete. We decided that, based on everything history had taught us, we ought to cooperate.

At a second conference in Philadelphia, during May of 1989, I met Eleanor M. Herbert, a National Park Service ranger at Independence Park, Philadelphia. Ms. Herbert had waged a campaign to have Native American contributions to democracy observed at the national urban park in Philadelphia, which includes Independence Hall. She also sought to have *Forgotten Founders* sold in the park bookstore, and succeeded, for a time, until her superiors ordered the book removed.

The fall of 1988 found me in Vermillion, South Dakota, after a short flight on a very small airplane which hopped over farm fields from Omaha. I delivered a presentation at "The Living Constitution," a conference at the University of South Dakota. I also met briefly with Warren Burger, retired Chief Justice of the U.S. Supreme Court and chairman of the U.S. Bicentennial Commission. He was the conference's keynote speaker. I approached him after the keynote speech, and offered a copy of *Forgotten Founders*. He was interested enough to stay up late the same night reading it. We were both staying at the Super 8 Motel. As it happened, we checked out at about the same time. Justice Burger walked rapidly down the hall and asked me to stop—he wanted to tell me how much he appreciated the new knowledge. He asked me to sign the book I had given him, and gave me a signed legal monograph of his own in return.

The influence idea began to appear in a number of general texts and anthologies during the late 1980s.[34] The idea appeared, for example, in a Canadian social studies textbook for middle school students, Adrian Seaborne and David Evans' *Canada and its Pacific Neighbours* (1989). The Great Law of Peace and the U.S. Constitution are compared.[35] The text quotes Canassatego's speech on July 4, 1744. The Iroquois League also is listed as one of five "Major World Peacekeeping Organizations and Agreements," with Pax Romana, the Geneva Convention, the League of Nations, and the United Nations.[36] The authors quote from the Great Law of Peace and the Constitution of the United Nations to show similarities.[37]

By the late 1980s, observations of Native American democracy were becoming standard Thanksgiving fare in some newspapers. In a piece titled "Pass the Turkey . . . and the Medicine, and the Laws . . . " in the *Los Angeles Times*, Johnny P. Flynn wrote:

> Both the French and American revolutions were advanced, in part, because colonists had seen, in Indian forms of government, how the democratic structure functioned when people elected leaders who debated issues in public forums. But scholars here and abroad still resist the conclusion that the Iroquois Great Law of Peace somehow contributed to the U.S. Constitution, the Bill of Rights, the bicameral legislature and the separation of powers. . . . Friedrich Engels wrote in 1879 that The Communist Manifesto "would have been far different" had he and Karl Marx known what they later learned about Indian forms of government.[38]

In July 1990, an article in the *Syracuse Herald-American* quoted Grinde regarding attendance of Iroquois at debates over the Declaration of Independence, as well as references to the Iroquois government in John Adams's *Defence of the Constitutions*. The article also described Native American concepts of federalism. In rebuttal to Grinde, Jan Wojcik, humanities professor at Clarkson University, Potsdam, New York, was quoted as saying "The evidence is flimsy at best. . . . [Franklin] was contemptuous of the Iroquois and referred to them as savages"—entirely missing the irony of Franklin's statement.[39]

In a November 1990 address during National Indian Heritage Month, Interior Secretary Manuel Lujan said, "When it came time to set up a government that has lasted for more than 200 years, we did not hesitate to borrow in part from a pattern that was working well for the Iroquois Nation."[40]

Eight days later, the influence issue came up in a *USA Today* debate over the banning of peyote. In light of laws that until 1994 banned use of drugs (such as peyote) in Native American religious rituals, Patrick Cox asserted, "It is ironic that the Articles of Confederation, the foundation of our Constitution, was based explicitly on the rules of the Iroquois Confederation. It is more ironic that so few people know it."[41] Also in *USA Today*, a short piece described "How the Indians Solve Their Problems":

> *Contrary to most movies and television, Indians have a proud history, not all primitive savagery. We borrowed from the Iroquois Confederation for our own Constitution. Today we can learn from the traditional Indian reverence for the land. We need to help preserve Indian culture.*[42]

By 1988, the influence thesis was being sucked into the giant rhetorical maw created by the nationwide debate over "multiculturalism" in school curricula. In the *Washington Post*, Charles Krauthammer, a conservative commentator, made a case against curricular reforms such as those adopted in the late 1980s at Stanford. Krauthammer bemoaned "the fact that Stanford emasculated its core curriculum in Western civilization . . . [in favor of] . . . 'cultural diversity' . . ." Bill King, a student leader of a protest there, was reported by Krauthammer to have said, among other things, that established college curricula ignore the fact that "the Iroquois Indians in America had a representative democracy which served as a model for the American system." Krauthammer scoffed at the assertion. Grinde wrote to the *Post*, citing the debt of American government to Iroquois precedents.[43]

Meanwhile, the idea was being aired in an international forum. Raul Manglapus, Philippine Foreign Secretary, challenged the industrial world's assumptions about its primacy in the theory of democracy at a ministerial meeting of the 21-nation Council of Europe in Strasborg, Germany. "The democratic value that is the heart of the constitution of the Council of Europe is indigenous not only to the northern societies, but to all human cultures . . ." Manglapus said, according to this account, "citing democratic republics like Licchavis, developed on the Indian subcontinent, 600 years before Christ, [and] the Iroquois Confederacy that preceded the United States Constitution . . ."[44]

In Oneida, Wisconsin, the Oneida Tribe of Indians observed the bicentennial of the signing of the United States Constitution to call attention to contributions of Native Americans to the document. The tribe held a Great Tree of Peace ceremony May 18, 1988 at the Norbert Hill Center in Oneida.[45] On August 26, 1988, more than 20,000 people gathered in Baltimore for one of the largest pow-wows on the East Coast. Barry Richardson, chairman of the pow-wow committee, said, "American Indians also celebrate the formation of the U.S. Constitution, which, he said, contains Indian principles such as initiative, recall, referendum, and equal suffrage."[46]

In the marketplace of ideas, however, not everyone was buying the idea that the Iroquois and other Native American democracies had played an important role in shaping the United States political system. In 1989, the academic debate over the issue that José Barreiro had proposed was about to begin in earnest as the Trolls mounted a counterattack.

NOTES

1. Bruce E. Johansen, "Philosopher as Savage: Benjamin Franklin and the Iroquois," *Northeast Indian Quarterly* 4, no. 3 (Fall 1987): 21–28.

2. "Iroquois Constitution: A Forerunner to Colonists['] Democratic Principles," *New York Times*, June 28, 1987, 40.

3. Allotment, implemented nationally in 1887, split up communal Indian land-holdings and allotted small areas (usually 80 to 160 acres) to Anglo-American-style nuclear families. The balance of the tribal lands, up to 90 percent in many cases, were then thrown open for non-Indian settlement. "Termination" was passed by Congress in 1953 to buy out title to entire Indian nations, so that they would cease to exist legally.

4. Elizabeth Shogren, United Press International, August 20, 1987. In LEXIS.

5. "Celebration Planned Here for Constitution's Bicentennial," *Cornell Chronicle* 19, no. 3 (September 10, 1187): 1, 7.

6. José Barreiro, *Indian Roots of American Democracy* (Ithaca, N.Y.: Cornell American Indian Program, 1988). This book went through several printings as *Northeast Indian Quarterly* split into *Akwe:kon Journal* and *Native Americas*.

7. José Barreiro, "Commentary," *Northeast Indian Quarterly* (Fall 1988): 52. See also, Barreiro, "The Iroquois Influence: Cornell Conference Showed Ties to U.S. Constitution," *Syracuse Post-Standard*, October 12, 1988, A–11.

8. Andrew L. Yarrow, "Weekender Guide," *New York Times*, September 11, 1987, C–1. See also: "Arts Scene," *Christian Science Monitor*, August 20, 1987, 22. As it had been by the Bread and Puppet Theatre in New York, the influence idea was later utilized by the In the Heart of the Beast Puppet and Mask Theatre's "alternative look at pre-and-post-Columbus America" in Minneapolis. A reviewer called this children's puppet show "devilishly witty and seductively charming." The show develops American history from a non-European point of view, taking its audience through history, illustrating Native American civilizations that "are anything but savage and often quite creative and complex—the Iroquois experimented with democracy long before royal Europe thought of it."

9. Dan Andrews, "City Officials Pay Tribute to 'the Great Experiment,'" United Press International, September 17, 1987.

10. "From One Sovereign People to Another," *National Geographic* (September, 1987): 370–373.

11. Jonathan Ferziger, "Special Constitution Package," United Press International, August 25, 1987, in *LEXIS*.

12. Harold Faber, "Indian History Alive at New York Site," *New York Times*, July 26, 1987, 36.

13. Jerry Fresia, *Toward an American Revolution: Exposing the Constitution and Other Illusions* (Boston: South End Press, 1988), 75–76.

14. Charles L. Mee, *The Genius of the People* (New York: Harper & Row, 1987), 237.

15. John Denvir, "A Book for the Bork Debate," review of Mee, *The Genius of the People*, in *Los Angeles Times*, September 20, 1987, 16.

16. Jeffrey St. John, "Constitutional Journal," *Christian Science Monitor*, July 24, 1987, 28.

17. Hanni Woodbury, *et al.*, trans., *Concerning the League: The Iroquois League Tradition as Dictated by John Arthur Gibson* (Syracuse: Syracuse University Press, 1993).

18. Walter F. Naedele, "An American Constitution Much Older Than 200 Years," *Philadelphia Inquirer*, May 7, 1987.

19. Correspondence, Sally Smith to John Kahionhes Fadden, October 1, 1987. Copy in author's files.

20. Senate Concurrent Resolution 76, September 16, 1987, 100th Congress, First Session. Copy in author's files.

21. Marybeth Farrell, untitled States News Service dispatch, September 30, 1988.

22. Marybeth Farrell, untitled States News Service dispatch, September 22, 1988.

23. Don Tewkesbury, "NW Tribes Angry at Reagan's Remark," *Seattle Post-Intelligencer*, June 1, 1988, A–9.

24. Robert W. Venables, "Reagan Remarks Insult Native Americans," letter to the editor, *New York Times*, June 23, 1988, A–22.

25. Bruce Johansen, "President's Remarks Showed Ignorance of the Past," *Alliance* [Nebraska] *Times-Herald*, June 20, 1988; see also *Omaha World-Herald*, June 16, 1988, 19.

26. *Advertising Age*, "Global Gallery: Creative Advertising from Around the World," October 10, 1988.

27. Daniel Kahn, "Agency Takes Up Challenge for Free," *Newsday*, August 1, 1988, 5.

28. Philip H. Dougherty, "American Indian Group Sponsors Ad Campaign," *New York Times*, July 27, 1988, D–18.

29. Maybeth Farrell, States News Service, October 26, 1988. In LEXIS.

30. Letter, Holly Tank, program officer, NEH, to Phil Lucas, president, Native Images, Inc., August 15, 1989.

31. Ira Peck, "The People of the Longhouse," *Junior Scholastic*, October 21, 1988, 12–14.

32. Ross Garon, "Pow Wow! Native American Indians' Contributions to Society," *Scholastic Update*, May 26, 1989, 4.

33. Howard Goodman, "An Age-old Ceremony of Peace for the Planet," *Philadelphia Inquirer*, May 2, 1989, B–1, B–2.

34. One example was Robert D. Marcus and David Burner, *America Firsthand: Readings in American History* (New York: St. Martin's Press, 1989). This book of historical readings included one from Elias Johnson, a Tuscarora sachem. The preface to Johnson's statement declares: "When the first European settlers reached North America, they encountered people who themselves had complex values and traditions." The authors cite the Iroquois Confederacy as an example and go on to say that it was able to create an effective confederacy without sacrificing tribal autonomy. The idea was briefly described in a political science textbook, Lowi and Ginsburg's *American Government: Freedom and Power* (1990), which states that "at least one clear link" indicates that Iroquois ideas were incorporated into Euro-American political philosophy—the 1754 Albany conference and Franklin's Albany Plan. (Theodore J. Lowi and Benjamin Ginsburg, *American Government: Freedom and Power* [New York: W.W. Norton, 1990].) Ironically, the authors' major cited source was Elisabeth Tooker's essay on the Iroquois in *The Handbook of North American Indians*. The discussion in this textbook is marred by a mangled spelling of "Seneca" as "Secca."

35. Adrian Seaborne and David Evans, *Canada and Its Pacific Neighbours*, (Edmonton, Alberta: Weigl Educational Publishers Ltd., 1989), 154.

36. Seaborne and Evans, *Canada and Its Pacific Neighbours*, 161.

37. Seaborne and Evans, *Canada and Its Pacific Neighbours*, 173.

38. Johnny P. Flynn, "Pass the Turkey . . . and the Medicine, the Laws . . . ," *Los Angeles Times*, op-ed pages, November 23, 1989, B–11.

39. Mike Hendricks, "Does Constitution Copy Confederacy?" Associated Press in *Syracuse Herald-American*, July 18, 1990.

40. "Interior Kicks Off Indian Month Celebration," *Indian News: Week in Review* 14, no. 13 (Washington, D.C.: Department of Interior, Bureau of Indian Affairs, November 2, 1990): 2.

41. Patrick Cox, "Banning Peyote Use Would Be Injustice." *USA Today*, November 10, 1989, 14–A.

42. "How the Indians Solve Their Problems," *USA Today*, February 9, 1989, 8–A. By the late 1980s, some press accounts also were noting the similar uses of the eagle as a national symbol by the United States and the Iroquois Confederacy. In the *St. Petersburg Times*, Gabriel Horn described his new book, *The American Eagle*, which was being considered by the Bush administration as a "gift of state," to be presented to visiting dignitaries. Horn, who writes under the name White Deer of Autumn (which his parents gave him at birth), said of the American Eagle: "Few people know that the Eagle Symbol of the United States of America . . . was originally the symbol of the Ho-de-no-saunee, or Iroquois. . . . [The United States] also borrowed ideas of democracy from the People of the Longhouse." See Tammerlin Drummond, "Inauguration Is Time of Opportunity . . . Native American Writes Poetically of U.S. Emblem," *St. Petersburg Times*, January 20, 1989, 1. In the *Buffalo News*, Richard Huntington, the *News* art critic, began a review of a show by twenty-four Iroquois artists at Niagara University by noting that the United States adopted the eagle that soars over the Iroquois Great Tree of Peace "as its symbol for freedom and democracy." See Richard Huntington, "A View of the World from the Iroquois Perspective," *Buffalo News*, January 11, 1995, Lifestyles, 7.

43. Charles Krauthammer, "A Battle Lost at Stanford," *Washington Post*, April 22, 1988; and Donald A. Grinde, Jr., letter to the editor, *Washington Post*, April 30, 1988.

44. "Philippine Minister Challenges North on Democracy," Interpress Service, May 5, 1988.

45. "Northeast Wisconsin News Briefs," United Press International, May 19, 1988.

46. "Pow Wow Opens in Baltimore," United Press International, August 26, 1988.

4.

To Whom Shall We Listen?

BRUCE E. JOHANSEN

ttacks on the influence thesis began in earnest in 1988, a year after copious publicity had been created by mention of the idea in association with the bicentennial of the Constitution, as well as the conference at Cornell, and the U.S. Senate resolution acknowledging an Iroquois role in the establishment of democracy in the United States.

We were being joined in a debate regarding a specific issue, and also about the general ground rules of academic and popular debate. What were the standards of fact suitable for admissibility in the court of public and scholarly opinion? We would encounter many instances of abusive argumentation—the *reductio ad absurdum* tactics, appeal to authority, *ad hominen* attacks, and paternalism mentioned earlier. The fervor of the debate would also spread awareness and curiosity about Iroquois and other Native American confederacies' influence on the evolution of democracy: As the debate spilled out of academia into the general public discourse the ensuing debate tested credentials and expertise: old power carefully built and husbanded was challenged by a new way of looking at Native Americans and their history. Briefly stated, it was a test of who would be allowed to talk and who would listen.

The first detailed rebuttal in a scholarly journal was Elisabeth Tooker's lengthy essay in *Ethnohistory*. Tooker alleged that proponents of the thesis believe the founders "copied" the Constitution from the Iroquois League. This obviously was not the case, Tooker found, because U.S. government is based on majority rule, not on unanimous consensus, and U.S. senators are not nominated by their clan mothers. Tooker wrote that the founders were almost entirely ignorant of Iroquois and other native political systems.[1]

Tooker generally used only the scholarly material of anthropology for her analysis, assuming that her discipline was the sole custodian of historical truth. The anthropological record begins in the 1840s with the works of

Henry Lewis Morgan and Henry Schoolcraft, who, it is said, were the first non-Natives to discover that the Iroquois Grand Council comprised fifty seats. This reading of history ignores observations made several decades earlier by many of the United States' founders. Astonishingly, Tooker seemed oblivious to the copious (but not usually "systematic") observations of Thomas Jefferson, Benjamin Franklin, Thomas Paine, John Adams, and others that were recorded during the founding of the United States. Adams described the "fifty families" of the Iroquois in some detail in his *Defence of the Constitutions of the United States*, which was used by delegates to the Constitutional Convention. Jefferson wrote to John Rutledge during August of 1787, "The only condition on earth to be compared with ours is that of the Indians, where they still have less law than we. The Europeans are governments of kites over pigeons."[2] This is but one example of many in which founders of the United States repudiated European authoritarian precedents.

Professor Tooker's analysis, which ignores most of the historical evidence from the founding period in United States history, established to her satisfaction that the influence thesis is "a myth."[3] Her analysis seemed to settle the question also for the editors of *Ethnohistory,* and for James Clifton and James Axtell, who had reviewed her paper before the journal published it. According to Tooker, the "myth" was initiated by a press release issued on Smithsonian letterhead dated March 26, 1936 by ethnologist J. N. B. Hewitt. Having apparently done little research herself, Tooker admitted that she "relied heavily" on *Forgotten Founders* for statements attributing political influence to the Iroquois, while attempting "no consideration of all the questionable interpretations of the data such authors as Johansen and Grinde make . . ."[4]

Tooker was skeptical that the founders knew much about the League of the Iroquois and then failed to acknowledge that Benjamin Franklin's papers clearly show that he attended an Iroquois Condolence ceremony less than nine months before the creation of the Albany Plan of Union. She also failed to address established research by scholars two generations earlier, such as Julian P. Boyd of Princeton University (editor of Franklin's Indian treaties and Thomas Jefferson's papers). In 1942, Boyd asserted that Franklin in 1754 "proposed a plan for the union of the colonies and he found his materials in the great confederacy of the Iroquois."[5] Tooker also ignored a statement by Richard K. Matthews, in *The Politics of Thomas Jefferson,* that in Jefferson's mind, "American Indians . . . provided the empirical model for his political vision."[6] Tooker asserted in her *Ethnohistory* piece that "The idea figures not at all in the standard histories of the Constitution, nor in the documents on which they rest."[7]

At some points in her article, Tooker contradicted historical data. She wrote that the Iroquois League and the United States Constitution are so structurally dissimilar that there is no relationship at all between them. She stated that there is a "lack of resemblance between the forms of government contained in the Albany Plan of Union and in the Articles of Confederation."[8] This statement is not only factually unsubstantiated but also contrary to accepted scholarship and other evidence.[9]

Ethnocentric bias salted Tooker's article from its very first sentence, where she states that the Iroquois Confederacy is only four centuries old. Why four centuries? She doesn't say how she knows this, so we can only suppose that the date coincides with the first mention of the Confederacy in archival records—as if the Confederacy could not have existed without evidence in European archives. Oral history accounts date the birth of the Confederacy much earlier, perhaps as early as 1000 A.D. This is not to argue that archives cannot be trusted, but that to depend on the written record to the exclusion of all else builds a Eurocentric bias into the exploration of our past.

The historical record is much richer, and often more subtle, than the version that Professor Tooker presented. To argue that American Indian polities helped shape our own is not to deny that the Iroquois system (and others) are unique unto themselves. Using Tooker's line of reasoning, the United States' system could not be compared to any other that went before it, since each was unique in its own way. The British "Constitution" is not even written, but that has not kept it from being included in our ideological genealogy. The founders of the United States examined all the examples they could find and fashioned their own.

Professor Tooker asserts that the treaty councils were "of a diplomatic character, hardly concerned with philosophical questions regarding the proper nature of political relationships between men."[10] That Franklin conducted diplomacy with the Iroquois and their allies is undeniable, of course, but it is equally true that the treaty councils provided a vital channel of communication between political opinion leaders of both cultures, and that Franklin and others drew philosophical sustenance from them.

If the idea that the Iroquois and other American Indian political systems provided an inspiration to colonial Americans is a "myth," as Professor Tooker contends, why did so many people utilize such images in so many different ways over such a large geographic area for nearly two centuries before, and, as the Constitution was written? If the Iroquois League was so much less democratic at that time than present-day Iroquois believe, why did so many colonials develop images of it, and other Native confederacies, as exemplars of liberty? If we have so over-romanticized the historical record, why does it brim over with references that agree with our thesis? Professor Tooker offered only a caricature of our argument, not an alternative explanation.

As Tooker's essay was going to press, the influence idea was attacked in the *New Republic*.[11] In the November 7, 1988 issue, Michael Newman mocked the idea (as he phrased it), that the Iroquois' "ancestors guided Madison's hand in writing the Constitution"—a claim that none of the "renegade historians" (as he called us) had made.

Newman went on to characterize an Iroquois ceremony on the Washington Mall as "hokey," and then expected American Indians to believe he was coming out against these ideas for their own good: "All the scholarly and political posturing tends to obscure the problems of modern-day Native Americans."[12] Newman maintained that assertions of Indian influence on the Constitution are a "myth [that] isn't just silly. It's destructive."

Part of what Newman called "political posturing" was the passage of a resolution in late 1987 by the Senate Select Committee on Indian Affairs observing Iroquois and other Native American contributions to democracy. The resolution associated an accurate history of Native contributions with enforcement of treaties, which could build the Native American economic base necessary to solve basic material problems of poverty and unemployment. Newman seemed to have missed the point of the resolution, drafted by Senator Daniel Inouye with Iroquois advice: history and today's material needs cannot be easily divorced.

Shortly after publication of the article by Newman condemning recognition of Native contributions to democracy, an oversimplification of the opposite kind appeared in the *National Enquirer*. Headed "Surprise! We Got Our Constitution from an Indian Tribe," the January 17, 1989 piece by Steve Grenard said: "The men who drew up the United States' Constitution modelled much of the historic document after the constitution of the Iroquois Indians, historians reveal," Grenard wrote, with typical *Enquirer* overstatement.[13]

The *Enquirer* article did contain a couple of historically accurate statements that both Tooker and Newman had missed: one was Thomas Jefferson's assertion (in a letter to Edward Carrington, January 17, 1787) that Indians govern themselves with "a much greater degree of happiness" than Europeans; the other was the fact that John Rutledge of South Carolina referred to the Iroquois Great Law of Peace as he chaired the Constitutional Convention's drafting committee.

To Tooker, Newman, and others who had not been prepared by a thorough study of the historical record, the idea that the political systems of Native American societies helped shape democracy in the United States seemed novel, even nonsensical. Our dominant Eurocentric culture certainly does not prepare us for the belief that our intellectual heritage is a combination of European and indigenous American ideas, nor that "life, liberty, and happiness" have Native American precedents. Some people with doctorates in history and anthropology dismiss the idea out of hand, with only the most cursory examination of the historical record. Although such people should know better than to prejudge the record, or to make up their minds before examining evidence, they are only responding to the perceptual prison their culture has erected around them.

Tooker, Newman, and other critics of the influence idea had a curious habit of assuming expertise they did not possess. *Ipso facto*, if they knew nothing about the influence of the Iroquois system on the aborning United States, evidence was assumed to be nonexistent.

Like Newman, Tooker sought to discredit the thesis by limiting the terms of debate to direct effects solely by the Iroquois only on the Constitution, as a document, and by ignoring nearly two centuries of ideological debates over life, liberty, and happiness from which this and other basic documents sprang. Operating with a woefully incomplete knowledge of history, both ignored the need to explore a larger cognitive map. For example, Newman blasted Donald A. Grinde for trying to tie the Iroquois into the Constitution by saying that a Philadelphia publication in August, 1787 printed a reference to the Iroquois Great Law of Peace which included the phrase "Unite, or die." "But the concept of national unity, it is safe to say, had solidified by that point in American history," Newman wrote. Newman did not mention that Franklin's "unite-or-die" came from the Iroquois sachem Canassatego's advice at Lancaster in 1744. Nor did he mention Franklin's printing of Canassatego's advice, his work as a diplomat to the Iroquois, and the Iroquois contributions to his Albany Plan of 1754.

This is hardly to say that Franklin copied the Iroquois. Thomas Paine, while he greatly admired the Iroquois political system, also acknowledged it could not be copied to govern people of European extraction in America. While it could not be copied, the Indian example could be utilized selectively, much as the founders borrowed from precedents in European antiquity. In fact, Jefferson wrote that Indian polities reminded him of what he believed his ancestors, the Celts, had practiced before the European age of monarchy.

By claiming that proponents thought the Constitution was "copied" from the Great Law of Peace, Newman and Tooker also erected an intellectual straw man, then proceeded to bash its brains out. One person did become a living "straw man," however, and his writings became a further pretext to discredit the thesis. Greg Schaaf framed the influence idea in a simplistic, overstated manner, drawing charges that he was ignoring all European contributions and producing one-sided history. Schaaf's booklet, "The Great Law of Peace and the Constitution of the United States of America," describes the Great Law of Peace, then places it side by side with the U.S. Constitution in an attempt to draw parallels in wording and other content. Instead of presenting what Grinde calls a "mosaic of history," Schaaf has contended that the Great Law was "the model" for the Constitution, and that the United States' founding document diverges from the Great Law only because the founders did not go far enough to emulate the Iroquois model.

Schaaf also advanced his ideas in an article, "From the Great Law of Peace to the Constitution of the United States: A Revision of America's Democratic Roots."[14] Erik M. Jensen, a professor of law at Cleveland's Case Western University, replied to Schaaf's argument, calling it "one of the more extreme presentations of the idea" of Native American influence on American political theory and practice. Jensen commented: "[T]he time for Professor Schaaf's theory has not come and will not come—if we care about historical truth. The proposition is nonsense . . . and recognized as such by nearly all serious historians."[15] Jensen wrote that Schaaf's work lacked primary documentation and was "grounded in quicksand."[16]

Jensen did acknowledge that founders such as Franklin and Jefferson discussed Indians copiously in their writings, and that the Indians influenced their view of natural rights. He rejected Indian influence on the constitution, however: "A people considered to be without law and government, as the founders saw the Indians, can hardly be considered a model for the U.S. Constitution."[17] Jensen was inclined to believe that oral renditions of the Great Law may have adopted the language of the Constitution, rather than the other way around.

In *Being and Becoming Indian* (1989) and *The Invented Indian* (1990),[18] James A. Clifton addressed the influence thesis in rhetorical terms similar to those of Tooker, William Starna, Robert Royal, and James Axtell. *Being and Becoming Indian* refers to the U.S. Senate resolution enunciating Iroquois contributions to American government as a "bizarre revision of history," in response to "a skillful pressure campaign by the national Indian-rights lobby."[19] Those awesomely influential Iroquois had been at it again, feeding a gullible public lies about history, according to Clifton. Claiming "There is not a whit of objective evidence to support this political myth,"[20] Clifton attributed the whole idea to a bunch of hacks and flacks, press-release packing Indians inventing useful political fables. In his rush to condemn the idea out of hand, Clifton cites no scholarly sources that oppose his view. Indeed, he rests his whole analysis on a footnote referring to Tooker's paper, in manuscript draft, calling it "an authoritative study of this invented tradition."[21] According to Clifton's version of historical reality, if Native Americans want to claim historical credit for something, there's always scalping.

At roughly the time he received Tooker's *Ethnohistory* paper for review, Axtell was weighing in on the political influence issue in his *After Columbus: Essays in the Ethnohistory of Colonial North America* (1988), where he discusses various troublesome "myths":

> Another myth that is very much before us during the bicentennial, is that the United States Constitution was closely patterned upon the League of the Iroquois. Each myth contains just enough truth to be plausible, but both are logically and historically fallacious. Should the scholar risk the displeasure of the disabused by constantly and forcefully saying so?[22]

Like the weather forecaster who slips in a 20 percent chance of snow, Axtell is just careful enough to keep his options open: something with "just enough truth to be plausible" could, after all, someday blossom into accepted fact, even if not wholly in the restrictive manner that Axtell defines the debate. He slams the door on that possibility with his ensuing words, however: "historically fallacious" seems a phrase etched in marble with a diamond tip.

Axtell's hint of uncertainty is understandable, given the short list of sources cited in defense of his statement: two of his own publications, a newspaper article from the *New York Times* (June 28, 1987), Tooker's *Ethnohistory* paper in draft form, and an M.A. thesis by a student in the College of William and Mary's History Department, where Axtell teaches. There is not one citation from the founders in the lot. Dr. Axtell did not break his back carrying books out of the library before leaping to the conclusion he trumpeted so "constantly and forcefully."

In *Beyond 1492: Encounters in Colonial North America*, Axtell wrote:

> Early Quincentennial issues of the *Northeast Indian Quarterly* were devoted to "Indian Roots of American Democracy" and "Indian Corn of the Americas: A Gift to the World." These subjects are typical of the "contri-

bution" approach that has been a dominant theme of Native American Studies [sic] since their inception in the late '60s, a phase that all minority studies tend to go through on their way to cultural assurance and self-definition.[23]

Axtell assumed that the Iroquois and other Native people advanced such ideas not because they were historically valid, but solely as a way of defining themselves by European political standards. Further, Axtell stated that studies of Native American contributions to American culture "marginalize their own group by making it conform or 'contribute' to the dominant culture and its standards of importance, rather than assert the integrity and value of their own cultures and histories."[24] By whose definition are these mutually exclusive? And why would Native Americans, who have been oppressed for so long by the United States government, make up a story that their ancestors helped shape the intellectual foundation of that oppressive institution? Axtell touches none of these issues. Instead, he creates his own image of what Native Americans should do and defines their motives for them. Such a position does not argue or debate. It states truths. Axtell, like the *New Republic*'s Michael Newman, cannot resist telling Indians what is good for them.

Woe be to anyone who argues that perhaps the influence idea has historical validity, for Axtell already has discredited that possibility by attributing the idea to Indian academic insecurity. Axtell's paternalistic attitude exemplifies Edward Said's observation (in *Orientalism*, 1978) that Europeans have written "the conquered" out of the "authorized" version of Western intellectual history.

The attacks on the influence thesis in the late 1980s spawned a counterwave of opinion in the years following. Ward Churchill, for example, took issue with Clifton's and Tooker's opinions in *Fantasies of the Master Race*.[25] One of the fantasies, Churchill writes, is that Europeans invented the entire ideological corpus of democracy. Concerning Tooker's participation in the influence debate, Churchill wrote:

> When questioned closely on the matter at a recent academic conference, this expert was forced to admit not only that she had ignored all Iroquois source material while forming her thesis, but that she was [also] quite unfamiliar with the relevant papers of John Adams, Thomas Jefferson, Benjamin Franklin, Tom Paine, and others among the U.S. founders . . .[26]

Vine Deloria, Jr. evaluated Tooker's argument in a review essay on Clifton's *Invented Indian* in *American Indian Quarterly*. Deloria commented:

Some years ago, Bruce Johansen published a little book entitled Forgotten Founders. . . . *A wave of nauseous panic spread through the old-boy's network of Iroquois studies since a commoner had dared to write in a field already dominated by self-appointed experts. Donald Grinde . . . published* The Iroquois and the Founding of the American Nation *[1977], elaborating on this heresy which was becoming an open scandal.*

Damage control measures went into effect, and soon Grinde and Johansen found their NEH grant proposals turned down by readers who emphasized the orthodox interpretation of Iroquois studies. Conservative newspaper columnists, learning of the controversy, promptly marched into historical debates of which they had no knowledge whatsoever and chastised Johansen and Grinde, and proposals by the two scholars to have an open debate over the topic were generally turned aside as if mere physical contact with the two would be a sign of incipient heresy.

Into the fray rode Elisabeth Tooker . . . [who] demonstrated, to her satisfaction, the impossibility of the Six Nations having any relevance at all for American constitutional thinking. Tooker's argument is so wonderfully naïve and anthro-centric that it makes the informed observer of the debate weep for her inability to free herself from the blinders which adherence to anthro[pology] doctrine has required she wear.

Recalling a meeting of the American Anthropological Association at which he and Tooker debated this issue, Deloria wrote that after he contended that John Locke's attempt to set up a landed aristocracy in North Carolina discredited him in the eyes of the colonists, "Tooker bolted into the aisle, shrieking, 'Tell that to your friends! Tell that to your friends!'"

Deloria concluded:

This debate has not really been joined properly because what Johansen and Grinde are saying is simply that considerably more material must be examined before hard and fast conclusions are drawn. Tooker's argument, it seems to me, is simply that materials, and arrangement of these materials which the entrenched scholars of anthropology have amassed, are sufficient to answer all questions regarding the Six Nations—period. The real debate, therefore, is over authority: to whom shall we listen—about anything? Here the credentials of the past, no matter how valiantly won, are just not enough to dominate or close debate on a subject—period.[27]

The contest of ideas that took place in journals and books was occasionally joined face to face. On May 2, 1989, Professor Tooker, who is a professor of anthropology at Temple University in Philadelphia, awoke to see her adversaries on the front page of the local-news section of the *Philadelphia Inquirer*. A news story described Jake Swamp, a traditional Mohawk sachem, planting a great white pine in Penn Treaty Park, as part of a conference that week titled "Forgotten Legacy: Native American Concepts and the Formation of United States Government." It was the second conference on this theme in Philadelphia, and this time there was more than talk and publicity: advocates of the idea were producing a curriculum for the state education department.

The curriculum was discussed the afternoon of the same day during a colloquium at the Atwater-Kent Museum in downtown Philadelphia. Don Grinde and I gave presentations of our work for the curriculum, and Mary Kinnaird reviewed progress on the Haudenosaunee curriculum in New York State. Grinde spoke on how the Iroquois had participated in some of the more important conferences in Philadelphia leading up to the signing of the Declaration of Independence and the writing of the Constitution, citing a rich tapestry of names and dates; I described the use of the American Indian as a national symbol of freedom in revolutionary art, songs, and other forms of late eighteenth-century culture.

After our talks, the floor was opened to questions from the audience. One man asked us to characterize the opposition to these ideas. Grinde talked of the established "Iroquoianists'" refusal to accept facts that had become evident through his examination of archival records—indeed, the "experts'" refusal even to allow Native Americans a role in interpreting their own history. "If this was tried before a group of blacks or Hispanics," he said, "it wouldn't be tolerated."

I said that our opponents seem to believe that whatever they don't know about can't exist. As students of history, I said, we should always be acutely aware that we do not know all there is to know. To research and write history is to discover these things. Believing that nothing new remains to be found, I said, our opponents rely on their own opinionated certitude, rather than a solid grounding in history.

Opposite us, across an array of tables set in a square, an older woman waved her arms emotionally and began to say: "As you know, I am on the other side of this issue." Since I had known Tooker only by her words, until that moment I had no idea that she was rising to a piece of intellectual bait I didn't even know I had cast. Immediately, a leisurely colloquium was transformed into an acerbic exchange of opinions on the issue. For the first time, advocates and opponents of the Native contributions thesis were locking horns face to face.

Grinde continued to cite the historical record in refutation of Tooker's *Ethnohistory* piece. Tooker at one point threw up her hands and exclaimed: "You historians can quote anything [to prove a point]!" She called Grinde's work "history-poo" and Grinde, losing his own temper, replied that Tooker's was "anthropology-poo."

Don and I hesitated to call the exchange a "debate," because Tooker seemed unable to carve out a position of her own. Instead, as she had in her *Ethnohistory* piece, Tooker fell back on her caricature of our position— insisting, for example, that we said the founders copied the Great Law of Peace into the Constitution, instead of addressing our ideas directly. Both of us replied that she ought to confront the real issue: the measure of importance that should be accorded to the Iroquois and other Native confederacies as one significant contributing factor. Compared to Don, I got off rather easily with Tooker. She seemed to acknowledge my analysis of art and symbols such as my belief that the "Mohawk" disguise used at the Boston Tea Party was adopted as a symbol of freedom and American identity. She also did not quarrel with tracing the bundle of thirteen arrows on the United States seal to Canassatego's 1744 speech in which he used a bundle of arrows as a symbol for the strength in confederate union. The problem, said Tooker, was that such symbols don't "prove anything," as if revolutionary symbols were picked at random, without any real thought of what they represented.

The exchange continued well into the evening, until the museum guard told us the room had to close. As she walked out the door, Tooker picked up a stack of conference posters (by John Kahionhes Fadden) depicting a meeting of Iroquois sachems and many of the most prominent founders in Independence Hall, a few blocks from the site of the colloquium. It was at this meeting on June 11, 1776, as independence was being debated, that an Onondaga chief gave John Hancock the name Karanduawn, or "Great Tree." Conference participants speculated all evening over what she did with the posters.

In the late 1980s, annual meetings of the American Society for Ethnohistory (ASE) became a forum for the debate, with the opponents arrayed against supporters. At the 1988 meeting of the ASE, in Williamsburg, Virginia, a preliminary conference schedule included a panel, "The Enduring Iroquois," at which Elisabeth Tooker presented a paper based on her 1988 article in *Ethnohistory*. Grinde was listed as a discussant for this panel, but was removed after conference organizer James Axtell said he could not find Grinde (who was doing research in the Washington, D.C. area) to confirm. When the final version of the program appeared early in the fall, Grinde's name was missing. He said he had been stiffed: issued an invitation that he never got, stricken from the program without his knowledge, then called a "coward" because he didn't appear. Axtell wrote Grinde on December 6, 1988, telling him: "Don't get your pants in a bunch. You seem to take umbrage at every breath a non-Indian scholar takes these days. Lighten up: there's no conspiracy and no affronts intended."

At about the same time, Grinde and his family were concluding a research trip on the East Coast and driving cross-country to San Luis Obispo. I had no trouble reaching him. As for umbrage at "every breath a non-Indian scholar takes," Axtell seemed to have forgotten that Grinde's coauthor is as white as the wind-driven snow of Scandinavia. Axtell's slap at Grinde's purported racism seemed wholly gratuitous.

At the 1988 ASE meeting, without Grinde present, Tooker was reported to have discussed Grinde's *Iroquois and the Founding of the American Nation* and my *Forgotten Founders*. According to a report in *Akwesasne Notes,* she said that Grinde's book contained only three primary references and that my work was "of poor quality."[28] "No serious scholar believes that the Iroquois influenced the U.S. government," Tooker said. "Only the bicentennial of the Constitution has brought attention to this."[29] When Grinde protested Axtell's removal of him from the 1988 program, he was invited to organize a panel at the next year's ASE convention, to be held in November, 1989 in Chicago.

The annual autumnal meetings of the Iroquois Research Conference also became a forum for discussion of Iroquois political practices and their effects on colonial society.

The debate was fully and formally joined for the first time on October 16, 1989 at the Iroquois Studies Conference near Albany, New York. Usually an event about but hardly for the Iroquois and other Native peoples, the 1989 conference was attended not only by the usual anthropologists and ethnohistorians, but also by a number of Iroquois people, who had previously been excluded. The result was an unusually lively exchange of opinions and an indication that the usual patrons of this conference had moved from outright denial of the influence thesis to absorbing, if still quite skeptical, interest.

An effort to open this conference to Native participation had begun in 1987, as Sally Roesch Wagner, who was studying the Iroquois impact on nineteenth-century feminism, worked out a strategy with Grinde. She recalled:

I wrote to Tooker asking that we have a sneak preview of the Ethnohistory panel at the Iroquois Conference, [asking that she] invite Grinde, and then kept on her. She was reluctant. We essentially "integrated" a conference that one of the planners allegedly said [should keep out] "Indians and amateur archaeologists" so that they could have true discussions.[30]

During this conference, Grinde spent nearly four hours in front of an audience that included most of the idea's harshest critics. At the Iroquois Studies Conference, Tooker was less personal in her comments than she had been during the impromptu confrontation in Philadelphia five months earlier. According to Grinde, she "tried to stick to the facts. She said 'I would love more than anything to teach this in my courses, but there isn't enough proof.'"[31] Tooker did recant her earlier assertion that no evidence exists after 1775 on which to argue that the Iroquois helped shape the United States Constitution. After the question-and-answer session, Tooker sought out Grinde at supper, and they discussed their differing approaches.

John Kahionhes Fadden, who watched Grinde's presentation, later wrote, "I take off my hat to Don Grinde. He stood here like a Lakota Dog Soldier with his academic lance driven into the earth . . ."[32] Grinde said the experience, a "trip into the 'lion's den,' . . . was not so bad. How many people can say that the question-and-answer session of their paper was three hours long, and it had a coffee break? We now know that they recognize that they have to deal with these ideas and facts."

Following Grinde's presentation, the debate was joined again before microphones offered by National Public Radio reporter Catherine Stifter, who interviewed several of the participants, questioning Grinde and the influence ideas' major antagonists extensively.

During his interview, William Starna began with a plea for examination of historical evidence in what he called a "scientific inquiry." Within a couple of sound-bites, however, he initiated a little intellectual mud-wrestling: "I'm afraid that the argument that Grinde's making is that the earth is flat." Starna likened the idea of Native influence on United States governmental institutions to the "story of Washington chopping down the cherry tree. It's about at that level."[33] Calling Grinde's work "awful history," motivated largely by the traditional Iroquois chiefs' desire for power, Starna continued:

"I think that if you brought in a class of undergraduates with majors in history, they would see the fallacy in what Grinde is doing, without even having to know the information, without even having to look at the documents" (emphasis added).[34]

In other words, as long as the students had been properly biased to begin with, they wouldn't need to trouble themselves with historical fact!

Later in the interview, Starna demoted Grinde's research from "awful history" to "simply not history" at all: "What would I call it? I thought his presentation this afternoon was surrealism. I heard a very glitzy, erudite-sounding individual who concluded something and then went out to look for the evidence."[35]

As Starna continued to contend that "no good evidence" existed to support the influence idea, I could only smile. Professor Starna had long ago fallen behind in the reading required of anyone who wanted to carry on an informed debate on this subject. Several hundred pages of documentation and as many footnotes had emerged since I first tested my own naiveté on Dr. Tooker in the late 1970s. Dr. Starna seemed like the poor sailor who wrapped an anchor around his leg before the tide came in. The ocean of evidence was up to his eyeballs by 1990, and he was still denying that he was wet.

Axtell took issue with the whole notion of influence of any kind. To contend influence, rather than cause and effect, is to do "weasel history," said Axtell. "The problem in intellectual history is that 'influence' is a word used to cover up lack of tight evidence. We've known for a long time in historiography that those are weasel words."[36] Axtell seemed in search of a "smoking gun," rather than a mosaic of historical evidence. If we could make our goose lay what Axtell regards as a single, very large golden egg, he might be impressed. Short of that, Axtell seems ready to ignore the whole idea. If and when such a golden egg comes into his intellectual pantry, Axtell indicated he would prize it: "I would love [the advocates of influence] to be right . . . it would be the best news since sliced bread."[37]

While Axtell said he would like to see the influence argument sustained, he outlined beliefs that would make it very difficult for him to accept such an argument without major surgery on assumptions that determine his view of history:

> We did not emulate the Indians so much as we formed our character against the Indians, by fighting them as enemies. I think there's very little intellectual debt to the Indian. They [the founders] were trying to build a very European-style civilization in this neck of the woods.[38]

In fact, the historical gospel according to James Axtell has the Iroquois smuggling ideas from the United States Constitution into the Great Law of Peace after an outline of it was first written in English by Seth Newhouse in the late nineteenth century. "The influence worked almost exactly the opposite from the way these people are arguing," Axtell told Stifter. He made this statement without qualification, and without evident factual (or even argumentative) support, offering no eggs to scramble, much less golden ones.

Furthermore, Axtell seemed to be wearing something of a racial chip on his white, male shoulders. "Frankly," he said, "some of us poor little white academics sitting in our little white ivory towers are jealous of the access that some of the Onondaga leaders and some of these so-called pro-Indian historians have had."[39] Axtell infers that such Indians and historians contribute to "lies passed off as history." He continued: "We'll be fighting this myth for bloody ever, with very little hope of expunging it totally."[40] So, is he in the market for a golden egg, or is he looking for a "final solution" that will permanently cleanse the public and historical mind of such notions? One wonders.

Among Axtell's galaxy of assumptions is one that assumes white, male historians have some inherent advantages over those of other races and gender. "There are very few Indian scholars who know the documentation of their past. . . . They don't know what it [was] like to [have been] an Indian in the seventeenth century," Axtell told Stifter. Besides, they carry perceptual baggage that attaches them to their "subject," the word Axtell used in the interview to describe his relationship with the Iroquois he studies. As a white man, Axtell seems to infer that he has the proper "professional and scholarly distance" to carry out a search for historical truth. Perish the thought that Axtell himself might hold cultural and ideological assumptions that prejudice and otherwise shape his particular view of history. "You know," Axtell told the radio network interviewer, "I think I have a better shot at getting at the truth about this constitutional issue because . . . I'm neither a descendant of a founding father [nor of] the Iroquois."[41]

At the November, 1989 meeting of the ASE in Chicago, Sally Wagner, Donald Grinde, and I met for the first time as a group, and suggested forming an informal scholarly network. Sally contributed the name "Coyote Collective" as we walked from an elevated railway stop to the lake-front Day's Inn during a light snow.[42]

Our panel took place on the nineteenth floor of the Day's Inn. In a room with a panoramic view of Lake Michigan and the downtown skyline, protagonists and antagonists on the influence issue met again in a panel entitled "Iroquois Influences on American Life." Grinde had twenty minutes to describe Iroquois influences on American government, followed by an equal amount of time for Wagner to discuss ways in which the Iroquois' matrilineal society shaped the vision of nineteenth-century feminists such as Matilda Joslyn Gage and Elizabeth Cady Stanton. Professor Tooker followed in rebuttal with a presentation entitled "The Iroquois League and the United States Constitution Revisited." Alice Kehoe of Marquette University provided commentary, and I then had fifteen minutes to summarize.

Perhaps forty people attended the session, which entertained questions from the audience for about forty-five minutes after the scheduled presentations. The audience included most of the noteworthy opponents of the influence thesis—Starna and Axtell among them. Unlike the marathon session at the Iroquois Studies Conference, the audience seemed rather subdued at this panel, with most of the debate taking place between panelists.

"There is absolutely no question of the importance of Indians in colonial history," Tooker told the audience. "And there is no question Indians have been used as a symbol by white Americans. I don't want to argue those issues." Without admitting it, Tooker was backing off some of the assertions in her earlier paper in *Ethnohistory*. As the scope of Tooker's knowledge expanded by checking sources we had provided her, however, she rushed to condemn our work as incomplete.

At the same time, Tooker sometimes seemed confused, as her preconceived notions about the primacy of European thought and values ran headlong into historical data she could not honestly ignore. At one point, she said: "I'm sure there's an influence somehow, but I am not sure we yet have it . . . someone has to do it. I'm not. I have other fish to fry." She seemed to contradict herself by saying, "We are driven to this conclusion [that the Iroquois did not help shape democracy] by the fact that they had a council of hereditary chiefs. Such ideas as freedom and democracy are Western [European] notions." To believe otherwise, she inferred, was to stumble over "common white misconceptions of Indian governments."

If concepts of freedom and democracy are so purely Western in origin, why did they blossom after Europeans discovered the New World and its societies? Why did these same Europeans so often use the image of the Indian, particularly the Iroquois, as an exemplar of the liberty they so cherished, and why did they so often use the imagery of the Native nations in their discussions of government?

As the two sides met in face-to-face debate during the late 1980s, the battle over influence was opening a new front in a sharp debate over an educational resource guide being developed by the Iroquois for the State of New York. A phalanx of Trolls were asked to review the curriculum. Some suggested it be killed, inferring that they knew the Iroquois' history better than the Indians themselves. Quite without intention on our part, the idea that the Iroquois Great Law helped shape longstanding democratic traditions was about to become a primary exhibit in what some conservatives would come to call the "culture war" over multiculturalism in American schools. One of the main battles in this "war" would be fought over the Curriculum of Inclusion in New York State.

NOTES

1. Elisabeth Tooker, "The United States Constitution and the Iroquois League," *Ethnohistory* 35, no. 4 (Fall 1988): 311: "Not until Lewis H. Morgan made it a special subject of study and published his findings did an account of the Iroquois form of government become available."

2. Jefferson to Rutledge, August 6, 1987, in Julian Boyd, ed., *The Papers of Thomas Jefferson,* vol. 11 (Princeton: Princeton University Press, 1950–1974), 701.

3. Tooker, "Constitution," 321.

4. Tooker, "Constitution," 330.

5. Julian Boyd, "Meet Dr. Franklin: Friend of the Indian," in *Meet Dr. Franklin,* Roy Lokken, ed. (Philadelphia: Franklin Institute, 1981), 239. Dr. Boyd, who taught history at Princeton University for two decades, acted as president of the American Historical Association in 1964 and presided over the American Philosophical Society between 1973 and 1976.

6. Richard K. Matthews, *The Radical Politics of Thomas Jefferson* (Lawrence: University Press of Kansas, 1984), 122.

7. Tooker, "Constitution," 306.

8. Tooker, "Constitution," 321.

9. Paul Smith, ed., *Letters of the Delegates to Congress,* Washington, D.C.: Government Printing Office, 1976, 4:99, 281. On June 11, 1776, Smith observes that plans for a confederation based on Franklin's 1754 plan of union were formulated in a committee of Congress and that the "4th, 7th, 8th and 12th of Franklin's Thirteen Articles are conspicuously incorporated into the committee's work." As an anthropologist, Tooker entered the debate on the Iroquois roots of American government without having a mastery of the factual data in the *Journals of the Continental Congress,* the *Letters of the Delegates,* and the *Papers of the Continental Congress.*

10. Tooker, "Constitution", 311.

11. Michael Newman, "The Iroquois and the Constitution: Founding Feathers," *New Republic,* November 7, 1988, 17–18.

12. Newman, "Founding Feathers," 17–18. For a more balanced report on the Iroquois tree-planting at the National Mall, which Michael Newman dismissed as "hokey," see Marybeth Farrell's reporting for State's News Service. She quoted Oren Lyons, Onondaga faithkeeper, and Grinde in support of the influence thesis, and Walter F. Berns, Georgetown University professor and author, against.

13. Steve Grenard, "Surprise! We Got Our Constitution from an Indian Tribe," *National Enquirer*, January 17, 1989, 36.

14. *American Indian Law Review* 14 (1989).

15. Erik M. Jensen, "The Imaginary Connection between the Great Law of Peace and the United States Constitution: A Reply to Professor Schaaf," *American Indian Law Review* 15, no. 2 (1991): 297.

16. Jensen, "Imaginary Connection," 301.

17. Jensen, "Imaginary Connection," 304.

18. James A. Clifton, *Being and Becoming Indian: Biographical Studies of North American Frontiers* (Chicago: Dorsey Press, 1989); and James A. Clifton, ed., *The Invented Indian: Cultural Fictions and Government Policies* (New Brunswick: Transaction Publishers, 1990).

19. Clifton, *Being and Becoming Indian*, 2.

20. Ibid., 2.

21. Ibid., 2.

22. James Axtell, *After Columbus: Essays in the Ethnohistory of Colonial North America* (New York: Oxford University Press, 1988), 252.

23. James Axtell, *Beyond 1492: Encounters in Colonial North America* (New York: Oxford University Press, 1992), 285–86.

24. Axtell, *Beyond 1492*, 285–86.

25. Ward Churchill, *Fantasies of the Master Race: Literature, Cinema, and the Colonization of American Indians* (Monroe, Me.: Common Courage Press, 1992).

26. Churchill, *Fantasies of the Master Race*, 168.

27. Vine Deloria, Jr. "Comfortable Fictions and the Struggle for Turf: An Essay Review of [James Clifton's] *The Invented Indian: Cultural Fictions and Government Policies* [1990]. *American Indian Quarterly* (Summer 1992), 402–4.

28. "Williamsburg Conference[:] Anthropologists Challenge Confederacy," *Akwesasne Notes* 21, no. 2 (Spring 1989): 18.

29. "Williamsburg Conference."

30. Letter, Sally Roesch Wagner to Bruce Johansen, August 23, 1995.

31. Letter, Donald A. Grinde, Jr. to Vine Deloria, Jr., October 25, 1989.

32. Letter, John Kahionhes Fadden to Bruce Johansen, October 17, 1989.

33. Catherine Stifter, radio transcripts, October 14–15, 1989, supplied to Grinde October 26, 1989, p. 3.

34. Stifter, radio transcripts, 15.

35. Ibid., 17–18.

36. Ibid., 28.

37. Ibid., 31.

38. Ibid., 29–30.

39. Ibid., 31.

40. Ibid., 33.

41. Ibid., 34.

42. At the same conference, Axtell provided some revealing insights into the way he regards Native peoples during his presidential address at the ASE meeting. Over lunch atop the Days Inn on Chicago's Lakeshore Drive, Axtell addressed what he called "humor in ethnohistory," including anecdotes about white men wondering whether Indian women had "fur" between their legs, the musical intonations of Native farts, and accounts of Indians given hoes for farming, only to wear them around their necks.

5.

"A Horror Story
of Political Correctness"

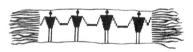

BRUCE E. JOHANSEN

When I began exploring the idea that the Iroquois Great Law helped shape ideas of the United States' founding generation, I had no idea that I was about to offend the cream of established anthropology in New York State. A decade later, I ambled naively into another mass of intellectual brambles in the same state, involving many of the same people. It was part of what a cadre of conservative critics came to call "the culture war," which would help to determine what the next generation will learn about history in school. During this "culture war," the idea of Iroquois influence on the political genesis of the United States became a flashpoint in a larger debate regarding multicultural education and "political correctness." The idea offended some prominent people, among them Patrick Buchanan, who tended to use the idea of Iroquois influence to symbolize all that he thought was wrong with American education in the late twentieth century. He was not alone.

The debate over different interpretations of history flashed intensely through the reviews written by both Coyotes and Trolls of a proposed New York State Education Department (SED) curriculum guide titled, "Haudenosaunee: Past, Present, Future." ("Haudenosaunee," the traditional name of the Iroquois, is pronounced *ho-de-no-sho-nee*.) The guide, written by a committee of Iroquois, was meant to be part of the New York State "Curriculum of Inclusion" which bedeviled critics of multiculturalism on a national scale. The entire Curriculum of Inclusion had several parts, each meant to redress historical ill-treatment (or nontreatment) of racial and gender minorities in the curricula of New York State's public schools. The Haudenosaunee curriculum was controversial in part because it contained assertions of Iroquois influence on the development of democracy. These assertions had been available to general audiences in books at the college level for several years. In New York State a phalanx of Trolls moved in, arguing that such assertions should be taken out, or the entire project junked. The Trolls, like many conservatives, seemed particularly sensitive when the influence issue filtered into school curricula. The idea seemed to be deemed too prurient for tender young ears.

Professor William A. Starna, chair of anthropology at the State University of New York College at Oneonta, was the most vocal of several "Iroquois experts" on the subject. He contended that "no evidence" existed to support the influence thesis; the idea, he said, was "bankrupt." Starna became a stalking horse for a small army of educational critics. In so doing, he spread the influence idea further than many of its advocates, as he spread misconceptions of it from sea to shining sea in *Time* magazine and the *New York Times.*

One of those misconceptions was that an Iroquois "pressure group" had lobbied the state into injecting an Iroquois perspective—including details of the Haudenosaunee political system—into the state curriculum for seventh, eighth, and eleventh graders. By the time William Starna, George Will, Arthur Schlesinger, Jr., *U.S. News & World Report,* and *Time* magazine were done with this story, they had created a conspiratorial tale of racial power politics that bore little resemblance to what actually happened. The effects of this exercise in mass-media fantasy are unclear. On one hand, the chorus of widely disseminated Bronx cheers for the influence idea certainly helped to scuttle the curriculum guide; on the other hand, Troll reactions to the guide spread the news that a debate existed to audiences that we Coyotes never could have touched ourselves.

The truth was far more prosaic than the epic tale of racial power-mongering that so many conservative critics would invent. The State Education Department itself asked for Iroquois help, realizing that its existing curricula were not complete.

The Haudenosaunee curriculum guide was born one September day in 1986 during the first week of classes at Saranac Central Junior High School in a conversation between two teachers. One of them was Philip Rice, who taught social studies; the other was Akwesasne Mohawk John Kahionhes Fadden, who had taught art at the same school for three decades. According to an account prepared later by Fadden: "[Rice] gave me a draft of a syllabus from the State Education Department . . . entitled Social Studies 7 & 8: United States and New York State History. Phil commented on what he perceived as weaknesses in the draft in regard to the Iroquois. After reading it, I couldn't help but agree."[1] Later, brief mentions of the Iroquois League as a precedent of the United States were inserted into the state's social studies syllabi for seventh and eighth, as well as eleventh graders.[2]

A few days later, Fadden was visiting the Oneida Territory to honor elders there; at the event, he broached the subject of a revised syllabus with Hazel Dean-John, coordinator of the Native American Education Unit at SED. She suggested that he contact Ed Lalor, director of the division of program planning at SED. Fadden wrote to Lalor on September 21, and on October 8 received a reply from Donald H. Bragaw, chief of SED's Bureau of Social Studies Education.

The alleged meeting with State Education Department officials at which Starna asserted that Iroquois "lobbyists" pressured the New York Education Department never occurred. Fadden stated:

> The idea for it was not the result of "lobbying" by the Iroquois as some of the detractors have written. The idea for the guide was brought up at a meeting at SED. The meeting resulted from a letter-writing campaign directed toward inaccuracies in a specific field-test draft, Social Studies 7 & 8: United States and New York State History. During that January 8, 1987 meeting the concept of a curriculum guide was suggested by Donald H. Bragaw . . . and was supported by Ed Lalor. . . . The idea [of a new curriculum] did not emanate from the Haudenosaunee "lobbyists" who were there to address the draft mentioned above."[3] [Emphasis in original]

A number of letters were written, meetings held, and a draft of "Haudenosaunee: Past, Present, Future" begun, following a five-day conference involving many of the participants from July 19 to 24, 1987 at the College of St. Rose in Albany. A second group meeting was held September 28 in Ithaca. This group was assembling the guide that would draw so much flak from conservative opponents of multiculturalism as well as the state's anthropological establishment.

For almost six years, Mary Kinnaird of the State Education Department would work as a guiding spirit for "Haudenosaunee: Past, Present, Future" inside the bureaucracy. Fadden recalled Kinnaird as an elementary school teacher with a doctorate in education who seemed to be "working her heart out on this project. She did her darndest to overcome the Troll attack . . . [but] within the hierarchy of SED Mary had little power, and her valiant efforts were to no avail."[4] Kinnaird's support of the guide led at least one of the "expert" reviewers, Laurence M. Hauptman of the State University of New York/New Paltz, to demand that New York Education Commissioner Thomas Sobol fire her. He called Kinnaird "a low-level incompetent bureaucrat."[5] Hauptman complained that Kinnaird had "helped select poor outside non-Iroquois consultants with little academic standing," but did not name them. Hauptman also recommended that the entire writing team be fired, and all efforts begun again "from scratch."

The committee of Iroquois traditionalists and scholars who drafted the proposed guide included Fadden (who often worked as a coordinator), Carol Cornelius, Michelle Dean-Stock, Steve Fadden, Rick Hill, Pete Jemison, John Mohawk, Kay Olan-Rotzler, Robert Venables, Denise Waterman, Irving Powless, Jr., Jake Swamp, Doug George, and Oren Lyons. The drafting committee labored through two drafts that a flock of conservative commentators later turned into a fantasy horror story of alleged political correctness. The first draft was sent to professional reviewers for a "field test" in the middle of 1988. "Due to naiveté on my part, I looked forward to constructive criticisms," Fadden recalled.[6] The Iroquois writers received little constructive criticism, however, as the Trolls mounted a concerted effort to erase many of the ideas expressed in the guide, including the notion that the Iroquois Great Law of Peace helped shape the fundamental law of the United States. The guide was slowly smothered inside the New York education bureaucracy as the storm raged around the Curriculum of Inclusion, fanned by misrepresentations of the Iroquois guide that reached audiences numbering in the millions on both sides of the Atlantic Ocean. Many of these people may still believe that the guide was an accomplished fact, long after the state cut 60 percent of its text and its Iroquois authors gave up in frustration.

Among a core of academics who called themselves experts on the Iroquois, the idea of Native American political influence, even in 1990, was still regarded as a subject best not discussed in polite company. As Vine Deloria, Jr. observed (in the Summer, 1992 issue of *American Indian Quarterly*), the ideological struggle was no longer over the historical record, which had been well illuminated. The center of the struggle involved redefinition of a power matrix. Who speaks for whom, Deloria asked—"Iroquois experts" for the Haudenosaunee, or the Haudenosaunee for themselves? The New York State resource guide "Haudenosaunee: Past, Present, Future" was to become a test case in a kind of intellectual decolonization, an opening to the possibility of the Haudenosaunee advancing a view that diverged from standard-issue ethnohistory.

New York was not the only state that had planned to release new curriculum guidelines on the subject of the Iroquois Confederacy. In September, 1991, a front-page story in the *San Francisco Chronicle* began:

> *Historic changes are happening to history. As students return to public schools throughout California today, many will learn stories that [neither] they nor*

their parents have heard before—that an African doctor named Imhotep made significant contributions to medical knowledge 2,000 years before Hippocrates; that the framers of the U.S. Constitution studied the bylaws of the Iroquois nation . . . [7]

While New York may have been the only state in which Native Americans undertook an entire curriculum guide, the idea of influence had extended far beyond the Iroquois home state's schools by the late 1980s and early 1990s. We were debating the same ideas in Nebraska, and curricula that contained them were being prepared in Kansas City and Oakland, California. A third-grade class at Weller Elementary in Fairbanks, Alaska, did a project on the Haudenosaunee and democracy.

The New York State Curriculum of Inclusion concluded that minorities' cultural contributions had been consistently downgraded in the past. It cited the failure of history textbooks to describe the role of black soldiers who fought on both sides in the American Revolution. Also mentioned was the scant attention paid to the Iroquois Indians, "whose system of government was said to have contributed significantly to New York State's constitution."[8]

A counterattack to the Curriculum of Inclusion developed quickly. Diane Ravitch, a professor of history at Columbia University Teachers College, was quoted in the Sunday *New York Times:*

> *Ravitch . . . who was enlisted by Mr. [Thomas] Sobol to comment on the [Curriculum of Inclusion] notes that the state's eleventh-grade syllabus is perhaps the only one in the nation that describes the two major influences on the United States Constitution as the European Enlightenment and the political system of the Iroquois Confederacy. The Iroquois role was added after an Iroquois delegation met with the state Education Department, she said.[9]*

Starna commented on Ravitch's views in a letter to the *Times* that was published three and a half weeks later. Starna's letter appeared under the headline "Whose History Will Be Taught, and What Is History Anyway?" Starna identified himself as "one of five university-based, non-Indian academics" who had been contracted to review the curriculum guide, which he said was plagued by "a large number of historical errors," including "that of alleged Iroquois influence on the United States Constitution." According to Starna, "no good evidence exists to support this popular idea, which did not become part of the United States historical myth until the 1860s . . . No informed, un-predisposed [a.k.a. 'nonconspiratorial'] historian makes this argument." According to Starna's reading of events, an Iroquois pressure group had "turn[ed] history on its head" by "special pleading."[10]

When Starna reviewed an early draft of the Haudenosaunee curriculum, he objected to the use of the term "Haudenosaunee" to describe the curriculum. While that is the traditional name of the people most of us call "Iroquois" (a French term), Starna argued that "Iroquois" had become a "cultural-linguistic marker." Later, in Mohawk Country, I heard a suggestion that the Haudenosaunee give Starna the name "Turkey Butt" in Mohawk, designate it his "cultural-linguistic marker," and see how he liked it.

The image of New York eleventh graders stuffing their heads with the tenets of the Iroquois Great Law popped up again in the April 1, 1991 issue of *Time* magazine in a cover story headlined "Upside Down in the Groves of Academe:"

> Increasingly, curriculums are being written to satisfy the political demands of parents and community activists. In some cases, expediency counts for more than facts. New York State officials, for example, have responded to pressure from Native American leaders by revamping the state high school curriculum to include the shaky assertion that the U.S. Constitution was based on the political system of the Iroquois Confederacy.[11]

It all fit so nicely, or so it seemed. With a surge of oversimplification, *Time* not only made an accomplished fact of a proposed curriculum, but shaved from it all the European antecedents that the curriculum guide included along with those of the Iroquois. The possibility that some of the Iroquois' assertions might be based on historical fact was not even considered. *Time* ignored the fact that "Haudenosaunee: Past, Present, Future" never made a comprehensive case that the Constitution was "based" on the Great Law. The *Time* article cites no names or sources for its allegations. Like many opponents of this idea, the authors of this article overstated the thesis as a way to discredit it.

Time magazine took up the subject again in a November 11, 1991 interview with New York Commissioner of Education Thomas Sobol, who took a cautious approach to the issue. In response to a question about the influence thesis, Sobol replied:

> Well, it depends on the way we teach it. It's very clear to me that our Constitution derives from the political traditions and thinking of Western Europe. Now it is a fact, I guess, that the Iroquois nations learned to live compatibly with one another. Whether or not they had any impact on the framers of the

Constitution, I don't know, but I am set to acknowledge its possible influence in part. It makes sense to me not to overemphasize it.[12]

The interviewer then asked: "Why teach it at all?" Sobol replied, "Why teach anything that's part of our history if there's only a few people involved? Why would you want not to teach it? . . . There's no harm in talking about it."[13]

Starna's second contribution to the influence debate was a response to the *Time* interview with Sobol,[14] repeating his well-worn assertion that "no good evidence" exists to support "Iroquois impact on the framers of the Constitution." He then appealed to the authority of "Years of research by non-conspiratorial scholars," which he said had disproved the idea. Starna cited no evidence from these "anti-influence" scholars. Indeed, he appealed to scholarly proofs that did not exist. Starna traced the roots of ideas the way Senator Joseph McCarthy identified Communists: It's what I say it is, not because I have proof, but because I say it's so.

Starna then made a more sinister charge, arguing, again with no cited factual support, that Iroquois who maintain influence are more than historical publicity hounds. He charged that they were engaged in ethno-historical blackmail. Starna alleged that "some of the native writers and their Iroquois allies" threatened to restrict access to Indian communities for Starna and others who criticized the Haudenosaunee curriculum guide in an apparent attempt to end their careers as "experts" on the Iroquois. Starna provided no specific evidence of such threats.[15]

As Starna's letters were published, I was exploring the historical record with Don Grinde on the book that would be published as *Exemplar of Liberty*. I had access to hundreds of sources that disproved Starna's brief barrage of buzzwords. I was watching journalists waive all pretense of verifiability when they quoted this self-proclaimed expert. I asked myself: has he read Franklin's or Jefferson's papers? How can he make a fool of himself in public like this? How far had the debate over an essentially historical issue become distorted by contemporary power agendas?

Starna's assertion involving unnamed "Iroquois leaders" and undocumented "threats" was turned into unquestioned truth at the peck of a keyboard by careless journalists. For example, *Washington Post* readers were told that "Indian leaders blacklisted . . . Starna for rejecting the idea that the U.S. Constitution was based on the Iroquois federation."[16]

In a letter to the New York State Education Department, however, Starna did name the architects of "this constitution nonsense." In a cover letter with a twenty-seven-page critique of "Haudenosaunee: Past, Present, Future," Starna wrote on November 20, 1992 that the second draft of the guide is "as badly flawed as the first. Most troublesome," wrote Starna,

> is the State Education Department's complete failure to address the erroneous views of American history, legal issues, anthropology and Indian-White relations presented in the guide. The most egregious of these is the bankrupt claim of Iroquois influence on the development and design of the United States Constitution.[17]

Starna complained that the curriculum guide reflected the views of "individuals who have a vested interest in seeing their peculiar views of history presented in the guide (Grinde, Johansen), or are allied politically with the writers ([Jake] Swamp, [Peter] Jemison, and [Sally] Roesch Wagner)." Starna demanded that his name be taken off the list of curriculum guide reviewers, and that passages describing Iroquois influence on American politics be removed.

Professor Starna's capsule critique of the influence thesis popped up again in the New York press during 1992 after Governor Mario Cuomo was reported to have

> credited the Iroquois people with developing the democratic principles that form the basis of the U.S. Constitution. . . . "The evidence is strong that the Founding Fathers were greatly influenced by the framework of the Iroquois Nation" [Cuomo said.][18]

Starna was quoted in rebuttal as saying that this is "one of the damnedest, silliest ideas I've ever heard. . . . The literature has absolutely devastated the argument that the Iroquois Constitution influenced the U.S. Constitution." Once again, Professor Starna had marshalled the authority of an uncited and largely imaginary "literature."[19]

Yet another political correctness horror story appeared in the November 12, 1990 edition of U.S. News & World Report, in an essay under the byline of John Leo titled "A Fringe History of the World." Leo assailed multiculturalism in school curricula, beginning with "Afrocentric" ideas as well as the Haudenosaunee curriculum in New York State. He asserted that the influence of the Iroquois on American statecraft was included in the curriculum only to appease the Iroquois, not because it was part of history. The Haudenosaunee guide to which Leo refers was under development at the time and not being used in New York schools. Nevertheless, he stated:

In Upstate New York, a Native American lobby demonstrated how a curriculum can now be altered by adroit special pleading. After a visit by an Iroquois delegation to the state education department, the school curriculum was amended to say that the political system of the Iroquois Confederacy influenced the writing of the U.S. Constitution. To the surprise of very few, this decision shows that some school authorities, eager to avoid minority-group pressure and rage, are now willing to treat the curriculum as a prize in an ethnic spoils system.[21]

I winced as I read this, and then nearly broke out laughing. Leo, of course, had no way of knowing that one of the primary proponents of this so-called prize in an ethnic spoils system was a middle-aged white man in Omaha. Leo's veiled reference to violence of a type that never happened was chilling.

Leo's paraphrase of Starna very concisely summarized the argument of influence thesis opponents: The idea is "a myth," that is being imposed on innocent school children by a small group of somehow awesomely powerful, media-hungry Iroquois who want to muscle this falsehood into "mainstream" history. Leo gave no hint that legitimate scholarly debate existed on the subject. To suggest that the idea is even debatable (and not "myth," or "the silliest idea I've ever heard") would have undermined the Eurocentric assumptions that fueled his argument.

Four years later, Leo again attacked the influence thesis, in *U.S. New & World Report*, this time in a column headlined "The Junking of History." Leo assailed "Afrocentrists," grouping them with those who deny the Jewish holocaust, as engaging in "pure assertion [and] a growing contempt for the facts." He included in his hit list of multicultural attempts to transform facts into opinion "the supposedly strong influence of Iroquois thought on the U.S. Constitution, now taught in many schools."[22]

Leo's column angered me viscerally. Through a chain of very loose associations, Leo was arguing that support of the Iroquois influence thesis was to be held on a par with the anti-Semitism of those who deny the Jewish holocaust. Having not a clue as to who I am or what I have written, John Leo, with an audience of millions, also had no way of knowing that I married into a Jewish family. The thickness of his ignorance and the certitude with which he ladled it out in full view of large numbers of people left me rather dumbstruck.

I replied to Leo in the April 8 issue of the magazine: "We have a genuine need to factor the accomplishments of nonwhite people into our history . . ."

In comparing advocates of Native American influence on American ideas to the debunkers of the holocaust, I wrote, Leo "has the debilitating problem for a social critic of not being able to tell historical wheat from chaff."

Among the clippings I received in 1991 was an editorial page column by George Will headlined "Therapeutic History Is Snake Oil," from the *Seattle Post-Intelligencer,* dated July 14, 1991. Will had written: "New York children are taught that the U.S. Constitution was decisively shaped by the political system of the Iroquois. Such fictions are supposed to nurture minorities' 'self-esteem' . . ."[23] In *Newsweek,* May 31, 1993, Will lambasted the influence idea again:

> *Religious fundamentalists try to compel "equal time" in school curricula for creationism and evolution. But they are less of a threat than liberals trying to maintain "fairness" for dotty ideas that make some "victim groups" feel good—ideas such as that Greek Culture came from Black Africa [an allusion to Martin Bernal's* Black Athena*],[24] or that Iroquois ideas were important to the making of the Constitution.[25]*

After Will called support for the idea "fiction," I began to refer to *Exemplar of Liberty* as the only novel in the world with 650 footnotes. Our work had been called a lot of things by a lot of people, but "fiction" was a first. Will's comment indicated how little he knew about the real debate over the issue.

By the time Arthur Schlesinger, Jr. published *The Disuniting of America* in 1992,[26] the arguments over the Haudenosaunee curriculum guide had been well rehearsed. Schlesinger's book spent several weeks on the *New York Times* best-seller list; through reviews of the book, misperceptions of the Haudenosaunee curriculum guide were spread throughout the English-speaking world. Schlesinger repeated the principal arguments of the "anti-influence" school: that the idea has no supportive evidence and that the "Iroquois lobby" is engaged in a self-aggrandizing public relations exercise:

> *In New York the curriculum for eleventh-grade history tells students that there were three "foundations" for the Constitution: the European Enlightenment, the "Haudenosaunee political system," and the antecedent colonial experience. . . . How many experts on the American Constitution would endorse this stirring tribute to the "Haudenosaunee political system"? How many have heard of that system? Whatever influence the Iroquois confederacy had on the framers of the Constitution was marginal; on European intellectuals, it was*

marginal to the point of invisibility. No other state curriculum offers this analysis of the making of the Constitution. But then no other state has so effective an Iroquois lobby.[27]

In his liberal bad old days, Schlesinger never would have written a book without footnotes full of attacks on people he did not name. Like many other books critical of our ideas, *The Disuniting of America* contained no footnotes or endnotes, so it is unknown what works he consulted. He had read *Forgotten Founders* in 1982[28] and praised it as "a tour-de-force of ingenious and elegant scholarship offering justice at last to the Indian contributions to the American Constitution."[29] A tolerable intellectual curiosity in the early 1980s, the idea of Iroquois influence on United States fundamental law a decade later became part of a tribalistic flame searing the "canon," our common political and historical heritage. Having acknowledged that the "Iroquois lobby" might have a modicum of political power in the contemporary world, critics of influence have portrayed it as part of the horde at the gates of Western civilization in the 1990s.

Such a perfect political correctness "horror story" was hard to stop. Lynne Cheney, who headed the National Endowment for the Humanities under President George Bush, incorporated Schlesinger's views as she offered her "spin" on the debate over multicultural education in *Change* magazine. Of Iroquois contributions to democracy, Cheney wrote: "This is not an idea accepted by reputable historians."[30]

The Disuniting of America also became a reference in the business press. In his column "Keeping Up," published in the April 19, 1993 edition of *Fortune*, Daniel Seligman took aim at "political correctness," which he described as "a movement driven by truly totalitarian impulses, [which] is embodied in thought police who endlessly endeavor to suppress data . . ." Seligman then hauled the issue of Iroquois influence on the Constitution out as his primary exhibit of "politically correct" thought, which he linked to a general decline in American educational levels.[31]

The theme that New York high school students were being force-fed lies about history in pursuit of minority self-esteem echoed from coast to coast. In New York City, John J. Miller, associate director of the Manhattan Institute's Center for the New American Community, a conservative think tank, decried attempts to build minority students' self-esteem with "pride-building curricula . . . pumping them full of stories meant to inflate racial pride."[32]

Although a desire to boost Native Americans' self-esteem did not create the assertions that the Iroquois helped shape the United States' political founding, the Iroquois contributions were sometimes used to boost the self-esteem of young Indians. In Kansas City, for example, an organization called Visible Horizons has been working "to help Indian youths claim their piece of the American Dream and reclaim pride in their heritage." An article in the *Kansas City Star* described a class taught by Carol Lee Sanchez-Allen at the Bader Memorial Christian Church, in which she outlined Native American contributions to American culture, including "that the Iroquois Confederacy's concept of the Grand Council influenced Benjamin Franklin's ideas for the U.S. Constitution."[33]

Schlesinger's *Disuniting of America* provoked self-satisfied applause among conservative critics who were overjoyed to see an established, classical liberal make common cause with their fears that "multicultural" education was causing American society to fragment hopelessly. Hungry for political correctness horror stories, many reviewers fell uncritically into line as Schlesinger represented a proposed curriculum guide as an established fact. Patrick Buchanan, perennial stump-preaching presidential candidate, bellowed:

> *The cultural war is already raging in our public schools. In history texts, Benedict Arnold's treason at West Point has been dropped. So has the story of Nathan Hale, the boy patriot who spied on the British and went to the gallows with the defiant cry, "I regret that I have but one life to give for my country." Elsewhere, they teach that our Constitution was plagiarized from the Iroquois, and that Western science was stolen from sub-Sahara Africa.[34]*

Buchanan went on to say, as quoted:

> *When you see the idiocy that somehow the American Constitution is a direct descendant of the Iroquois Confederation documents—this is all trash and nonsense. The effort is to turn future Americans into people who despise their own history and background . . .[35]*

What is a professor to do when he finds the subject of his Ph.D. dissertation munched as campaign fodder by a politician who has done something more than mangle the truth? How can Buchanan assume anyone who believes the Iroquois contributed to our political culture despises his own history and culture? Does Buchanan have a hidden racial agenda? Why does giving the Iroquois some credit denigrate other sources of our heritage, including those from Europe?

A close runnerup to Buchanan in the demagoguery department was

Rush Limbaugh, who wrote the following in his 1992 book *The Way Things Ought to Be*:

> Multiculturalism is billed as a way to make Americans more sensitive to the diverse cultural backgrounds of people in this country. It's time we blew the whistle on that. What is being taught under the guise of multiculturalism is worse than historical revisionism. It's more than a distortion of facts. It's the elimination of facts. In some schools, kids are being taught that the ideas of the Constitution were borrowed from the Iroquois Indians and that Africans discovered America.[36]

Reviewers looking for evidence that Dead White Males are an endangered species sprang to attention. In his review of *The Disuniting of America* in the *London Daily Telegraph*, Ambrose Evans-Pritchard came out in defense of DWEMs—Dead, White, European Males—who he says are suffering at the hands of "the American race-relations industry, [which is] amply subsidized by the public purse." Back in the United States, the *New York Post* published an editorial which took issue with Commissioner Sobol's decision to continue development of the proposed "Curriculum of Inclusion." The editorial included four subheads in bold-faced type: "Wide Condemnation," "Bizarre Priorities," "Wasting Our Money," and "Self-Esteem Pablum." On the subject of the Iroquois and the development of democracy, it said: "In one unit, students are taught that an obscure Indian tribe in upper New York state was in great part responsible for the ideas that underlie the United States Constitution. This, of course, is utter nonsense."[37]

National Review was more than happy to welcome Schlesinger into its conservative fold. Reviewer Richard Brookhiser took aim at purveyors of multiculturalism, "'Scholars' who claim that the Constitution was cribbed from the Iroquois, or that ancient Egypt was a black civilization whose wisdom was plundered by Alexander the Great and slipped to his tutor Aristotle."[38] In his book *In Defense of Elitism* (1992), William Henry III displayed his annoyance at the fact that the Heath anthology of American literature now "pointedly begins with Native American chants . . . rather than Pilgrim rhetoric." He also said that it is "wicked for the State of New York . . . [to teach] . . . that one of the two main sources for the U.S. Constitution was the organizing pact of the Iroquois Indian nation."[39]

Washington Times columnist Richard Grenier nearly split a gut over the issue. "New York State, as its official educational policy, now honors the Iroquois Nation as a prime cultural influence on American civilization. . . . Why does the U.S. Constitution, on which the Iroquois are now credited with having a powerful influence, not provide for such well-established former Iroquois traditions as raiding and murder of rival tribesmen, old people, and children too small to be useful? Why doesn't it guarantee the right to rape . . . ?" Grenier wrote that the Indians cast in the movie *Black Robe* were "bracingly authentic." He defined "authentic" as "Dirty, cruel, they brutalize, [and] torture."[40]

Grenier was recycling an older column on the same issue which had appeared a year and a half earlier. In that column, Grenier sparred with fantasy notions of multicultural education:

> *African-Americans claim that Queen Nefertiti of ancient Egypt was black*
> *. . . . Iroquois Indians have induced New York State education officials to*
> *include in their 11th-grade syllabus the dogmatic assertion that the Iroquois*
> *Confederacy was a major influence on the U.S. Constitution."*[41]

He labels such assertions unfactual and racist. If the Iroquois can claim to have influenced the Constitution, then people of Mongolian descent have the right to insist that Genghis Khan "was a principal influence on the United States Constitution."[42] This last illogical leap of reasoning is demonstrably silly, but also chilling. Is the man a columnist or a clown? Either way, he seems not to know much about American history, and nothing at all about the part the Iroquois played in it.

Grenier continued his attack on multiculturalism in a 1990 piece in *National Review*. He claimed "a new breed of treasonous clerks has emerged" who express "hostility to the ideals that underlie American democratic institutions [which] has become both blatant and grotesque." The "treason" is that standard European-derived fare in humanities departments now faces competition from "a hodgepodge of world cultures." First on Grenier's list of such high crimes was "the constitutional principles of the Iroquois." Now that support of the Iroquois influence thesis has been equated with treason, would Grenier argue that it should be punishable, like treason, by death?[43]

The "hordes at the gates" reaction to multiculturalism was epitomized in a 1991 *Forbes* cover story by Dinesh D'Souza, titled "The Visigoths in Tweed." D'Souza, a research fellow at the American Enterprise Institute, targeted "a new barbarism—dogmatic, intolerant, and oppressive" that he said has "descended on America's institutions of higher learning." This hideous intellectual monstrosity was said by D'Souza to be "a neo-Marxist ideology promoted in the name of multiculturalism."[44]

D'Souza considered the debate over Iroquois influence on democracy in his book *The End of Racism*, published in 1995. As if to prove that an appetite for wishful thinking is the world's best book sales agent, D'Souza contends that racism has ceased to exist, a novel idea to the many people who still suffer its effects in their everyday lives. Part of D'Souza's case that racism has ended rests on what he regards as liberals' "bogus multiculturalism." In this context, D'Souza finds "virtually non-existent" support for the idea that the Iroquois political system helped shape American concepts of democracy.[45]

Occasionally, the Haudenosaunee curriculum guide was treated as something other than a political correctness horror story. In Albany's *Metroland*, Jeff Jones summarized criticism of the guide:

> *Jack Wandall, an Albany writer and filmmaker and long-time supporter of the traditional Iroquois chiefs [said], "I see it [Starna's critique] as an escalation of the old-boy, mainly white network to shore up their entrenched advocacy of being the only ones who are in the know about Indians."*[46]

In the *St. Louis Post-Dispatch*, Margaret Johnson took issue with George Will's characterization of multicultural education. Johnson applauded the day when school curricula will be purged of Eurocentric bias, "and the Iroquois people are honored for the ideas of our Constitution as . . . [it] is based on the constitution of the Iroquois nation . . ."[47] Reviewing Schlesinger's book and several others on the theme of political correctness, in the *New York Times*, Frank Kermode commented: "Ms. Ravitch is wrong to deny the influence of the Iroquois (Haudenosaunee) of Upstate New York on the Constitution . . . with rancor substituting for argument."[48]

The debate over the Iroquois, democracy, and the Haudenosaunee curriculum continued to broaden. The debate grew with an animus of its own, losing all scholarly moorings, often reduced to capsule or buzzword form, with many distortions.

I read such commentary realizing that these observers knew next to nothing about the historical record, and less about the real debate over the historical validity of Iroquois influence. Why so much bombast, I wondered —why such abject shrieks of denial? One hears the pain of raw nerves being touched, of fear that the Iroquois are trying to put something over on the American people. I imagined John Wayne calling for a circling of the wagons, and then recalled the firestorm of Euro-American fear that brought trigger-happy troops to Wounded Knee Creek in 1890, four hundred miles and a lifetime and a half away from where I sat in Omaha.

The whole debate over "political correctness" has one very serious flaw:

it is a political struggle, not in the least about historical accuracy. We are not about to throw the Magna Carta in the ocean and make it swim back to England, or advocate the expunging of Socrates and Shakespeare from our history. European history is as valid a part of our heritage as it ever has been. As a middle-aged man whose ancestors immigrated to the United States from Norway and Scotland, I am rather fond of the English language, having written several books in it. I live in a pseudo-Shakespearian Tudor brick house in Omaha, and I own an English foxhound. How could I deny "our English heritage?" To assert, however, that all of our heritage came from England, or even from Europe, is a simplistic mistake. Any thinking person should welcome the addition of the many influences from different cultures that enrich our heritage.

Steve Phillips, president of the San Francisco Board of Education, weighed into the debate over multiculturalism, writing in the *San Francisco Examiner* that "While there exists a growing acknowledgment that education should reflect the cultural diversity of the student population, we rarely discuss the implications of such changes for whites." Phillips wrote:

> A narrow Eurocentric curriculum not only alienates, it does a significant disservice to white students. . . . A student who understands the annexation of the Southwest, Reconstruction, the Chinese Exclusion Act and the Iroquois influence on the U.S. Constitution will have a much better grasp of history than someone who studies only George Washington, Abraham Lincoln, and Andrew Carnegie.[49]

I watched this battle unfold in newsclippings sent to me by John Fadden and his father Ray from New York newspapers. Colleagues in Omaha would occasionally begin my day by asking whether I had seen the latest issue of *Time* magazine or *U.S. News & World Report*. I was amazed at how easily the title of "expert" was bestowed by the press, and how this title, once bestowed, seemed to confer unlimited license to say anything without factual support. How easily consensual truth was whipped up out of journalistic buzzwords and opinionated froth—and how it spread, like wildfire, through the journals of popular opinion. It was so easy to pander to a Eurocentrism that continues to narrow the focus of our history, and to stereotype the Iroquois as historical savages on the intellectual warpath. The whole debate was raising issues larger than the question of whether the Iroquois helped shape the genesis of democracy in the new United States. It was also causing people to raise questions about our history as a whole and about our national character. It was following the fault lines of major debates in society regarding who should be educated, and what they should learn.

The debate ultimately landed on my own doorstep, in Omaha. George Garrison, director of Black Studies at the University of Nebraska at Omaha, raised the subject (along with blacks' contributions) at a meeting of high school educators in Norfolk, a small city northwest of Omaha that is known as the home town of the entertainer Johnny Carson. A report on the meeting was published in the *Omaha World-Herald*, followed by an editorial in the same newspaper that repeated many of the assumptions I had heard in other states.

The headline on the editorial summarized its point of view: "Multi-cultural Law a Weapon for Indoctrination by Zealots." It began with a brief summary of Garrison's presentation in Norfolk, pointing out that he was the chair of a state advisory committee that was working on infusion of multi-cultural materials into state curricula following passage of a law to that effect. Garrison had said that the law would not force history to be rewritten, but would require the correction of some omissions and errors.

Contending that the case for Native American contributions to democracy is "overstated," the editorial cited a comment by Francis Jennings, senior research fellow at the Newberry Library, that Indians were excluded from the protections of the U.S. Constitution: "This . . . should be noted by the mythologists who insist that Indians strongly influenced the writers of the United States Constitution."[50] The *World-Herald* asked Garrison what errors and omissions concerned him:

> *Conventional American history, he said, teaches that the philosophical foundations of American democracy were laid by European thinkers and writers. Multiculturalism, on the other hand, teaches that some of the ideas discussed at the first Continental Congress originated with American Indians. A good multicultural class would teach about American Indian contributions to democracy, Garrison said.*

The editorial then compared this belief to another it said was being spread by people who had been "indoctrinated with the idea that Greek philosophers were plunderers of African thought." Without naming names, the editorial was taking issue not only with our ideas of influence, but also Martin Bernal's thesis that black Africa had a salubrious effect on the intellectual development of Europe.

Garrison also had made this point. He had said, as well, that one of the first people to die in the Boston massacre (1770), Crispus Attucks, was black (he had a black father and an American Indian mother), and that Asians had contributed significantly to the construction of the transcontinental railroads. "In the hands of people who are influenced by such rubbish, a legislative insistence on correcting 'errors and omissions' can be a powerful weapon indeed for molding the next generation of kids," the editorial continued.

By chance, six days after the *World-Herald* editorial was published, Don Grinde and I crossed paths with Jennings at the annual Iroquois Studies conference near Albany, New York. During a coffee break at the conference, I tried to give Jennings the *World-Herald* editorial that had quoted him. He waved it away, saying: "I get quoted everywhere. Who cares about Omaha?" I told him I lived and worked in Omaha, to which Jennings retorted: "You are not a scholar. You're a confidence man!" Minutes later, Grinde tried to start a separate conversation with Jennings and got the same treatment, in almost the same words, without the Omaha local angle. Late that Saturday evening, as Don and I rose to give our presentations, Jennings walked out of the room. We had originally been scheduled for midday Sunday, after I was scheduled to be on an airplane back to Omaha. We were moved to 9 P.M. Saturday night, hardly academic prime time.

Back in Omaha, Garrison and I both replied to the editorial.[51] One day, as this exchange was going on, I walked into a study area in our office and greeted Margorie Chambers, a black student, as she thumbed through the *Norton Anthology of English Literature*. "Catching up on your dead white men?" I asked. She assented. I said: "I can't be too hard on them. I'm going to be a dead white man some day." We shared a multicultural chuckle.

NOTES

1. Letter, John Kahionhes Fadden to Bruce Johansen, December 31, 1992.

2. Letter, John Kahionhes Fadden to Bruce Johansen, July 31, 1995; New York State Department of Education, Social Studies: United States and New York State History, 7 & 8, Tentative Syllabus (Albany: 1987), ix, 50; New York State Department of Education, Social Studies: United States and New York State History, 11, Tentative Syllabus (Albany: 1987) ix, 25.

3. Letter, John Kahionhes Fadden to Bruce Johansen, November 28, 1992. Bragaw raised the idea of a Haudenosaunee-composed guide in a letter to Fadden October 8, 1986, as well. Letter, Fadden to Johansen, April 6, 1993, and personal communication, Bragaw to Fadden, October 8, 1986, in Johansen's files.

4. Letter, John Kahionhes Fadden to Bruce Johansen, September 5, 1995.

5. Letter, Laurence Hauptman to Thomas Sobol, August 31, 1988. Hauptman also criticized Kinnaird for making public all reviews of the guide by critics

supporting and opposing it. Hauptman took this to be a compromise of confidentiality, not an exercise in free and open debate.

6. Letter, John Kahionhes Fadden to Bruce Johansen, December 31, 1992. Copy in author's files.

7. Nanette Asimov, "Multicultural Approach: History Rewritten for the New School Year," *San Francisco Chronicle*, September 3, 1991, A–1.

8. John Hilderbrand, "Anti-minority Bias Seen in State Education Guides," *Newsday*, July 29, 1989, 7.

9. Joseph Berger, "Now the Regents Must Decide If History Will Be Recast," *New York Times, Week in Review*, February 11, 1990.

10. William A. Starna, "Whose History Will Be Taught, and What Is History Anyway?" *New York Times*, letter to the editor, March 7, 1990.

11. Anne Hopkins and Daniel S. Levy, "Upside Down in the Groves of Academe," *Time*, April 1, 1991, 67.

12. George Russell, "Reading, Writing—and Iroquois Politics," *Time*, November 11, 1991, 20.

13. Ibid., 20.

14. William A. Starna, "Iroquois Constitutional Influence?" letter to the editor, *Time*, December 2, 1991, 10.

15. William A. Starna, "Whose History Is It," *New York Times*, March 7, 1990.

16. Larry Witham, "Indians' Political Muscle Flexed over Past 20 Years," *Washington Post*, July 23, 1991, A–5.

17. Letter, William A. Starna to George M. Gregory, Supervisor of Educational Programs, New York State Department of Education, November 20, 1992. A chronology of developments related to the curriculum guide (September 1986 through March 1, 1993), compiled by John Kahionhes Fadden, illustrates how complex the chain of events associated with the SED guide became, especially when compared with Starna's simplistic account.

18. Karen Nells. "PEF Officials Confront Cuomo at State Museum," *Albany Times-Union*, October 6, 1992, B–1, B–6. Those confronting Cuomo were leaders of the New York State Public Employees Federation, who, according to Nells's account, "were protesting their union's lack of a contract and the loss this month of some health benefits."

19. Jack Campisi, associate professor of anthropology at Wellesley College, Massachusetts, characterized the resource guide (excepting its first seventy pages) as "worthless" and "racist." Hazel W. Hertzberg, professor of history and education at Columbia University, said the Iroquois-composed guide was "one-sided and narrow." She also rejected out of hand the idea that the Confederacy provided "a model" (not the model) for the Constitution, but she did not recommend completely excising such statements. William T. Hagan, distinguished professor of history at SUNY

Fredonia, argued, "I know of no evidence that the delegates to the Constitutional Convention were influenced in any significant fashion by the example of the Iroquois Confederacy."

20. John Leo, "A Fringe History of the World," *U.S. News & World Report*, November 12, 1990, 26.

21. Ibid., 26.

22. Leo, "On Society: The Junking of History," *U.S. News & World Report*, February 28, 1994, 17.

23. George Will, "Therapeutic History Is Snake Oil," *Seattle Post-Intelligencer*, July 14, 1991. See also Bruce Johansen, "The Search Goes on in America for Complete, Credible History," *Omaha World-Herald*, November 6, 1991, 27.

24. Martin Bernal, *Black Athena: The Afroasiatic Roots of Classical Civilization*, 2 vols. (London: Free Association Press, 1985). Bernal, through an exceedingly complex analysis of language, builds a case that African civilization importantly influenced Greek and, in turn, Western European civilization.

25. George Will, "'Compassion' on Campus," *Newsweek*, May 31, 1993, 66.

26. Arthur M. Schlesinger, Jr., *The Disuniting of America* (New York: W.W. Norton), 1992.

27. Schlesinger, *Disuniting of America*, 97.

28. Bruce E. Johansen, *Forgotten Founders: Benjamin Franklin, the Iroquois and the Rationale for the American Revolution* (Ipswich, Mass.: Gambit), 1982.

29. Letter, Arthur Schlesinger, Jr. to Lovell Thompson, publisher, Gambit, Inc., July 14, 1982.

30. Lynne W. Cheney, "Multiculturalism Done Right," *Change*, January, 1993, 8.

31. Daniel Seligman, "Measuring PC: Those Influential Iroquois," *Fortune*, April 19, 1993, 159.

32. John J. Miller, "The Moonbeam of Self-Esteem," *Newsday*, June 2, 1993, 84.

33. Julius A. Karash, "Program Helps Indian Youths," *Kansas City Star*, August 20, 1995, A–1.

34. Patrick J. Buchanan, "America's Cultural War," *Atlanta Constitution*, September 15, 1992, A–15.

35. Peter Mitchell, "A Conversation with Buchanan," *Orlando Sentinel*, February 27, 1992, A–5.

36. Rush Limbaugh, *The Way Things Ought to Be* (New York: Pocket Books, 1992), 204.

37. *New York Post*, editorial, "The Sobol-Jeffries Victory," May 14, 1990.

38. Richard Brookhiser, review of Schlesinger, *The Disuniting of America*, *National Review*, May 11, 1992, 49.

39. Cited in Edwin M. Yoder, review of William Henry III, *In Defense of Elitism*, 1994, *Atlanta Journal and Constitution*, October 9, 1994, N–8.

40. Richard Grenier, "Revisionists Adrift in a Sea of Ignorance," *Washington Times*, November 15, 1991, F–3.

41. Grenier, "Historic Identity Crises," *Washington Times*, March 27, 1990, F–3.

42. Martin W. Seneca, who lives on the Cattaraugus reservation in upstate New York, replied to Grenier's allegations that the Iroquois were primitive, violent, and ignorant. Referring to the influence of the Iroquois political model on the United States, Seneca wrote: "This powerful Iroquois influence was known even . . . in 1776 when Benjamin Franklin was drafting the Constitution [Articles of Confederation]. . . . Any articulate historian, honest and unbiased, should not have to ask about Iroquois influence. We are well-documented on this." See *Washington Post*, November 24, 1991, B–5.

43. Richard Grenier, "The New Treason of the Clerks: Criticism of American Liberal Intellectuals," *National Review*, July 23, 1990, 42.

44. Dinesh D'Souza, "The Visigoths in Tweed," *Forbes*, April 1, 1991, 81.

45. Dinesh D'Souza, *The End of Racism*, (New York: Free Press, 1995), 356.

46. Jeff Jones, "Capitol Intensive: Indian Guide," *Metroland*, January 28, 1993.

47. Margaret Johnson, A Historic Year," *St. Louis Post-Dispatch*, January 1, 1990, 2–B.

48. Frank Kermode, "Whose History Is Bunk?" *New York Times*, February 23, 1992, Section 7, Page 3 [Book Review].

49. Steve Phillips, "'Multicultural' Must Include Whites," *San Francisco Examiner*, May 20, 1996, A–19.

50. Francis Jennings, *Founders of America*, 292.

51. George Garrison, "Multicultural Education Makes Up for Past Errors," *Omaha World-Herald*, September 30, 1993, 21; Bruce Johansen, "Defending Multiculturalism," *Omaha World-Herald*, October 8, 1993, 23.

6.

Expanding the Scope
of "Permissible Debate"

BRUCE E. JOHANSEN

We have gone back to ancient history . . . all around Europe, but find
none of their constitutions suitable to our circumstances.

Benjamin Franklin

By the early 1990s, the idea that Native American societies helped shape
United States political history was spreading into "mainstream"
academia, as well as public schools, motion pictures, and other media.
As these ideas spread, they lost none of their remarkable ability to cause
certain "Iroquois experts" to suffer near-total meltdowns of their gray matter.
I felt a perverse temptation to cheer every time I watched a Troll lose his
or her intellectual lunch over the idea. I imagined Joseph McCarthy
being asked to consider the lighter side of Communism, or Adolph Hitler
absorbing a lecture on the contributions of Judiasm to our European heritage.
As I explored this subject I was reminded repeatedly of Noam Chomsky's
notion that certain subjects lie beyond the bounds of "permissible debate."
As I watched, the debate regarding Iroquois influences on democracy was
straining to expand those limits.

By 1990, the Trolls' wildly simplistic caricatures of our work became a con-
venient foil, rather than a matter of academic life and death, because
the Trolls no longer controlled nearly all access to publication. By 1990,
Exemplar of Liberty was on its way to press through the American Indian
Studies Center of UCLA;[1] shortly afterwards, a trade press, Clear Light Publishers, of Santa Fe, published *Exiled in the Land of the Free*. Both are dense,
complex treatments of the influence idea, surpassing older, shorter treatments
that Donald Grinde and I had published a decade and more before. Akwe:kon
Press also republished José Barreiro's *Indian Roots of American Democracy*.[2]
Very suddenly, Trolls who had complained of a scarcity of documentation on
the issue had a load of richly annotated reading waiting for them.

As notions of Native American intellectual influence worked into the general fabric of history, a variety of perspectives on the idea emerged. Robert Venables looked at the cultural interchange through a lens of European history and imperialistic motives: "In [the] Roman wars of conquest, the Founding Fathers' Northern European [tribal] ancestors had played the role of Indians. This time, the Founding Fathers were determined to be the Romans."[3]

At the Cornell Conference, Venables had reminded us that many of the founders (Franklin included) speculated in Native lands at the same time that they borrowed Iroquois political constructs. In his writing, Venables asserts that the founders borrowed from the Iroquois and other tribes out of their own self-interest in creating an empire.

In *Voices from the Battlefront: Achieving Cultural Equity* (1994), Peter G. Jemison, who is Seneca, described "the Indian roots of American democracy." He observed that "strong counterforces were at work" to retain slavery and to favor some established interests, resulting in a Constitution that did not adhere strictly to Iroquois law, but contained vestiges of it.[4]

For seventeen years as a historian of feminism, Sally Roesch Wagner wrestled with a mystery. She was trying to answer the question of where nineteenth-century radical feminists such as Elizabeth Cady Stanton and Matilda Joslyn Gage got their utopian ideas regrading sexual equality and transformation of the patriarchal society in which they lived.

"For seventeen years, I searched for the answer to this question, which was not being addressed by the material in libraries of suffragism," Wagner recalls. Finally, while she was studying the papers of Gage in the late 1980s on a fellowship from the National Endowment for the Humanities, Wagner solved the intellectual riddle. "The answer was right there," said Wagner.

> It wasn't hidden. It was in my face, and I had not seen it. What was operating were my own notions of white supremacy, the idea that white women could not learn anything from Native women. I didn't even know I had thought that. I had in place a system of seeing the world that was so tight . . . that I didn't even know it was there.[5]

What Wagner had found was that both Stanton and Gage, while living in Upstate New York, had drawn inspiration from the matrilineal structure of the Iroquois Confederacy. In the first chapter of Gage's *Woman, Church and State*, she acknowledges that "the modern world [is] indebted" to the Iroquois "for its first conception of inherent rights, natural equality of condition, and the establishment of a civilized government upon this basis."[6]

"What was it like for white women in the nineteenth century to come suddenly into a society in which they did not have to fear rape?" Wagner asked herself. "Gage was surprised because she could walk around Onondaga without fear—she felt released from that constant, nagging fear. She felt a sense of freedom." Wagner asked herself how Gage and Stanton reacted to a society in which women, especially elderly women, were respected, not shunned. As Wagner spent time with Iroquois women, she remarked on "the experience of being really listened to by men." As Wagner was growing into what she called "the age of dismissal in [European-American] culture," she also was growing into "the age of being attended to most seriously" in many Native American cultures, including the matrilineal Iroquois.

> When I experience the reality of being heard in that way, I realize that these are echoes for me of what my nineteenth-century foremothers experienced— they had a vision of what it would be like if your kids belonged to you and couldn't be ripped off by their fathers. What it felt like to be with women who owned property, and who had rights to their own children. They didn't live in constant fear of male violence, and they had real authority—not token, romanticized Mother's Day-type respect.

Wagner described the excitement of the intellectual journey that she undertook once she realized that the Iroquois had helped to inspire Matilda Joslyn Gage:

> Gage was describing the Iroquois. This is what had been staring me in the face for seventeen years. Now I had the time to dedicate to figuring out what she was talking about. . . . I went to the library at California State University Sacramento, and began a scavenger hunt. . . . I began with the sources that Gage cites, such as Cadwallader Colden, Morgan, Lafitau. Those led to others. I started going through the newspapers to see what she was reading. The Onondaga Historical Association had a hundred-year collection of clips [of the] the New York Herald-Tribune and the Syracuse papers. These were the papers that Gage read. It took me about six months of research before I could understand those stories. The level of understanding of the average reader of the Onondaga Standard [about the Iroquois] was higher than or probably comparable to scholarship today. The question of "What did Gage know about the Iroquois" opened a Pandora's Box. Two dozen white women in Onondaga Country were writing about the Iroquois. Many of these women had Indian names and spent a lot of time with the Iroquois. What began as a question of what did Gage know, what did Stanton know, quickly turned into "Look at what everyone knew!"[7]

Through her research, Wagner rediscovered what Gage and Stanton had known: "They studied the Iroquois . . . and found a cosmological world that they believed to be far superior to the patriarchal one of the white nation in which they lived."[8] Gage had been surprised to find Iroquois women playing important roles in political affairs at a time when women in the United States were property of their husbands and could not vote. Gage was adopted into the Mohawk wolf clan. "These women were amazed to learn that Native American women had rights long before white women in this country had them. The women in Iroquois tribes owned property and voted. They controlled the rights to reproduction and the rights to raise their children," Wagner stated.[9]

Other feminists, including Paula Gunn Allen, were discovering what Wagner had found, and at about the same time. "Neither Greece nor Rome had the kind of pluralistic democracy as that concept has been understood in the United States since Andrew Jackson, but the tribes, especially the gynarchial tribal confederacies, did," she wrote.[10] In the *American Indian Law Review*, Renee Jacobs cited Wagner's work as she made a case that while the founders adapted some aspects of Iroquois law, they were essentially blind to the equity of the sexes that was woven into Haudenosaunee fundamental law and political life.[11] The founders who associated with the Iroquois generally did their business with diplomats, who were men. Their writings display no knowledge that they knew women were key to deciding who among the men sat on the council and did the Iroquois' diplomatic business.

Gail Landsman described the ways in which Native American (particularly Iroquois) examples helped shape the ideology of the women's movement from 1848 to 1920 in *Ethnohistory*, the same journal that had been so hostile to arguments of Iroquois influence on democracy generally. Landsman argued that while the early suffragists utilized the Indian image extensively, they were activists who formed their opinions "not through the discovery of objective truth but in the context of validating and/or advancing the story of woman suffrage."[12]

Our first copies of *Exemplar of Liberty* arrived in the mail around Christmas, 1991. *Exemplar of Liberty* greatly expanded the scope of our published work. First and foremost, the book was a pooling of work both of us had done since publication of our first books on the subject, between nine years (for me) and fourteen years (for Don) of additional research. By uniting our efforts, Don and I also gained the intangible benefits of partnership in a struggle. We could bounce ideas between us and critique each other's work.

Finally, our decision to pool efforts established a friendship that has seen us through coauthorship of several subsequent books. *Exemplar of Liberty* was our first, and with the help of several other books by other authors, it established a dense matrix of published knowledge regarding how and why the Iroquois political system figured importantly in the thinking of the United States' founders.

Reviews began rolling in shortly after New Year's. Expressing a consensus view in *The American Historical Review*, Yasuhide Kawashima found *Exemplar of Liberty* to be "a challenging book," and "a penetrating study of how Native American nations practiced their democracy," with a "succinct portrayal" of Roger Williams' use of Native precedents for political freedom and religious toleration. Kawashima said that Grinde and I had "meticulously collected" historical information to build a case that Native American political institutions had an impact on the founding of the United States, but that we "seem overly zealous in claiming more than their evidence can substantiate. . . . Many of their statements are overdrawn."[13] The reviewer took exception to *Exemplar*'s tracing of feminism, the Northwest Ordinance, judicial review, and the Bill of Rights in part to Native American origins. Concluding, Kawashima wrote that the central question was no longer whether Native American precedents helped shape democracy, but to what extent.

Elisabeth Tooker took her licks at *Exemplar of Liberty* in *Northeast Anthropologist*. She had obviously read the book, but most of the evidence had slid off her metaphorical back like water off a duck. Still ignoring most of the relevant sources, and still citing unnamed authorities, she was escalating her accusations to the point of contending that we were perpetuating a hoax.

Tooker opened her review saying that "most scholars have dismissed" Grinde's *The Iroquois and the Founding of the American Nation* and Johansen's *Forgotten Founders*. She also summarily dismissed *Exemplar of Liberty*. Tooker, who does not identify the scholars who purportedly agree with her, wrote, "the result is no more convincing than their previous efforts."[14] Tooker repeated her contention that Benjamin Franklin did not admire the Iroquois political structure because he called Indians "ignorant savages" in his 1751 letter to James Parker in which he advised the colonists to form a union on the Iroquois model. She seemed to have humorlessly missed the ironic nature of Franklin's statement. Tooker concluded that "what Grinde and Johansen have written is an elaborate hoax. . . . Indians were unimportant in shaping events on this continent that led up to the founding of the United States."[15]

Reviewing *Exemplar of Liberty* in the *Canadian Historical Review*, J. A. Brandao found little merit in the book; the reviewer's analysis closely resembled that of Elisabeth Tooker, who was cited by Brandao as an authority on the issue.[16] When Don Grinde and I tried to rebut the review, the editor of the journal told us to "go easy"—the reviewer was one of her graduate students. After we composed an appropriately soft-shoed rebuttal, the editor then rejected it on grounds that the journal's format had been changed.[17]

Exemplar of Liberty received an enthusiastic reception in Native American journals and magazines. Alan Tack, in *Native Peoples*, wrote:

> Clearly, the pervasive and persistent influence of American Indian political systems on modern democracy and the American character lend this book its life and power. The authors' hope is that some day we may all "join hands and celebrate the diverse roots of the American democratic tradition without the blinders of indifference and cultural arrogance." This book nurtures that hope by helping us understand American democracy as a unique synthesis of Native American and European ideas.[18]

In the *American Indian Culture and Research Journal*, Wilbur Jacobs, professor emeritus of history at the University of California, Santa Barbara, maintained that the Iroquois were "great peacemakers as well as warriors."[19] He wrote:

> We can learn much from the Indians' world-view of peacemaking and their concern for the welfare of future generations, as well as their ability to live together in harmony. . . . Perhaps the greatest debt America owes to Native American people is for our magnificent traditions of freedom and democracy. I scarcely need mention the volume Exemplar of Liberty by Donald A. Grinde and Bruce E. Johansen, which for the first time gives us widespread documentation of this indebtedness. Equally significant is the fact that the book is an exemplar of the fighting spirit in the front lines of knowledge, counteracting the cadre of well-meaning but misled scholars who call themselves "Iroquoianists," although the Iroquois themselves often decline to be identified with them. Against this formidable phalanx of academic shock troops, Grinde and Johansen have skillfully penetrated firing lines of generalities with barrages of understory factual research that toppled the opposition. Grinde and Johansen proved that the Indian people of North America left a legacy of freedom and democracy that is world-wide in its influence.[20]

In another article for the *American Indian Culture and Research Journal*, Jacobs examined *Exemplar of Liberty* in light of his readings in history while a research scholar at the Huntington Library:

Grinde and Johansen are doing pioneering work in Indian history, correcting the misdirected thinking of certain colonial historians and anthropologists. In so doing, they are spreading a new light of understanding and setting forth new themes for general American history and government.[21]

In the same article, Jacobs critically examined the writings on the subject by Professor Tooker, and found support for our construction of history in the works of Lawrence H. Gipson. Jacobs also called on his readings of Carl L. Becker and William Brandon as he observed that European colonists were exposed to Native American diplomacy and forms of governance on a repeated basis from the earliest years of settlement, setting a precedent for Benjamin Franklin's use of an Iroquois confederate model in his Albany Plan of Union and Articles of Confederation.

The Iroquois precedent for democracy (and its model of decentralized decision-making) was embraced within the environmental movement during the early 1990s. During the third week of April, 1992, between four thousand and five thousand citizens of Kansas City and surrounding areas observed Earth Day by assembling a large mosaic of materials to be recycled in the shape of a turtle, after the Iroquois reference to North America as "Turtle Island." The mosaic, which occupied the space of roughly a football field, was constructed in Kansas City's Penn Valley Park, and dismantled the next day. Information on Iroquois life, including constitutional influence, was distributed at the event. Participants reenacted the story of the Peacemaker with twenty-five-foot tall puppets. Programs handed out at the event on Sunday, April 24 observed that the Peacemaker had formed a league that was a "model for our own democratic form of government."

Jerry Mander's 1991 title *In the Absence of the Sacred* called for a return to a sense of sacredness of the earth expressed in many American Indian religious philosophies as an alternative to the "techno-utopian" thinking that has created an economic system that is devouring the last indigenous niches of the earth and polluting the entire planet. At a time when toxic levels of PCBs have been found in Inuit (Eskimo) mothers' milk thousands of miles from their sources, Mander called for a revolution in philosophy and economics. Mander wrote that learning how Native Americans helped shape democratic thought was his most exciting discovery while researching his book.[22]

Among overenthusiastic portrayals, any complete history of the influence idea should acknowledge the front page of the first issue of *The New England Pilgrim*, which was headlined "U.S., Soviet Constitutions Stolen

From the Iroquois: But Our Founding Fathers, Engels Bungled the Theft."[23] As one who once made a living writing headlines, I know this one's main virtue: it fit the space allotted for it. Otherwise, it vastly overstated the issue. Besides, all the evidence I have seen indicates that the Great Law was freely offered, not "stolen."

The influence idea was filtering into textbooks by the early 1990s. In the 1992–1993 edition of a college-level introductory political science textbook, a sidebar asked: "Did you know . . . that the federal government of the United States was modeled, in part, on the sixteenth-century Iroquois Confederacy . . . ?" The idea is later developed in more detail.[24] The source is listed as "Jerry Stubben, Iowa State University." Stubben, who is a professor of political science at Iowa State and part Ponca, appeared on a 1991 Organization of American Historians panel with Grinde and me, and exchanged information with us. In the 1994–1995 edition of the textbook, all references to the Iroquois and democracy were excised, for reasons unknown to any of us.

Two books by Jack Weatherford, *Indian Givers: How the Indians of the Americas Transformed the World* (1988) and *Native Roots: How the Indians Enriched America* (1991), helped to popularize the influence idea; I read and marked up early drafts of *Native Roots*, and provided Weatherford with a draft of *Exemplar of Liberty*.

In the *Whole Earth Review*, Donald Johns reviewed Weatherford's *Native Roots*, noting that "the book describes the Native American origins of 2,000 words in American English, as well as government (the Iroquois model of democracy) . . . [and] half our food crops." Such things "ought to be the stuff of school curricula," remarked Johns.[25]

Weatherford himself wrote, in the *Minneapolis Star-Tribune*,

In the realm of politics, the Indians not only gave us the word "caucus," but they taught us how to make a caucus, and from this developed a major part of our political system and the convention system by which we nominate presidential candidates. Other parts of Indian political institutions were incorporated into the constitution, including impeachment of elected officials, the separation of military and civilian personnel, and the admission of new states as equal members into the union.[26]

Thomas Altherr criticized *Indian Givers* in *American Indian Quarterly* maintaining that Weatherford's analysis was too simplistic, and said he "would have profited enormously from reading Elisabeth Tooker's and Bruce Johansen's exchange on the subject in 1988 and 1990 volumes of *Ethno-*

history."[27] Altherr had forgotten that in a book published in 1988, Weatherford could have had no knowledge of the *Ethnohistory* articles, which appeared in 1990.

Other reviews of books that engaged the influence thesis were rolling in. In his review of José Barreiro's *Indian Roots of American Democracy,* Howard L. Rheingold observed that the Iroquois "social contract—the Great Law of Peace—almost certainly informed the creators of the U.S. Constitution."

Five years after the bicentennial of the U.S. Constitution, the five-hundredth anniversary of Columbus's first voyage to America provided a forum for historical debate involving the state of Native America and the portrayal of its history. The early 1990s witnessed an outpouring of writing on the "cultural encounter" and its aftermath, during which the Native American origins of democracy were common intellectual currency.

David E. Stannard, an historian of holocausts, made a case in *American Holocaust: Columbus and the Conquest of the New World* that the half-millennium following the voyages of Columbus brought to the New World the longest, most devastating holocaust in the annals of human history. According to Stannard, European immigrants absorbed Native notions of liberty and federalism as they pushed westward:

> *Probably the most common association that is made with the congregations of northeastern cultures concerns their sophisticated domestic political systems . . . such as the Five Nation Confederacy of the Iroquois. . . . Many writers, both historians and anthropologists, have argued that the League was a model for the United States Constitution, although much controversy continues to surround that assertion. The debate focuses largely on the extent of Iroquois influence on Euro-American political thought, however, since no one denies that there was some influence.*[28]

Stannard's view of the issue—that the question was not whether the Iroquois had helped shape democracy, but to what extent—was becoming the consensus view by the early 1990s. "In any case," Stannard wrote, "however the controversy over Iroquois influence is decided, it will not minimize the Iroquois achievement."[29]

In *Stolen Continents: The Americas Through Indian Eyes Since 1492* (1992), Ronald Wright provided a similar analysis. The Iroquois Confederacy, wrote Wright, "still survive[s], still fighting for recognition of a nationhood that they believe they never surrendered to the parvenus who built the United States and Canada around them. They also feel ironic pride that European colonists took the Iroquois Confederacy as a model when contemplating a union of their own."[30]

Also during the quincentennial year, People Against Sexual Abuse of New York City, in conjunction with the Church Avenue Block Association, developed and produced a workshop for formerly undocumented aliens applying for citizenship that explains the Bill of Rights. The program, called "Roots of Democracy," was developed in observance of the bicentennial of the Bill of Rights, and stresses the relationship of the U.S. Constitution to the Iroquois Indians' Great Law of Peace.[31]

In an edition of the *American Indian Culture and Research Journal* that was entirely given over to the Columbian encounter, Patrick C. Morris, professor of liberal studies, University of Washington (Bothell), described the first encounters between Columbus and the Tainos. Morris took issue with "narrow Eurocentric view[s] of discovery and its aftermath."[32] Part of an effort to alleviate this narrowness, argued Morris, is inclusion of Native American political traditions in histories of Columbus' voyages and their aftermath. Toward this end, Morris says that Donald Grinde's article in the same issue of AICRJ

> sets out evidence for substantive contributions by American Indians, particularly the Iroquois, to the form of federalism adopted by the United States through its Constitution. The academic debate precipitated by the injection of Indians into the authorship of this most precious of all United States historical documents is indicative of the intellectual climate surrounding scholarship related to Indians and other indigenous peoples. After 500 years, it is time we have this debate.[33]

Treatments of the quincentenary abounded in the popular media. *U.S. News & World Report* briefly noted Iroquois contributions to democracy in its cover story on the Columbus quincentenary. The article surveyed Native American life before the arrival of Columbus. It said: "Three centuries before the U.S. Constitution took shape, the Iroquois League ran a Congress-like council, exercised the veto, protected freedom of speech, and let women choose officeholders."[34] Gannett News Service released "A Primer on the First People" on the five-hundredth anniversary of Columbus's first landfall in the Americas. This newswire piece contained a detailed account of the circumstances that compelled Benjamin Franklin and other colonial leaders to meet Iroquois sachems and adopt some of their political practices.[35]

The *Dallas Morning News* published a three-thousand word survey of the five centuries since Columbus's first landfall in the Americas, in which Suzan Shown Harjo characterized Columbus Day as "a holiday that represents native national, cultural, and family genocide":

> *It was here, in the Iroquois, Muscogee, and other confederacies, where Benjamin Franklin, Thomas Jefferson, and other Founding Fathers found longstanding working models of Native nations united for peacetime purposes .... The basic precept of democracy—inherent sovereignty of the individual—was found here.*[36]

Ironically, wrote Harjo, today the system to which Indians so vitally contributed refuses to recognize many Native American religious rights.

The influence issue also was examined extensively in *Omni*, a popular science magazine. Jane Bosveld surveyed the debate, then concluded, borrowing from Jack Weatherford:

> *the Indian model of democracy was replaced [after 1800] by the Greek model, in which slavery was permitted. It was a shift in thinking that rationalized the fate of African-Americans and laid the foundation for displacement and genocide of Native Americans. Perhaps it is time to include the Great Law of Peace in American textbooks.*[37]

The idea that Iroquois democracy helped shape subsequent political developments was aired in some unusual places during the quincentennial year of 1992. One of these was *Sassy*, a magazine aimed mainly at teenage girls. Tucked among articles with titles such as "Axl Rose: Clothes Horse," and "Beauty Tips for Procrastinators," Mary Kaye contributed an article titled (on the magazine's cover) "Why Our Screwed-up Planet Needs Native Americans." While most of the article relates the author's personal experiences among the Navajo, she writes: "These days the brainwashing is more insidious . . . textbooks virtually ignore Native American contributions (did you know, for example, that parts of Iroquois law were incorporated into the American Constitution?)"[38]

The Iroquois example was being discussed in Africa as well as in the United States. In the context of a discussion of African tribes thrown together in European-designated nations, Jason W. Clay wrote in *Utne Reader*: "There has been intriguing talk in Uganda of a confederation of tribes based on the League of the Iroquois, where local power would be left to the tribes and state politics would be decided by a joint council in which each tribe, regardless of size, has an equal vote."[39]

Exemplar of Liberty began to attract an audience abroad. By September of

1992, Alexander Sudak wrote that he had completed a Polish translation, and that he had forwarded the manuscript to the Polish-American Historical Society in Warsaw to be considered for publication. In the meantime, a condensation of *Exemplar of Liberty* into article form by Grinde was published in the Spring, 1993 issue of *Historia*, the journal of the Polish Historical Association.[40] An article in *The Warsaw Voice* described the activities of the Polish Friendship Society, a group of Poles who study American Indian history and issues, publish books, and edit a journal. The group also organizes peaceful protests on behalf of Native American people and causes, such as freedom for Leonard Peltier. The publishing house, called Tipi, has issued about a half-dozen titles, and the journal, *Tawacin Quarterly*, has published since 1986.

> The quarterly includes materials about the Great Peace Law, which is a discovery for the Polish reader. The law made it possible for the confederation of five Iroquois nations to function in harmony for several centuries. The editors stress that this law was taken by white colonists as a model for the United States constitution . . . and a model for democracy, but later the colonists forgot for long years both the Indian original and its authors.[41]

The quincentenary year also witnessed the release of several biographies of Native Americans. One of them was Nancy Bonvillian's *Hiawatha: Founder of the Iroquois Confederacy*, which quotes Benjamin Franklin's 1751 letter to James Parker.[42]

The Columbus quincentenary also provoked some searching examinations of the last five hundred years in the Americas. In *The State of Native America: Genocide, Colonization, and Resistance*, Rebecca L. Robbins began a chapter with a brief description of the Iroquois Confederacy. Robbins observed that precontact political systems in the Americas were sophisticated and complex. She added:

> Certain of the structures and principles of indigenous governance, notably those drawn from the Haudenosaunee (Iroquois) Confederacy . . . were so advanced that they were consciously utilized as a primary model upon which the U.S. Constitution was formulated and the federal government created.[43]

Exiled in the Land of the Free also was published during the quincentenary year and received extensive praise in the trade-review press. "These impressive essays by eight Native American leaders and scholars present persuasive evidence that the American colonists and the U.S. founding fathers borrowed from the Iroquois Confederacy and other Indian political institutions in drafting the U.S. Constitution," wrote an unnamed reviewer in *Publishers Weekly*.[44] By 1995, the book had sold ten thousand copies in hardback, and was being prepared for publication in paperback.

Exiled presented a sophisticated analysis of how the Iroquois system of government interacted with the embryonic United States. Principal author Oren Lyons told reviewer Robert L. Smith of the *Syracuse Post-Standard* that the United States adopted only parts of Iroquois and other Native democratic systems. The founders compromised with their European heritage by permitting slavery in the southern states and ignoring the rights of women, as well as making the vote initially contingent on property ownership. In his review, Smith noted that most of the book's contributors subscribed to the "influence school": he identified "Iroquois concepts, such as federalism, untested in Europe, that found their way into the Constitution."[45]

Oren Lyons also addressed the United Nations on the subject of Native American influence on democracy, as part of the proceedings to begin the 1993 Year of Indigenous Peoples.[46] Appearing on "Bill Moyers' Journal" (Public Broadcasting Service), July 4, 1992, Lyons discussed Iroquois ecological and political traditions and asserted Iroquoian precedents for United States government.

In the *New York Times*, Rodney A. Smolla wrote that *Exiled in the Land of the Free* "explores the relationship of Indians to the Constitution from two directions. . . . First, how Indian traditions may have influenced the creation of the Constitution, and second, how subsequent interpretations of the Constitution have affected the lives of Indians over time." On the subject of influence, Smolla, director of the Institute of Bill of Rights Law at the College of William and Mary, wrote that *Exiled* makes a good case for Iroquois influence on the Constitution from the Albany Congress (1754) through the Philadelphia Convention in 1787, that Benjamin Franklin and other Founders were students of the Iroquois as well as of other political systems, and that European philosophers such as Locke and Rousseau also drew upon Native precedents.

Smolla also reviewed the case against "influence," including the purported lack of written credit to the Iroquois per se. He continued:

> In one profound sense, however, the resolution of this debate does not really matter, for it is not necessary to establish through documentation a linear chain of cause and effect . . . the authors make a compelling case for the existence of an Indian civilization of participatory democracy rich in its respect for individual human dignity, yet steeped in values of community.[47]

In the *American Indian Culture and Research Journal*, Wilbur Jacobs called *Exiled* "a splendid new book." Jacobs observed that "Donald Grinde's penetrating analysis of Iroquois political theory stresses the impact of the Six Nations upon emerging American concepts of governance leading up to the Constitutional Convention. . . . Non-Indian Iroquois researchers have consistently ignored the impact of Indian people upon the growth of American concepts of freedom and liberty."[48]

Not all the reviews were positive, however. Richard Haan, writing in *The Journal of American History*, found that "There is not much new," in *Exiled's* assertion of Iroquois influence on the development of the democratic tradition. Haan contended that the authors "fail to ask how much of the present-day Iroquois tradition of the Iroquois League has been influenced by contact with mainstream American culture."[49]

A year after publishing *Exiled in the Land of the Free*, Clear Light brought out another title that utilized the influence idea, Frank Waters's *Brave Are My People*, a collection of essays on Native American leaders. In his biography of Deganawidah, the Peacemaker, whose vision is preserved in the Iroquois Confederacy, Waters wrote that "the Peacemaker . . . had a dream: a wonderful, practical dream that came true for all America." He concluded:

> The influence of the League of the Iroquois upon the course of this nation, the United States of America, has been in the highest degree. For it is believed now that because the framers of the Constitution were familiar with the League, the charter for the government of the United States was modelled upon many of its principles. Whether or not this is true, the symbols of the great pine and the eagle, and the concept of a number of separate peoples united in a federation for the good of all, were derived from American roots and given practical expression through the Peacemaker and Hiawatha.[50]

David Maybury-Lewis's *Millennium: Tribal Wisdom and the Modern World* was published within months of *Exiled in the Land of the Free*. *Millennium* is a survey of aboriginal cultures around the world, prepared by Cultural Survival of Cambridge, Massachusetts, which Maybury-Lewis and his wife founded. The book contains a well-developed description of the Iroquois League's origins and operations. It also mentions Canassatego's advice to the colonies on unification in 1744, and Benjamin Franklin's use of the theme in the early 1750s. Maybury-Lewis writes:

> There is an argument raging currently over whether or not the founding fathers of the United States of America consciously modelled their new nation

*on the Iroquois Confederacy. It seems to me, however, that the important
thing is not whether they did or did not, but the fact that they could have.
There were, after all, no models in Europe at that time for the kind of federal
republic that the Americans established.*[51]

Maybury-Lewis considered the problems of modern states that include a
large number of nationalities. He wrote that solutions to these problems
"require us to have a different idea of the state, a kind of new federalism
which, after the manner of the League of the Iroquois, permits each people
in the nation to keep its council fire alight."[52]

According to Jerry Mander, author of *In the Absence of the Sacred* (1991),
Millennium was "an immensely valuable collection of rare information about
dozens of the world's still-viable native societies." Mander wrote that *Millennium* "takes us through native medical practice and pharmacology, religious
philosophy, and numerous examples of democratic forms of governance,
notably the Iroquois,' whose Great Law was surely the main model for the
U.S. Constitution."[53]

Of all the academic fields in which the influence thesis has been
discussed and debated, the "winner," in terms of column inches of academic-
journal type, is law. At least three-dozen law journals have treated the issue
in one way or another. Don Grinde, Oren Lyons, Kirke Kickingbird, and I
were invited to speak at the 1990 American Bar Association convention in
Chicago.

The influence thesis has been most often used in legal journals to support arguments for Native self-determination. Milnar Ball, Caldwell
Professor of Constitutional Law at the University of Georgia School of Law,
wrote that American Indian tribes existed as legal entities "long before the
state and federal governments were formed." Ball notes "persuasive evidence
that American democracy began between 350 and 500 years before the
American Revolution with the Iroquois Law of the Great Peace." Ball uses
this fact to support his assertion that "tribes, unlike local governments, have
inherent authority to govern; they need not rely on outside legislative power
to give them authority to act."[54]

In the *Wisconsin Law Review*, Robert A. Williams, Jr., a professor of law
at the University of Colorado and a Lumbee Indian, supports his case for
Native American self-governance by describing the Iroquois Confederacy
and its historic influence on the formation of the United States.[55] Writing in
the *California Law Review*, Williams argues that the Iroquois have an
effective model for a multicultural society, as he strives to "avoid overt

engagement in the needlessly acrimonious debate about the degree of influence of Iroquois political ideas on the 'Founders' of the United States and
their drafting of this nation's Constitution."[56]

Although the general reception of the influence idea had improved in
academia by 1992, the debunking brigade was out for the quincentenary, as
well. One of the more superficial treatments of the idea appeared in Robert
Royal's *1492 and All That: Political Manipulations of History*. Royal maintained that "a few—very few—passages"[57] in historical records indicate
Iroquois influence. Royal borrowed from Tooker the belief that no one in-
vestigated the structure of the Confederacy until the founding of American
anthropology in the 1840s, ignoring the observations of Franklin, Jefferson,
Adams, and others. Consequently, Royal wrote, the Iroquois role "in shaping
the Constitution in any serious way is doubtful to say the least."[58]

Similarly, in *Culture of Complaint: The Fraying of America*, Robert
Hughes wrote:

> *American ideas of liberal democracy are only to be nourished at their sources,*
> *which lie absolutely within the European tradition; and it is far more*
> *important that the young should know about them before they go on to acquire*
> *whatever acquaintance they may wish to have with the ancient culture of the*
> *Dogon or the political institutions of the Iroquois.*[59]

While Hughes may choose to remain ignorant of the African Dogon,
David Maybury-Lewis wrote in *Millennium* that the Dogon have been studied
by so many European and American anthropologists that they have incorporated an anthropologist figure into some of their ritual dances. It is
possible, therefore, that the Dogon know much more about Hughes' culture
than he knows of theirs. The same might be said of the Iroquois, who are so
close to Hughes—yet, in affairs of the mind, still so far away.

NOTES

1. Donald A. Grinde, Jr. and Bruce E. Johansen, *Exemplar of Liberty: Native America and the Evolution of Democracy* (Los Angeles: UCLA American Indian Studies Center, 1991).

2. José Barreiro, *Indian Roots of American Democracy* (Ithaca, N.Y.: Akwe:kon Press/Cornell University), 1992.

3. Robert Venables, "The Founding Fathers: Choosing to Be the Romans," *Northeast Indian Quarterly* 6, no. 4 (Winter 1989): 31.

4. Peter G. Jemison, "Setting the Record Straight," in *Voices from the Battlefront: Achieving Cultural Equity,* ed. Marta Moreno Vega and Cheryll Y. Greene (Trenton, N.J.: Africa World Press, 1994), 26.

5. Interview, Johansen with Sally Roesch Wagner, Omaha, Nebraska, June 2, 1995. See also: Sally Roesch Wagner. "The Iroquois Confederacy: A Native American Model for Non-Sexist Men," *Changing Men* (Spring–Summer 1988): 32–33; Wagner, "The Root of Oppression Is the Loss of Memory: The Iroquois and the Early Feminist Vision," *Akwesasne Notes* 21, no. 1 (Late Winter 1989): 11; Wagner, "The Iroquois Influence on Women's Rights," *Akwe:kon Journal* 9, no. 1 (Spring 1992): 4–15.

6. Matilda Joslyn Gage, *Woman, Church and State* [1893], ed. Sally Roesch Wagner (Watertown, Mass.: Persephone Press, 1980), 10.

7. Interview, Johansen with Sally Roesch Wagner, Omaha, Nebraska, June 2, 1995.

8. Maureen Nolan, "Iroquois Women Serve as Models," *Syracuse Post-Standard,* April 8, 1995, B–3.

9. Lois Vesburgh, "Roles to Fill: South Dakota Researcher's Work, Performances Connect to CNY," *Syracuse Herald-American,* January 1,\ 1995.

10. Paula Gunn Allen, "Who Is Your Mother? Red Roots of White Feminism," in *The Graywolf Annual Five: Multicultural Literacy,* ed. Rick Simonson and Scott Walker (St. Paul: Graywolf Press, 1988), 23.

11. Renee Jacobs, "The Iroquois Great Law of Peace and the U.S. Constitution: How the Founding Fathers Ignored the Clan Mothers," *American Indian Law Review* 16 (1991): 497–531.

12. Gail H. Landsman, "The 'Other' as Political Symbol: Images of the Indians in the Woman Suffrage Movement," *Ethnohistory* 39, no. 1 (Summer 1992): 252; Landsman, "Portrayals of the Iroquois in the Woman Suffrage Movement," paper presented at the annual Conference on Iroquois Research, Rensselaerville, New York, October 8, 1988.

13. Yasuhide Kawashima, review of Grinde and Johansen, *Exemplar of Liberty,* 1991, *American Historical Review* 98, no. 3 (June 1993): 941.

14. Elisabeth Tooker, review of *Exemplar of Liberty,* 1991, *Northeast Anthropologist* 46 (Fall 1993): 103.

15. Tooker, review of *Exemplar of Liberty,* 107.

16. J.A. Brandao, review of *Exemplar of Liberty,* 1991, *Canadian Historical Review* 74, no. 3 (fall 1993): 436.

17. We wrote, in part:
   History sometimes tells us as much about power relationships as about facts. Our intellectual architecture is built on assumptions about domination and subordination as much as on the actual facts of any particular matter.

When Donald A. Grinde, Jr., and Bruce E. Johansen assemble a mosaic of historical evidence to support their assertion that the political societies of Native Americans helped shape the evolution of democracy in America, debate often rises less over the facts than over assumptions and motivations, such as the authors' assumed deprecation of our "British" (or "European") heritage. At a time when English is the *lingua franca* of the world, and economic systems which originated in Europe are invading even the most remote areas of the earth, the idea that non-Europeans contributed significantly to our shared intellectual history is sometimes deemed to be (to use Noam Chomsky's phrase) "beyond the scope of permissible debate."

Viewing history through the intellectual filters of dominance can cause distortions. Historians may forget that although the Founders were of European heritage, many of them were searching history and their own experiences for an entirely new mode of government. Benjamin Franklin remarked at the Constitutional Convention that "We have gone back to ancient history . . . all around Europe, but find none of their constitutions suitable to our circumstances." James Wilson concurred: "British government cannot be our model."

The colonists did not go to the trouble of a revolution merely to reconstruct a purely British system in America. Instead, the Founders of the United States created a unique non-monarchial state that synthesized European heritage and thought with Native American societies that many of the Founders (most notably Franklin and Jefferson) knew well. Any history of this time which subscribes to European roots exclusively is a product of racial arrogance and fantasies of empire. [*Exemplar of Liberty*, 191]

18. Alan Tack, review of *Exemplar of Liberty*, 1991, in *Native Peoples*, Summer 1992, 72.

19. Wilbur Jacobs, "Columbus, Indians, and the Black Legend Hocus-Pocus," *American Indian Culture and Research Journal* 17, no. 2 (1993): 178.

20. Jacobs, "Columbus, Indians," 184.

21. Wilbur Jacobs, "The American Indian Legacy of Freedom and Liberty," *American Indian Culture and Research Journal* 16, no. 4 (1992): 185–93.

22. Jerry Mander, *In the Absence of the Sacred* (San Francisco: Sierra Club Books, 1991). In his rush to embrace the idea, Mander made several factual errors. One of the more intriguing was his placement of Benjamin Franklin at the scene of Canassatego's 1744 speech at Lancaster as the Onondaga sachem advised the colonists to unite on an Iroquois model. Franklin made his acquaintance with Canassatego's words as a printer of Indian treaties. His diplomatic contact with the Iroquois and their allies began after 1750.

23. John Kaminski, "U.S., Soviet Constitutions Stolen from the Iroquois: but Our Founding Fathers, Engels Bungled the Theft," *The New England Pilgrim* 1, no. 1 (December 1991): 1, 8–9.

24. Barbara Bardes, et al., American Government and Politics Today: The Essentials (St. Paul, Minn.: West Publishing Co., 1992), 66, 140.

25. Donald Johns, "Native Roots: How the Indians Enriched America," Whole Earth Review, December 22, 1993, 110.

26. Jack Weatherford, "A Year to Discover Rich History of the Very First Americans," Minneapolis Star-Tribune, October 13, 1991, 21–A.

27. Thomas Altherr, review of Jack Weatherford, Indian Givers, American Indian Quarterly (Spring 1992): 259–61.

28. David E. Stannard, American Holocaust: Columbus and the Conquest of the New World (New York: Oxford University Press, 1992), 28–30.

29. Stannard, American Holocaust, 30, emphasis in original.

30. Ronald Wright, Stolen Continents: The Americas Through Indian Eyes Since 1492 (Boston: Houghton-Mifflin, 1992), 115–16.

31. "Manhattan Neighborhoods," Newsday, January 13, 1992, 21.

32. Patrick C. Morris, "Who Are These Gentle People?" American Indian Culture and Research Journal 17, no. 1 (1993): 8.

33. Ibid., 8.

34. Lewis Lord and Sarah Burke. "America Before Columbus," U.S. News & World Report, July 8, 1991, 2.

35. Chet Lunner, "A Primer on the First People," Gannett News Service, October 12, 1992, in LEXIS.

36. Suzan Shown Harjo, "Columbus: Discoverer or Despoiler? American Indians Still Reeling from Genocide," Dallas Morning News, October 11, 1992, 1–J.

37. Jane Bosveld, "Forgotten Founders: Did the Great Law of Peace, the Constitution of the Iroquois Nation, Help Shape Democracy and Federalism?" Omni, February, 1992, 33.

38. Mary Kaye, "The Road to Beauty," Sassy, October, 1992, 76–78, 90–91.

39. David Maybury-Lewis, "Tribal Wisdom: Is it Too Late to Reclaim the Benefits of Tribal Living?" Utne Reader, July/August 1992, 76–77. This is a sidebar to the main article by Jason W. Clay, originally published in Mother Jones, November/ December, 1990.

40. This article was first published in English as Donald A. Grinde, Jr., "The Iroquois and the Nature of American Government," American Indian Culture and Research Journal 17, no. 1 (1993): 153–73.

41. Waleria Mikolajczyk, "Poland and the American Indian: Friends of the Red Man," The Warsaw Voice, January 17, 1993.

42. Nancy Bonvillian, Hiawatha: Founder of the Iroquois Confederacy, (New York: Chelsea House, 1992), 103.

43. Annette Jaimes, ed., The State of Native America: Genocide, Colonization, and Resistance (Boston: South End Press, 1992), 87. See especially chapter 3, "Self-

Determination and Subordination: The Past, Present, and Future of American Indian Self-Governance" by Rebecca L. Robbins.

44. Review of Oren Lyons et al., Exiled in the Land of the Free, 1992, Publishers Weekly, September 14, 1992, 92. The book was actually a cooperative effort between Native American and non-Native scholars, not Native Americans alone, as this review states. Six of the coauthors are Native American (Oren Lyons, John Mohawk, Vine Deloria, Jr., Howard Berman, Donald Grinde, and Curtis Berkey); two are not (Laurence Hauptman and Robert Venables).

45. Robert L. Smith, "Democracy, Indian Style," Syracuse Post-Standard, December 28, 1992, B–1, B–5.

46. Alexander Ewen, ed., Voice of Indigenous Peoples: Native People Address the United Nations (Santa Fe: Clear Light Publishers, 1994), 31–36.

47. Rodney A. Smolla, "Last in War, Peace, and the Supreme Court," New York Times Book Review, April 11, 1993, 22.

48. Wilbur Jacobs, review of Lyons et al., Exiled in the Land of the Free, 1992, American Indian Culture and Research Journal 18, no. 1 (1994): 177–79.

49. Richard Haan, review of Lyons et al., Exiled in the Land of the Free, Journal of American History 81, no. 2 (September 1994): 641–42.

50. Frank Waters, Brave Are My People (Santa Fe: Clear Light Publishers 1993), 7, 22–23.

51. David Maybury-Lewis, Millennium: Tribal Wisdom and the Modern World, (New York: Viking, 1992), 245.

52. Maybury-Lewis, Millennium, 264.

53. Jerry Mander, "Wisdom from Other Cultures," review of Maybury-Lewis, Millennium, San Francisco Chronicle, April 26, 1992, 3.

54. Milnar S.Ball, "Legal Storytelling: Stories of Origin and Constitutional Possibilities," Michigan Law Review 87 (August 1989): 2280. For coverage of the ABA panel, see Maria Morocco, "Rediscovering the Roots of American Democracy," Human Rights 17, no. 3 (Fall 1990): 38–39.

55. Robert A.Williams, Jr., "The Algebra of Federal Indian Law: The Hard Trail of Decolonizing and Americanizing the White Man's Indian Jurisprudence," Wisconsin Law Review (March 1986): 219.

56. Robert A. Williams, Jr., "Linking Arms Together: Multicultural Constitutionalism in a North American Indigenous Vision of Law and Peace," California Law Review 82 (July 1994): 981.

57. Robert Royal, 1492 and All That: Political Manipulations of History (Washington, D.C.: Ethics and Public Policy Center, 1992): 152–53.

58. Royal, 1492 and All That, 152–53.

59. Robert Hughes, Culture of Complaint: The Fraying of America (New York: Oxford University Press, 1993), 150.

7.

"You've Made a Cliché of It!"

Bruce E. Johansen

D uring early August, 1994, Pueblo anthropologist Alfonso Ortiz discussed the evolution of the debate over the influence issue with me at the Picuris Pueblo's annual feast day. We talked as we watched a traditional ceremony in which four clowns assisted each other in pursuit of a fat lamb at the top of a thirty-foot pole. The same four clowns had been doing this for several years, and they had grown rather older and fatter than before. After an hour of frustration as the crowd watched the lamb dangle in the breeze, one of the clowns went to fetch an extension ladder that shortened the climb to about fifteen feet.

I wondered aloud what Elisabeth Tooker might make of this. "Post-contact phenomenon," she may have snorted. Alfonso chuckled, and admonished me not to judge all anthropologists by those who claimed to be experts on the Iroquois. He reflected that, despite the resistance of such experts, the influence idea had become intellectual elevator music in some quarters. "You've made a cliché of it," he told me.

On June 12, 1995, a warm, humid Monday morning, I made my way to the University Library of the University of Nebraska at Omaha to return two books. While there, I sat down at a terminal for LEXIS, a database for several hundred newspapers, other publications, and transcripts. On a whim, I typed in "Iroquois and Constitution" as keywords for a data search. I was surprised by 425 "hits," and intrigued as I started to read them, since I was finding item after item that I did not have in my annotated bibliography. New entries were rolling in by the dozens. When Alfonso Ortiz told me we had made a cliché of it, I never suspected how right he was until I carried a two-inch thick stack of printouts out of the library.

The next day I returned to the library, and became so entranced at the machine that one of the librarians told me: "You're using that thing like an

IV!" I found more than one hundred more new "points" in the debate. Barely any of them named any major participants in the debate by name. The print-outs took me to every major city in the United States and Canada, to England, to Poland, and the Philippine Islands. I had a renewed sense of how large and varied the world is, and how so many voices could be raised, with so many very divergent perspectives, on a single, well-defined issue.

After I had exhausted the newspaper files of LEXIS, a legally inclined friend reminded me that the database also contains law journals. I tapped them next, and watched the idea of Native American influence on democracy spread over roughly a decade (1985 to 1996) through a maze of legal journals.

During the summer of 1990, Oren Lyons, Donald Grinde, Kirke Kickingbird, and I were invited to present our case for Native American philosophical and legal precedents to the annual meeting of the American Bar Association in Chicago. Maria Morocco, a copy editor of the *ABA Journal,* described the panel in that daily legal newspaper, which was distributed to the roughly twenty thousand lawyers, judges, and legal scholars who attended the convention.[1] In its fall 1990 issue, Morocco expanded her account in the ABA magazine *Human Rights.*[2]

No paradigm shift in thinking affects everyone at the same time. Even in 1995, while some of the self-defined experts still thought we were making it all up, the idea that Native American confederacies helped shape concepts of democracy was being worked into elementary school curricula by the same group that had authored the Pledge of Allegiance a century earlier. The second National School Celebration in 1992 (the centenary for the first, celebrated in 1892), stressed America's patriotic heritage. A booklet published by the National School Celebration contains an essay by Elizabeth Christensen ("Our Founding Grandfathers"), observing the Iroquois roots of American democracy. The book lists month-by-month themes for celebration. The theme for October is "How did the political and social order of Native Americans influence American democracy?"[3]

The idea also reached children through more elementary school texts and workbooks.[4] An elementary school workbook, Jan Maher and Doug Selwyn's *Native Americans: Grades 3 and 4,* also discussed the Iroquois Great Law of Peace, Benjamin Franklin, and the writing of the Constitution.[5] High school history textbooks were criticized for excluding the influence idea. In James W. Loewen's *Lies My Teacher Told Me* (1995), a survey of the twelve leading high school history textbooks, one of the themes discussed is "the influence of the Iroquois' system of government on the framers of the Constitution." Loewen devotes a chapter to textbook portrayals of Indians, and calls them "the most lied-about subset of our population."[6] He devotes considerable space to the historical circumstances that initiated Iroquois influence on U.S. political institutions. In a footnote, Loewen takes issue with Arthur Schlesinger, Jr.'s argument in *Disuniting of America* (1992) that Europe "was also the source—the unique source—of those liberating ideas of individual liberty." Loewen comments: "He offers no evidence, only assertion, for this claim, and apparently does not know of Europe's astonishment not only at Native American liberty but also at religious freedom in China and Turkey."[7]

The influence idea was raised in diverse debates aimed at solving very large social, political, and ecological problems. The idea was raised, for example, by Tom Hayden, a founder of Students for a Democratic Society in the 1960s and a California state senator in the 1990s, as he invoked political decentralization as a way to disassemble the "special interest state." In *Tikkun*, a progressive Jewish journal, Hayden called for a decentralization on "a Jeffersonian, or Quaker, or Iroquois" model in an economy based in an ecosystem balanced for generations to come.[8]

The use of the Iroquois as an exemplar of eco-correct participatory democracy drew a retort from Martin W. Lewis in *Green Delusions:*

> *The Iroquois Confederacy is a particularly ill-considered exemplar [of direct democracy]. Admiring the Iroquois political system . . . for its democracy is like praising Nazi Germany for its enlightened forestry. The Five Nations not only engaged in a highly successful campaign of ethnocide against their competitors in the fur trade, the Hurons, but they also raised the torture of war captives (those they chose not to adopt . . .) to an art.*[9]

In the early and middle 1990s, the influence thesis also spread through a proliferating number of books on multicultural themes. One example was James A. Joseph's *Remaking America: How the Benevolent Traditions of Many Cultures Are Transforming Our National Life* (1995). Joseph was president of the Council on Foundations when he wrote this book; in 1995, President Clinton nominated him as ambassador to South Africa. This collection of multicultural readings begins the first page of its first chapter by quoting from *Exemplar of Liberty:* "The native peoples lived in confederations so subtle, so nearly invisible, as to be an attractive alternative to monarchy's overbearing hand." Joseph, who is African-American, then writes, "The advanced democratic

practices of the Iroquois, for example, fitted very well with the abstract principles of democracy already forming in the minds of the European settlers."[10]

Also in the multicultural field, Joseph Coburn *et al.* contributed a
thirty-page essay on American Indians to *Educating for Diversity*, an "anthology of multicultural voices." In the essay, the authors wrote:

> *The U.S. government was heavily influenced by the League of the [Iroquois].*
> *Democracy and communist governments were influenced by the "Village*
> *Council" governing practices utilized by the majority of tribes in*
> *pre-Columbian America. Forms of this practice survive today."*[11]

Debate over American Indians' role in the history of democracy has
risen as Native American studies programs proliferate across the United
States. Such programs were virtually unknown in the United States before
1970. The influence debate has intensified as Native peoples have attempted
to express their own views unhindered by certain ethnohistorians, anthropologists, and other "friends of the Indian," who have bestowed upon
themselves the authority to define the Indian world to the rest of us—even
to Native peoples themselves. This is an exercise in what James Clifford
called "monological" authority, a major aspect of European ethnocentri-
cism.[12] The "experts" define the terms of debate and do most of the talking.
The very nature of monological authority denies Native voices equal access
to the mechanisms by which the general society defines and sanctions truth,
and in turn, power relationships.

When a group is not allowed a self-defined voice, it has no face, except
that defined by others. The decolonization of history is only one part of what
needs to be done. Native people in the United States (and around the world)
have been struggling for much of the twentieth century to decolonize their
entire lives. For example, what might happen to Native Americans rights to
occupy their homelands if Native nations were accepted legally, politically,
and culturally as having predated European-American occupancy of the
Americas? This is only one example of many ways in which the power to
define "truth" determines conditions of life for both the colonizer and the
colonized.

Any debate which so much as challenges the format (not to mention the
substance) of monological authority creates intellectual tensions both in the
academy and in the political arena. The debate over influence has, for
example, spilled into debates over the return of Native remains and burial
objects. In upstate New York, the same lines of conflict permeated the debate
over return of wampum belts to the Haudenosaunee. Thus, the debate over

Native American influence on the evolution of democracy has become part of a broader effort by Native Americans to decolonize their own history. In its totality, this debate may be less about "multiculturalism" than about the de-Europeanization of North America's history.

From a Native American perspective, the facts of the last five centuries have been those of living (and often dying) in confrontation with aggressive and often destructive cultures imported from Europe. This point is sometimes lost on European-Americans who are not accustomed to thinking of themselves as living in an imperial state. The rhetoric of decolonization may not seem to apply to history written by the victors in the war in which much of North America changed hands. The invader looms large, however, in any history written by Native Americans, because developments set into motion by the invader affected their peoples and cultures so fundamentally. The fact that Native American political systems helped shape the developing institutions and official ideology of this imperial state is no small irony. The adopting of cultural elements of a conquered people is not unprecedented, however. Almost half a century ago, Felix Cohen compared the European-American use of Native American political ideas to the use the Romans made of Greek political culture.

To maintain an empire requires habits of mind that justify its existence. Academic inquiry is often called into service to provide reasons why one nation, or one group of people, should be deemed superior to another. A century ago, some scientists supported assertions that a man's intelligence can be determined by his cranial capacity. (Women had no rights in the dominant society at that time and were therefore not considered.) The theory was expounded by Europeans who, it was found, had the biggest skulls. Today the intellectual tools of oppression are not quite so crude. Instead, we hear learned individuals worrying about whether new knowledge offered by non-European people will crowd out "the canon," that singular body of knowledge describing "Western civilization" that all of us are supposed to share.

Edward Said has speculated on the "relationship between anthropology . . . as an ongoing enterprise and . . . empire as a going concern."[13] As an academic discipline, anthropology was born in the heyday of unquestioned empire building justified by the doctrine of Manifest Destiny, which sanctioned expansionist policies. The work of anthropology's founder, Lewis Henry Morgan, fit squarely within a Eurocentric framework, as he tried, in his last book *Ancient Society* (1877), to rank all cultures in three categories: civilized, barbarian, and savage. Even after years of association with Iroquois people, Morgan set forth standards of evaluation that are exclusively European. Morgan found the Iroquois to be "barbarian." Morgan's classifications have informed the conduct of anthropology ever since. On Morgan's value judgments have been built a social-scientific method of observing Native Americans as subjects, not as equals. In the "observer-subject" dichotomy on which traditional anthropological method rests, there is no room for the "subject" (usually Native people) to talk back to the "observer" in Native terms, viewing history through Native eyes. Thus, the debate over influence began, and continues, mainly outside the academic province of anthropology or ethnohistory, which provides no perceptual framework in which to appreciate it.

One knows he's reached clichédom when he sees the subject matter of his Ph.D. dissertation popping up in history quiz books. On the back cover of John Malone's *Native American History Quiz Book* (1994), the first question is: "What confederation, first formed in 1570, had significant influence on the United States Constitution?"[14] In Jack Utter's *American Indians: Answers to Today's Questions* (1993), under the question "Who are the Six Nations?" Utter provides a brief description of the Iroquois League and its Great Law of Peace, and compares its structure to that of the United Nations.[15]

In the early 1990s, the idea was spreading into the broadcasting media and film. The idea made an appearance on the National Public Radio show "The Engines of Our Ingenuity." Hosted by University of Houston Engineering Professor John Lienhard, the show celebrated its one thousandth broadcast in 1995. Lienhard, who mastered a stutter, broadcasts over thirty NPR affiliates nationwide. A *Houston Chronicle* article lists a number of segment titles, mentioning one that "dealt with what the U.S. Constitution owes to the political system of the Iroquois nation. . . . the transcript of [this segment] is the most requested Lienhard episode to date."[16]

The idea was widely accepted enough by 1993 for "Larry King Live" to use it as a news hook for celebrating Independence Day. With Pat Mitchell sitting in for King, Oren Lyons on July 5 talked about Native American precedents for United States fundamental law. Lyons described Iroquois consensus-making practices, the story of the Peacemaker, and colonists' early encounters with Native Americans that provided channels of communication for Native American ideas. Lyons described one student of his in Buffalo who was "very angry" because, at age thirty-two, with four children, he had never been told of the Iroquois influence on U.S. fundamental law. "My children are going to hear about this," the student told Lyons.[17]

During 1993, researchers for the Turner Broadcasting Network visited the Six Nations Indian Museum in Onchiota, New York, where John Kahionhes Fadden gave them a copy of *Exemplar of Liberty*. That book and other suggestions of influence that researchers heard along the way figured prominently in the documentary "The Broken Chain," one of several programs that Turner's network aired on Native American subjects during 1994. These programs were part of a general surge in tele-documentary efforts on Native American history at this time, but their focus was different from most. "The Broken Chain" and several other segments in the series Turner titled "The Native Americans," were produced entirely by Native American talent, on camera and behind the scenes. As much as the format permitted, they were told from a Native point of view. In the non-Indian press, reviews were mixed, with the influence idea alternately exalted and panned.

Reviews of "The Native Americans" were so diverse that they started a mini-debate on their own. In the *New York Times*, television critic Walter Goodman faulted "The Native Americans" for "romantic pictures and expositions that mix fact with myth," one such mixture being "the view . . . [that] the political arrangements of the Iroquois Confederacy, a union of tribes in upper New York State, was a model for the framers of the United States Constitution. One Indian historian reports that 'the fundamental beginning of Western democracy as we know it' can be found in the Iroquois wampum belts. So much for John Locke."[18] Goodman apparently is not a student of Locke. Otherwise, he would realize that Locke also was influenced by Native American conceptions of liberty and natural rights, especially conceptions expressed by Roger Williams in the seventeenth century.

In *Newsweek*, Harry F. Waters took issue with the series' assertion that the Iroquois helped shape democracy:

> As an exercise in history, "The Native Americans" may not escape scholarly challenge. For openers, its claim that the Iroquois Confederacy provided the model for the U.S. Constitution will come as a revelation to those who thought the Magna Carta had something to do with it.[19]

Waters overstated the case to discredit it, a common tactic of opponents; the film asserts that the Iroquois provided *a* model, not *the* model. There is an enormous difference, one that Jefferson, Franklin, Paine, and others among the founders appreciated. Waters seemed not to fathom the possibility that the Iroquois and Magna Carta *both* could have had influence on the United States' formative ideology.

Time magazine's Richard Zoglin applauded the idea: "The acting is more wooden and the drama more sketchy than in *Geronimo* [a TV movie broadcast on TNT]. Yet the history lesson—that principles of the Iroquois Confederacy were an important influence on the American Constitution—is well told."[20] John Freeman, in the *San Diego Union-Tribune*, said that Ted Turner, "the Mouth of the South," is spending $60 million "to raise awareness of Indian history and culture." Freeman continued:

> To its credit, "The Broken Chain" does portray Iroquois as thoughtful and peace-loving—until provoked. But once they're provoked, watch out! The movie also carries this important message: that the U.S. Constitution is based on the Iroquois tenet of many diverse nation-states being bound together as one nation.[21]

While other writers in the *Orlando Sentinel* had panned the influence idea, Greg Dawson liked it. "The Broken Chain," he said, "recounts a fascinating chapter of American Indian history surely unfamiliar to most viewers—the story of the Iroquois Confederacy, a sophisticated organization of six Indian nations in the Northeast that became a model for the U.S. Constitution."[22] Dawson noted that the founders failed to observe the power of clan mothers in the confederacy, and did not include Iroquois-style women's rights in the Constitution.

As it spread in broadcast media and film, the influence idea also was raised by several entertainers during interviews on the road. It became part of singer Buffy Sainte-Marie's road show in the early 1990s. According to a piece in the *San Francisco Examiner*, she talked about the Indian concept of consensus building, which was practiced long before it became popular in modern organizations. She said, according to the *Examiner*'s account, "The Iroquois Confederacy used the kind of decentralized decision-making that modern 'network' organizations use today, just as the founding fathers of the United States borrowed key ideas from Iroquois statecraft when they framed the Constitution."[23]

Sainte-Marie also raised the subject during an interview in Toronto. She is quoted as saying, "Right now, people all over the world are dissatisfied and looking for new ways of government. They could learn, for instance, from the Iroquois Confederacy, from which the American Constitution derives." Sainte-Marie said the Constitution "didn't go far enough. The Europeans couldn't handle the female roles in the Iroquois system and chose to ignore them. From there, it's a short jump to ignoring the rights of females altogether."[24]

The influence issue also made its debut on the rap circuit. Litefoot, a twenty-six-year-old member of the Cherokee Nation, played Little Bear, an

Onondaga who is taken from 1761 to the present in the movie *The Indian in the Cupboard*. Litefoot, who calls himself the "first Native American rap artist/motivator," was described in an interview as "fiercely devoted to promoting cultural identity and awareness among young Native Americans." Author Bonnie Britton wrote, "He's no fan of Custer (a punk) or George Washington (an Indian killer) or Benjamin Franklin, who he says plagiarized from the Iroquois Confederacy 'and put it in the Constitution.'"[25] The influence issue also is mentioned briefly in the script of the movie.

Litefoot may have been the first Native American rapper to espouse Iroquois influence, but a Chicano did it two years earlier. In 1993, *Toronto Star* entertainment writer Peter Howell described the stage act and thoughts of vocalist/lyricist Zack de la Rocha, lead singer of Rage Against the Machine, who said that American society, "is a machine that will do anything to keep going. It has no moral understanding or any true sense of the word 'freedom,' or 'democracy.' The only true democracy ever experienced throughout the Americas was the one the Iroquois Indians had."[26]

Oneida folksinger Joanne Shenandoah shared Iroquois democratic ideas with roughly 250,000 people as she took part, with several other Iroquois, in the opening of the 1994 Woodstock music festival. She was joined on stage by Tadadaho Leon Shenandoah and Jake Swamp, traditional Mohawk sub-chief.

In the early and middle 1990s, some authors began to factor Iroquois political precedents into general histories of the British colonies in America. For example, Arthur Quinn, a professor of rhetoric at the University of California, outlined the founding legend of the Iroquois Confederacy in his *New World: An Epic of Colonial America from the Founding of Jamestown to the Fall of Quebec* (1994). He also described how the Iroquois example helped shape the United States. Quinn presented events involving Franklin and the Iroquois in some detail, beginning with Canassatego's advice that the colonists unite on an Iroquois model in 1744. Quinn makes a point of the fact that Franklin publicized the Onondaga sachem's advice by printing the treaty on his press. Quinn points out that Franklin's 1751 letter to his printing partner James Parker advising the colonists to unite as had the Iroquois was not simply private correspondence—it was published and publicized. "The Iroquois, strange to say, were not only providing the opportunity for this [colonial union]; they had long been providing by their example the method—or so Franklin thought."[27] Quinn says that the Iroquois model provided proof that confederation need not result in the type of oppressive centralized authority that was much feared in the colonies.

Even as the idea that the Iroquois and other Native American confederacies helped shape the ideology of democracy became so well known that it was called a cliché in some quarters, it had hardly reached the playing field of permissible debate in other arenas. Into the influence debate, like a bull, lumbered columnist Charley Reese of the *Orlando Sentinel,* who wrote that ideas such as Iroquois influence on democracy lay a claim on gullible Americans because they don't know their own history. His version of history was simple: "All the institutions of American government are derived from our European culture. None comes from Africa or Asia or American Indians." Reese called "ignorant" assertions in the recent Turner Broadcasting series "The First Americans" that "our forefathers derived the idea of the U.S. Constitution from the Iroquois Confederation."[28]

With this statement, Reese was barely getting warmed up. "It's not even worthy of comment, except to point out that only a person 100 percent ignorant of American and European history could make such a dumb statement." Before leaving the scene, our bull leaves a twenty-four-carat nugget of absolute denial at the door: "The superbly educated authors of the American Revolution had nothing to learn from a primitive tribal alliance."[29]

In 1995, Laurence Hauptman took aim, as his title indicates, in *Tribes and Tribulations: Misconceptions About American Indians and Their Histories.* Hauptman rues the pervasive "misconception" that the Iroquois and other Native American confederations helped shape democracy. "Despite the highly speculative nature of the evidence . . . this misconception has become a shibboleth," writes the author, citing the U.S. Senate resolution of 1988 supporting the idea.[30] Using what we could call the "Iroquois publicity-hound thesis," Hauptman speculates that the Iroquois created oral history to assert that key ideas were borrowed from them. Speaking of misconceptions—this one is straight out of the Trolls' book of shibboleths.

Hauptman rests his argument first on the writing of the Constitution itself, and second on the life of James Wilson, a man whose influence was minor at best. Wilson, he claims, was too materialistic and too Eurocentric to appreciate the Iroquois example. Hauptman fails, however, to deal with an important statement that Wilson made at the Constitutional Convention June 7, 1787, which calls this attitude into question: "The British government cannot be our model. We have no materials for a similar one. Our manners, our laws, the abolition of entails and primogeniture, the whole genius of our people are opposed to it."[31]

Having rather ineffectively chipped at one tree in our forest of argument, Hauptman declares that every tree in the woods has been felled. He then closes by declaring that Canassatego was "hardly part of Wilson's mind-set."[32] He does not examine Benjamin Franklin's relationship with the Onondaga leader. Hauptman argues that Wilson's appetite for Indian land rendered consideration of Indian intellect impossible for Wilson, despite the fact that history tells us that some colonists appreciated Native polities and at the same time speculated in Native American land, Franklin having been a prime example.

Reviewing *Tribes and Tribulations* in the *American Indian Culture and Research Journal*, Jerry Stubben praised Hauptman's collection of nine essays as well written and documented, but said that "Hauptman's use of the psychological profile of James Wilson to rebut Donald Grinde's and Bruce Johansen's argument that the Iroquois and other Native American nations influenced the founding fathers in their development of democracy in America is less than convincing." By concentrating on Wilson, "a minor player in Iroquois/colonial relations," writes Stubben, "Hauptman overlooks the influence of Native American political thought on major players such as Franklin, Jefferson, and Rutledge."[33]

The idea that Native Americans lived in complex polities that helped inspire democratic ideas emerged as an issue in Canada's debate over a new Constitution in the early 1990s. A 1993 report of the Royal Commission on Aboriginal Peoples considered alternatives to Canada's present confederation, and Native American peoples' roles in Canadian governance. Iroquois models of government were presented. The report argued that the Canadian confederation has come more to resemble the Iroquois League over time, moving gradually from exclusive reliance on its British origins.[34]

Relations between European-Canadians and Native peoples were especially taut in Quebec, because that province was asserting its sovereignty while denying similar claims of Mohawks and others within its borders. In the *Vancouver Sun*, Stephen Hume addressed the question of Quebec's claim for "special status" in a newly defined Canadian confederation. He wrote that advocates of Quebec's sovereignty were being hypocritical when they refused to allow sovereignty for First Peoples (Indigenous Peoples, such as the Inuit) inside the province's borders. Canadian Native leader Ovide Mercredi, a Cree chief, was said to have recently made this argument, for which he was criticized by several Quebec politicians.

Consider the monumental insult Mercredi must feel in downtown Montreal where the first encounter between the founders [of Quebec] and the Iroquois is

celebrated with a disgusting depiction of Paul de Chomeday blowing out
a chief's brains with his pistol. . . . The Indian he killed already had a con-
stitution so sophisticated that the United States borrowed it . . .[35]

Joe Clark, Canadian Minister for Constitutional Affairs, used the
Iroquois heritage as evidence of Native peoples' ability to govern themselves
in a speech to the Canadian Manufacturers Association: "Aboriginal self-
government . . . was here when Thomas Jefferson and Benjamin Franklin
looked to the Iroquois Confederacy when they were designing the American
Constitution."[36] Clark reiterated his position in another speech; he said that
the recognition of natives' right to govern themselves is "no less fundamental than the recognition of Quebec as a distinct society." In a speech at
Queen's University in Kingston, Ontario, attended by a standing-room only
audience, Clark said that both issues "will determine whether this country
will succeed or fail." To support his contention that aboriginal people should
govern themselves, he said, according to this account, that "elaborate and
sophisticated systems of native self-government existed long before European
settlers arrived. The Iroquois Confederacy, for example, was a model for the
American constitution."[37]

Voyce Durling-Jones, a member of the Canadian diplomatic corps as
consul general to Liberia, also raised the Iroquois model of democracy in a
speech in Vancouver, B.C. titled "Doing Business with Aboriginal Canada."
He mentioned several Native American contributions to general North
American culture and went on to say, "In the United States, the Iroquois
Confederacy served as a model for the new colonial government's federal
system—paradigm shift—though the true history of the Americas has still
not been truly comprehended or proper acknowledgement yet given to the
First Peoples of the Americas . . . "[38]

A book published in Canada during 1991, *Occupied Canada: A Young*
White Man Discovers His Unsuspected Past, brings the idea of Iroquian contributions to democracy into the personal story of Robert Calihoo, who was
raised in Edmonton under the name Robert Royer by a very proper but racist
white grandmother.[39] After her death, when he was ten years of age, Calihoo
called on his father, Albert Calihoo, whom he had not previously met. He
discovered that Albert is a Native American, a Mohawk, whose family hailed
from Kahnawake, near Montreal.

Young Calihoo is introduced to reservation life and its privations as
he discovers what Canada has done to the people whose identity he is
now assuming. Part of the book comprises his autobiography; the rest, by

professional writer Robert Hunter, is an exposé of conditions faced by First Peoples in Canada. Hunter also surveys Native contributions to many cultures, including the impact of the Iroquois on the likes of Locke, Thoreau, Tolstoy, their effect on American democracy, Marxist communism, and the French Revolution.

In 1993, the two-hour Canadian film *Kahnasatake: 270 Years of Resistance*, developed the influence idea in the context of the 1990 confrontation between Quebec police and Canadian army troops at the Mohawk settlement of Kanesatake, near Oka, Quebec. The film, which was made for the National Film Board of Canada by Alanis Obomsawin, won an award as Best Canadian Film at the 1993 Toronto Film Festival. It describes Iroquois history and governmental structure, including an assertion that the Iroquois system "influenced the adoption of a democratic charter in North America."

The influence idea reached a substantial New Age audience, and sometimes became exaggerated along the way. Robert Hieronimus treated the idea extensively (but not always entirely accurately) in *America's Secret Destiny: Spiritual Vision and the Founding of a Nation* (1989). This New Age history considered the Iroquois contribution at the beginning of its first chapter. Hieronimus noted Canassatego's 1744 speech and Franklin's popularization of it. In another New-Age title, *Mother Earth Spirituality* (1990), Ed McGaa briefly described Canassatego's advice to the colonists (1744), Benjamin Franklin's use of Iroquois models in the Albany Plan (1754), and the Founders' use of a federal system similar to the Iroquois Confederacy.

Another New Age treatment, Jean Howard and Margaret Rubin's *Manual for the Peacemaker* (1995) attempts to give advice on how to practice the Great Law of Peace on a personal level. This book traces the story of Deganawidah and Hiawatha and includes exercises designed to make the Peacemaker's teachings useful to all. In its introduction, *Manual for the Peacemaker* discusses ways in which Iroquois political thought helped shape that of Franklin, Jefferson, and other founders of the United States, as well as French and British philosophers.

Applications of the influence idea continued to proliferate. Late in 1993, Jewell Praying Wolf James wrote "The Indian Pledge of Allegiance," which was read by Joseph de la Cruz, former president of the Quinault Indian Nation, at the National Congress of American Indians (a tribal-states relations panel), Reno, Nevada, December 2, 1993. The pledge was "dedicated to American Indian and Alaska Native veterans, leaders, people, and children."

I pledge allegiance to my tribe,
To the democratic principles
    of the republic;
    and to the individual freedoms
Borrowed from the Iroquois
    and Choctaw confederacies,
As incorporated into the
    United States Constitution,
So that my forefathers
    shall not have died in vain.

President Clinton incorporated the influence thesis into a speech that he gave to several hundred Native American tribal leaders at the White House on April 29, 1994. He said: "So much of what we are today comes from who you have been for a long time. Long before others came to these shores there were powerful and sophisticated cultures and societies here—yours. Because of your ancestors, democracy existed here long before the Constitution was drafted and ratified."[40] Clinton was probably referencing *Exemplar of Liberty;* Lummi representative Jewell James had asked me to donate two copies of the book for this event. The book was presented to President Clinton with other gifts the day before the speech.

Later in 1994, the influence issue became a factor in a published debate between Mohawk editor and activist Doug George-Kanentiio (Joanne Shenandoah's husband) and State University of New York anthropology professor Dean Snow. In a letter to the editor of the *Albany Times-Union,* George took issue with statements attributed to Snow in a feature article printed on November 3. The feature story had praised Snow's *The Iroquois* (1994), as "a sweeping narrative that traces the Iroquois culture from its beginnings a thousand years ago to its survival in today's United States and Canada." According to this piece, Snow believes that the idea that the Iroquois influenced the patriots who drew up the U.S. Constitution is a "myth."[41]

George replied: "It seems the anthropologists have once again managed to pick our bones for their own individual academic and economic gains." He continued: "We Iroquois have grown weary of having our culture, history and traditions taken apart by these social scientists. They have a nasty habit of treating us like bugs in a jar . . ."[42] Regarding Snow's dismissal of the idea that the Iroquois' political system helped shape American democracy, George wrote:

While the anthropologists grudgingly concede that our people exercised
a revolutionary influence on the world through our foods, technology and

architecture, they illogically insist that we had little or no influence on the minds of the American colonists. . . . Of course the authors of the U.S. Constitution were profoundly impressed by the democratic traditions of the Iroquois. Where else in the world could they have looked for examples of the free nation they were creating? Autocratic England? Dictatorial France? Serf-ridden Russia?[43]

During the fall of 1995, Donald Grinde and I were challenged to a "forum" on the influence idea in *William and Mary Quarterly*, one of the United States' most venerable historical journals. At first I thought it merely coincidental that WMQ is published on James Axtell's home campus, but I realized that coincidence was not the issue after reading papers by Philip A. Levy and Samuel Payne criticizing *Exemplar of Liberty* to which we had been asked to respond. Both thanked Axtell for assistance; Levy was a Ph.D. student at William and Mary. The circumstances compelled Grinde to speculate that we were being set up. "Sure we are being set up," I e-mailed him. "We should make the most of it." This forum appeared in the July, 1996, issue of WMQ.[44]

At about the same time, Alvin Josephy, Jr. published *500 Nations: An Illustrated History of North American Indians*, a companion volume to a 1995 CBS television series on Native Americans that was being hosted by the actor Kevin Costner. Josephy was no new convert to the influence thesis; he first mentioned it in *The Patriot Chiefs* as early as 1958, when I was eight years of age, and my Ph.D. dissertation was two decades in the unknown future. Following a brief description of the Haudenosaunee (Iroquois) League, Josephy wrote, "The Confederacy envisioned by the Peacemaker . . . influenced enlightened seventeenth and eighteenth century philosophers and writers in the colonies and Europe who were seeking just ways for their people to be governed." Josephy says that Benjamin Franklin's Albany Plan of Union "drew inspiration" from the Iroquois League, and that its example had an "indirect influence" on debates during the Constitutional Convention in 1787. Josephy says that the way in which the two houses of the U.S. Congress use conference committees to reconcile differences resembles the procedures of the Iroquois League.[45]

As the present book went through its paces at the press, the influence idea continued to pop up in unexpected places. One of them was the U.S. Navy, where Chief of Naval Operations Jeremy Boorda advocated the idea in a memo to all commands on shore and at sea. Boorda was ridiculed by conservative sailors and newspaper columnists alike.

Columnist John McCaslin of the *Washington Post* ridiculed Boorda's directive to honor Native American contributions to democracy in observance of Native American Heritage Month, November 1995. "And you thought the great genius of our form of government was bequeathed by that race of kings across yonder ocean—the Magna Carta, the common law, and all that? But it wasn't, according to eminent historian and political scientist Jeremy Boorda, who moonlights as Chief of Naval Operations." Admiral Boorda encouraged all commands to "support programs and exhibits, publish items of interest in command bulletins, and promote maximum participation by military and civilian personnel." McCaslin quoted an unnamed "senior veteran" as calling this the silly season of politically correct admirals. The veteran was quoted by McCaslin as saying "I don't know whether to laugh or cry."[46]

Another "Inside-the-Beltway" treatment of the idea emerged after editors of the *Washington Post's* "Outlook" (opinion) section asked three novelists to write President Clinton's "ideal" acceptance speech at the 1996 Democratic National Convention. One of the three was Louise Erdrich, who is Chippewa. She used Iroquois political and ecological concepts in her version of Clinton's acceptance speech:

> *Brothers and sisters, let us bend eagerly to the task before us and not allow the partisanship of the campaign to deter us from our essential work. The men and women of the League of the Iroquois, our earliest political organization, from which Benjamin Franklin drew inspiration for our form of government, based decisions not on short-term political gain, but considered what the effect of each act would have upon the seventh generation.*"[47]

During the winter of 1996–1997, I crossed paths with Dean R. Snow's new history of the Iroquois. Again Snow interjects the influence idea at about 1750 on his timeline. Snow seems to rue the fact that "this idea is very popular with the general public and most politicians." He writes, "There is . . . little or no evidence that the framers of the Constitution sitting in Philadelphia drew much inspiration from the League." However, concludes Snow, "the temptation to demonstrate that the United States Constitution was derived from a Native American form of government, for ephemeral political purposes, is too strong for some to resist." Resisting an urge to take this comment personally, I flipped to a footnote, in which Snow references *Exemplar of Liberty*. Additionally, Snow remarks that "I trust that, in the short term, but only in the short term, this paragraph will be the most controversial offered in this book."[48]

These occurrences signalled a kind of finality for me in the debate over Iroquois precedents for democracy—the idea had reached the desks of chief petty officers in the Navy, and the pages of the *William and Mary Quarterly*. It had been shouted from the rap stage, and factored into a dizzying array of books. By 1996, the Library of Congress cataloguing system introduced a new subject heading: "United States—Civilization—[American] Indian Influences." All of this indicated to me that the time was about to arrive when the active phase of the debate over this issue would end—for the most part. After two decades of struggle to have the idea accepted as viable history, my reward has become evident in Native American studies class, from students who ask me why there was a debate at all—isn't the Iroquois role obvious?

By the middle 1990s, reflecting on the journey of the influence idea during the previous two decades, I increasingly thought that I had been given the honor of a ringside seat in one particularly pointed example of the ways in which history is made, with all its distortions, denials, and various exercises in wish fulfillment. The making of history is an imperfect process involving a grand cacophony of voices. In books, in scholarly articles, in the popular press, documentaries, talk shows, and in popular entertainment, a new consensus on the origins of democracy was emerging—day by day, person by person.

I sometimes feel a sense of satisfaction at having helped to inject a set of ideas into popular and academic consciousness. That feeling is tempered by the knowledge that ideas are only part of history. The rest is experience. The struggle over this explicit issue may fade by the year 2000, because these ideas have been considered and accepted. How much will the acceptance of these ideas reduce racism, which continues to fester in our culture (whatever Dinesh D'Souza may think)? How much of a role will acceptance of these ideas play in the adoption of a broader multicultural curriculum? The debate over the Iroquois influence thesis is a small event next to the continuing struggle to create a society that truly and justly accommodates all peoples, including the land's first inhabitants. All of these struggles continue.

The assertion of Native voices will continue to help shape debates which will determine the place of these ideas in the broader history of the Americas as we enter the twenty-first century. The present debate is preparing America, at large, to accept a far broader and richer portrait of history than the limited version which posits all-European origins of democracy, with its implicit undertone of Western European (especially English) superiority. Within another generation, we will be free of the "Saxon myth" that limits the scope of democracy's origins solely to Anglo-American tradition. The whole story of American history is much richer, more complex, and diverse than that.

NOTES

1. Maria Morocco, "Indians Reclaim Legal History," *American Bar Association Journal*, August 6, 1990, 5.

2. Maria Morocco, "Rediscovering the Roots of American Democracy," *Human Rights* 17, no. 3 (Fall 1990): 38–39.

3. Christina S. Reeve, *Documents of Freedom: National School Celebration* (Costa-Mesa, Calif.: Celebration U.S.A., 1994), iii, 36–37.

4. Evelyn Wolfson's *The Iroquois: People of the Northeast* (1992), as well as another book, *Keepers of Life: Discovering Plants Through Native American Stories and Earth Activities for Children* (1994).

5. Jan Maher and Doug Selwyn, *Native Americans: Grades 3 and 4* (Seattle: Turman Publishing, 1991), 15–16.

6. James W. Loewen, *Lies My Teacher Told Me*, (New York: The New Press, 1995), 92.

7. Loewen, *Lies*, 328. See also Mary Mackey, "Everything Your American History Textbook Got Wrong," review of James Loewen, *Lies My Teacher Told Me*, *San Francisco Chronicle*, February 12, 1995, 3.

8. Tom Hayden, "Running in Place: Pushing Past the Market in the Clinton Era . . . " *Tikkun*, January, 1994, 33. While at an academic conference at UCLA (December 3, 1994), Grinde was approached by Hayden, who indicated that he had read *The Iroquois and the Founding of the American Nation*, and *Forgotten Founders*. Hayden then learned of the coauthored *Exemplar of Liberty*. He bought the entire stack of the book offered at the conference by the UCLA American Indian Studies Center, the book's publisher.

9. Quoted in J. Baldwin, review of *Green Delusions: An Environmentalist Critique of Radical Environmentalism*, *Whole Earth Review* 78 (March 22, 1993): 121. For a concise treatment of the Iroquois' wars with the Hurons, see William Brandon, *The Last Americans* (New York: McGraw-Hill, 1974), 217–21.

10. James A. Joseph, *Remaking America: How the Benevolent Traditions of Many Cultures Are Transforming Our National Life* (San Francisco: Jossey-Bass Publishers, 1995), 23, 25–26.

11. Joseph Coburn et al., "American Indians," in *Educating for Diversity*, ed. Carl A. Grant (Boston: Allyn & Bacon, 1995), 239.

"American Indians," in *Educating for Diversity*, ed. Carl A. Grant (Boston: Allyn & Bacon, 1995), 239.

12. See James Clifford, *The Predicament of Culture* (Cambridge: Harvard University Press, 1988), especially 52–53.

13. Edward Said, "Representing the Colonized: Anthropology's Interlocutors," *Critical Inquiry* 15 (Winter 1989): 217.

14. John Malone, *The Native American History Quiz Book* (New York: Quill/William Morrow 1994), back cover.

15. Jack Utter, *American Indians: Answers to Today's Questions* (Lake Ann, Mich.: National Woodlands Publishing Co., 1993), 42–43. In 1995, the influence idea was included in a survey of Native American history for the previous century in the *American Historical Review*, in which R. David Edmunds wrote, "Recently, claims by some Native American historians that the Constitution of the United States was modelled after the Iroquois Confederacy have attracted the public's attention and engendered considerable controversy." R. David Edmunds, "Native Americans, New Voices: American Indian History, 1895–1995," *American Historical Review* 100, no. 3 (June 1995): 729.

16. Todd Ackerman, "Being Creative about Others' Creativity: University of Houston Professor John Lienhard celebrates the Human Side of Technology . . .," *Houston Chronicle*, March 12, 1995, A–33.

17. "Larry King Live," Transcript #863, "Independence Day: Our Indian Legacy," Cable News Network, July 5, 1993.

18. Walter Goodman, "A Romantic Tribute to the First Americans," *New York Times*, October 10, 1994, C–16.

19. Harry F. Waters, "On the Trail of Tears," *Newsweek*, October 10, 1994, 56.

20. Richard Zoglin, "Ted Turner Goes Native," *Time*, December 6, 1993.

21. John Freeman, "'The Broken Chain' is Honorable, but Devoid of Passion," *San Diego Union-Tribune*, December 12, 1993, 8.

22. Greg Dawson, "Turner Retells the Story of Indians . . . ," *Orlando Sentinel*, December 5, 1993, D–1.

23. Howard Rheingold, "Singer On-line With Indian Culture," *San Francisco Examiner*, July 13, 1994, C–2.

24. Lenny Stoute, "Buffy's Back With First Album in 15 Years," *Toronto Star*, March 17, 1992, C–4.

25. Bonnie Britton, "'Indian' Out of the 'Cupboard,' Into Motivation," *Indianapolis Star*, July 21, 1995, E–1.

26. Peter Howell, "Rock-Rap Rage Hammers at 'Elitist Wall,'" *Toronto Star*, January 14, 1993.

27. Arthur Quinn, *New World: An Epic of Colonial America from the Founding of Jamestown to the Fall of Quebec* (Boston: Faber & Faber, 1994), 450–52.

28. Charley Reese, "Americans: Knowledge of Past Is Key to Retaining Your Liberty," *Orlando Sentinel*, February 1, 1994, A–8.

29. Reese, "Americans."

30. Laurence Hauptman, *Tribes and Tribulations: Misconceptions About American Indians and Their Histories* (Albuquerque: University of New Mexico Press, 1995), 27.

31. Adrienne Koch, ed. *Notes on Debates in the Federal Convention of 1787,* reported by James Madison (Athens: Ohio University Press, 1966), 85.

32. Hauptman, *Tribes and Tribulations,* 38.

33. Jerry Stubben, Review of Hauptman, *Tribes and Tribulations, American Indian Culture and Research Journal* 20, no. 1 (1996): 253–56.

34. Royal Commission on Aboriginal Peoples, *Partners in Confederation: Aboriginal Peoples, Self-Government, and the Constitution* (Ottawa: Government of Canada, 1993).

35. Stephen Hume, "Bigotry Wrapped in Nationalist Banner," *Vancouver Sun,* February 21, 1992, A–13.

36. Transcript, "Notes for a Speech by the Right Honorable Joe Clark . . . President of the Privy Council and Minister Responsible for Constitutional Affairs" [At the annual meeting of the Canadian Manufacturers Association], Toronto, June 12, 1992 (in LEXIS).

37. Edison Stewart, "Grant Natives 'Real Power,' Clark Says," *Toronto Star,* September 10, 1991, A–13.

38. Voyce Durling-Jones, "A Paradigm Shift in the Americas: Biopolitics and Bioeconomics," *Tekawennake* [Brantford, Ontario], July 7, 1993, 5, 14.

39. Robert Hunter and Robert Calihoo, *Occupied Canada: A Young White Man Discovers His Unsuspected Past* (McClelland and Stewart, 1991).

40. Bunty Anquoe, "President Offers Hope," *Indian Country Today,* May 4, 1994, A–1, A–2. See also: William Clinton, "Guest Essay," *Native Peoples* 7, no. 4 (Summer, 1994): 5.

41. Rick Karlin, "Exploring Cures from the Iroquois . . . Author Shares Iroquois Discoveries," *Albany Times-Union,* November 3, 1994.

42. Doug George (Kanentiio), "Indian Reservations Have Reasons for Not Welcoming Anthropologists," *Albany Times Union,* November 15, 1994, A–14.

43. George, "Indian Reservations."

44. Donald A. Grinde, Jr., Bruce E. Johansen, Philip A. Levy, and Samuel Payne, "Forum on Iroquois Influence on the Formation of the American Polity," *William and Mary Quarterly,* July, 1966, 587–636.

45. Alvin Josephy, Jr., *500 Nations: An Illustrated History of North American Indians* (New York: Knopf, 1994), 50, 52–53.

46. John McCaslin, "Inside the Beltway: The Great Pumpkin Speaks," *Washington Post,* October 26, 1995, A–5.

47. Louise Erdrich, "Read Their Lips! Three Novel Ideas for a Clinton Speech," *Washington Post,* June 23, 1994, C–1.

48. Dean R. Snow, *The Iroquois* (Oxford, U.K.: Blackwell, 1994), 154, 238.

Euro-Forming the Data

BARBARA A. MANN

This book has focused on the unacknowledged influence of Native American thought on modern American government. The unexamined flip side of the "influence" debate is the distortion built into the data by scholars who, however unconsciously, impose their own Western norms and values on their study of "Other" cultures. The result "Euro-forms" the data, forcing it into conformity with Western frames of reference, whether or not it fits. A full consideration of "influence" therefore requires an examination of the other side of influence—Euro-formation. Built-in assumptions of Euro-forming include:

1. A predisposition to monotheism, yielding
2. A belief that "Truth" is unitary, leading to
3. A fixation on "Purity" of descent, resulting in
4. A contempt for Native culture.

The Western frame of reference is constructed around cultural metaphors of One, which derive directly from a prior supposition of monotheism: There is but One Truth, and it speaks in a monologue that is not to be interrupted. Competing "truths" are necessarily fraudulent in the either/or universe of the West. Truth in the singular requires an ongoing quest for "purity."

Purity was once calmly construed as racial, a matter of "blood." Anxiety over racial purity pre-existed the United States. Definitions of blood impurity are contained in colonial laws dating back to the seventeenth century, at least. In the overtly racist nineteenth century, ferocious miscegenation laws were passed, both North and South. Contrary to popular opinion, these racial laws did not exclusively target Africans, but included Native Americans, Jews, and later Asians, as well.

As recently as 1887, with the passage of the eugenics Dawes Act and associated legislation, Congress sought to define the "quantum," or proportion, of red blood it took to be legally Other in America, using a "scientific" system based on Lamarckian genetics, which allowed for the inheritance of acquired characteristics (a "half-blood" could be re-categorized as a "full-blood," should the family "degenerate"). Despite their anecdotal nature, "full-blood" and "half-blood" were legal terms used to determine the level of competence an Indian enjoyed before the bar. The non-Indian "half" had better not be African, Jewish, or Asian, however, as competence derived exclusively from "Anglo-Saxon blood." Under slavery, half-Anglos called "mulattos" had customary standing in certain places, but "zambos," the official term for someone like the Seminole leader Osceola, with one African and one Indian parent, were judged to be legally incompetent.

Thus, "blood quantum" terminology was really just a continuation of the long-standing African identity tests, which had used the terms "mulatto," "quadroon" and "octoroon" to specify your level of European ancestry. These older racial terms having fallen into disuse after slavery, Dawes-era legislators looked to Francis Galton's new "science" of eugenics for more modern terminology, adopting his "quantum" terms of "half-blood," "quarter-blood," "eighth-blood," and so forth. These terms were equivalent to "mulatto" (half), "quadroon" (quarter) and "octoroon" (eighth). They simply sounded more up-to-date and could be applied exclusively to Native Americans.

By the late 1950s, blood purity laws governing Asian and African Americans were being struck down in the wake of the Civil Rights Movement. Purity concerns did not die in 1964 with the passage of the Civil Rights Act, however. They were merely driven deep underground, where they remain to this day, albeit obscured by the newly self-conscious vocabulary of public America—except when it comes to Native America. With Indians, and Indians alone, racist language is still perfectly acceptable in mainstream venues. While no reporter would dream of asking Toni Morrison whether she is a quadroon or an octoroon, much less demand that she "prove it" by presenting her federal "Negro Registration Card," editors and reporters regularly ply Native Americans with precisely these questions. Because Indians are the only people in America who need federal permission to say who they are, Native activists like the Keetowah Band Cherokee Ward Churchill are regularly subjected to invasive demands that they document their "blood quantums." Any refusal to comply with this outrageous requirement is portrayed by reporters as a "controversy" over identity, rather than what it is, resistance to government oppression.[1]

Such blatant racism is possible in the national news media because quantum counting remains federal Indian law. To this day, the U.S. Bureau of Indian Affairs assigns—or, more often, denies—legal "status" using a flawed process that rules out as many legitimate candidates as it lets in. The artificial in-crowd thus created is pitted against federally unrecognized—but no less real—Indians in this perfectly played game of divide and conquer.

Academia gingerly sidesteps the nastiness of identity disputes. Race is theoretically left by the wayside in the ongoing purity debates over influence but, while the verbiage may sound more refined, establishing the "pure" descent of ideas from a wholly European progenitor is no less the goal. The pulse of debate quickens with the same frank horror that animated earlier eugenicists when the possibility of consorting with some inferior Other comes up. Interestingly enough in this influence debate, only the European monoculture is presumed to be in danger from the addition of multicultural "impurities." The sense of European cultural supremacy prevents Euro-additives from being seen as adulterating the culture of the Other. No less with ideas today than with human beings yesterday, mixed genesis is interpreted as a moral evil by a monoculture that sees addition as defilement.

To protect European intellectual "purity," Western scholars must ensure that its central themes endure. If one is dealt a blow, it will be temporarily withdrawn from academic discussion, only to be reintroduced in a new key. Although transposed, it remains the same old song. For example, Western philosophy has traditionally held that soul or mind and matter or body are separate. Before multiculturalism challenged the right of Christians to call every tune, one of Christianity's jobs was to expound on this Western theme of body-soul separation, inserting it into all spiritual discussions. Now that heavy-handed missionary tactics are no longer extolled, at least not in academia, at least not out loud, basing a theory on Christian theology is frowned upon as outmoded, "unscientific."

Just because Christianity is no longer the primary vehicle of articulation does not mean that Western scholars have abandoned the old theme of body-soul duality, however. Western psychology has inherited the task of articulating this particular duality theme of the divided self, dressed up anew as a "scientific" (and therefore unimpeachable) philosophy. Instead of the weak flesh of a corrupt body leading sinners astray, scholars discuss "urban alienation" that flourishes in "the youth culture" leading "Generation X" astray, but we should note that, whether secular or sacred, the message remains the same: The self is divided and without expert guidance is likely to run amok. Modern counselors seek to "free" alienated "Xers" from their "debilitating apathy" no less ardently than missionaries once worked to "save sinners" from the "moral infirmities" of their "weak flesh."

Pretenses aside, this is really neither a theological nor a psychological debate; it is a power struggle. On the practical level, the explanations of Christianity and psychology work equally well to provide a rationale for social controls imposed from above. The weak self of antiquity required the regulation of the Church; the damaged self of modernity needs the guidance of Therapy. Neither the Christian claim on the "immortal soul," nor psychology's claim on mental health should blind us to pragmatic results. Conceding the right of either the clergy or mental health workers to intervene in our lives effectively gives them invisible authority over us. Note that mental health professionals now have what clergymen had before them, the moral authority of their social status to coerce patient/penitent cooperation. All that has changed is the name of the oracle.

Native spirituality is a threat to this cultural theme, in either incarnation, because it concedes no such soul/body division. On the spiritual level, this means that, for Native America, there is no such thing as a governing theology. Individual judgment prevails. On the political level, this means that Native culture allows no outside authority to impose its definitions on individuals through the exercise of police powers. It actively denies the truth of the West's basic rationale that individuals, trapped in their soul/body duality, need wiser heads to tell them how to behave. Native spirituality thus explodes a primary social control mechanism of the West. Thought policing is hard to justify to people who do not believe themselves to be "out of control" or in need of supervision.

However subliminally, Europeans recognized this threat to their culture at once. It is no accident that one of the very first traits Europeans criticized in Native Americans was their independent judgment. In the words of Giovanni Verrazano in his 1524 "Rapport" ("Report") to King Francis I of France, summing up one of the first voyages to North America, *"il nous parût qu'ils n'avaient aucune loi"*—"it seemed to us that they didn't have any law"—and therefore *"vivent en tout liberté par suite de leur totale ignorance"* —"they live in complete liberty because of their total ignorance"—by which he meant ignorance of Christianity.[2] What Verrazano, and all European observers after him, meant by the lack of "any law" in Native America was the absence of any controlling church-state hierarchy.

In fact, Native America "lacked" neither governmental nor spiritual precepts. Both existed in mature abundance, just not in any form Europeans recognized easily then or now. Native spirituality actively unifies soul and body while recognizing that anyone who is ready can access the extra-human, amaterial dimension of *orenda*, that is, spirit force. The "spirited" individual is in direct, unmediated contact with any visions she or he may seek or need. Such ideas naturally resist the authoritarianism Europeans considered "natural," leading Christian missionaries to pronounce Native American religions "stupid" and "childish." Today, with missions to "save the savage soul" having long since gone out of style, psychology has taken up the cause, now defined as "freeing the Native psyche from superstition." Like Christianity before it, psychology impatiently dismisses those Native philosophies so dangerous to Euro-style hierarchy by vilifying Native religion as quixotic, a delusional state, or an outright fraud. Whereas Christianity once debunked *orenda* as childish or satanic, psychology now downplays *orenda* as "anti-intellectual," deriding it as "magical" thinking. Once more, all that has changed is the mechanism of official scorn.

Interpretive biases such as these constitute what I call "Euro-forming." They inhere in all the founding philosophies of the arts and sciences, where they continue, quietly, to guide analysis. We have but to pull up the original sources of the various academic disciplines to see Euro-forming in progress, looking as transparent, perplexing, and crude to us today as twentieth-century biases will someday look to posterity. Euro-scholars may naturally wish to avoid returning to the scene of the crime, but conscience requires no less of us all. Turning our attention away from primary sources before honestly evaluating—and rooting out—their biases only ensures that built-in notions of European bio-cultural supremacy will go on jerking the strings from behind the scenes.

One of my favorite pastimes is to pull up old dictionaries, encyclopedias, and other authoritarian tracts masquerading as helpful records of fact, and ponder the unassailable myths of 1851, 1901, 1949, or even, the 1960s and 1970s. This is an excellent cautionary exercise that never fails to give me due pause concerning the worth of conventional wisdom. Since the vision of each generation has a different vanishing point, circumlocutions that worked to disguise the unspeakable truth in earlier eras will fail to dodge the point in the present. Continuing biases become painfully apparent.

For example, I am especially fond of one entry in the 1949 *Encyclopedia Americana* (EA). Despite the fact that the Holocaust was, by then, a known quantity, the EA featured an entry entitled, "Eugenics." Lauded as a "branch of learning,"[3] eugenics was still deemed crucial enough to warrant nine single-spaced columns covering five pages of precious space. If eugenics was a disgraced science by 1949, it would be hard to discover that fact from this article, which concedes only, in the final paragraph, that due to the "World War," eugenics had "lost the services of many brilliant minds that, had peace continued, would have made notable contributions to the subject."⁴ Such was the state of reputable scholarship in 1949.

Revisiting Lewis Henry Morgan on the Iroquois provides another such object lesson in the submerged pillars of Western scholarship. The 1901 reissue of Morgan's 1851 classic expanded the original *League of the Ho-de-no-sau-nee or Iroquois* with footnotes and appendices compiled by its editor, Herbert M. Lloyd. Lloyd's "up-to-date" annotations are almost comical at times, steeped as they are in smug "Saxon" theories of "historical progress" and "social evolution." Lloyd accepted in 1901 what Morgan had accepted in 1851, that cultures "evolved" through "stages of history" from "barbarism" and "savagery" (found in Africa, Asia, and Native America) to "civilization" (found in Europe). Morgan spent a wearying amount of print indulging in rhetoric that compared the Iroquoian culture to the cultures of ancient Greece and Rome, the better to demonstrate the orderly progression of history to its "Saxon"⁵ climax. He sought to tie Iroquoian thought to that of "primitive" Greco-Roman polities to demonstrate that Europeans had reached the "highest intellectual elevation" possible, as opposed to the Iroquois, who remained "in the infancy of his mental growth."⁶

Morgan was hardly alone in these arguments, which had been common-place since the Renaissance. For instance, in his famous 1580 essay, "Cannibals," on (most probably) the Iroquois, Montaigne also traced the "similarities" between Native Americans and "the ancients." Thus, the very triteness of the argument may help explain why Morgan *et al.* failed to note the inconsistency of maintaining, on one hand, that the ancient Greeks could have "fathered" American democracy while denying, on the other hand, that the ancient Iroquois were capable of the same feat. When these arguments were coined, the difference between the "primitive" Iroquois and the "primitive" Greeks was obvious: the Greeks came from the "racial stock" that European scholars had already voted most likely to succeed, while the Iroquois came from an "inferior race" that needed to be "civilized and christianized." Modern Euro-formers are less eager to name race as the great divide between ancient Greeks and Iroquois but nonetheless cling to the old contention that anything Indians could do, Greeks could do better.

In his explication of Iroquois government, despite the fact that he insists, erroneously, on calling Iroquoia an oligarchy—a mistake Elisabeth Tooker doggedly perpetuates—Morgan manages to show that Iroquoia was a func-tioning democracy.⁷ He ignores the embarrassing question this raises, based on the very theory he so ardently supports: If the Iroquois are "savage" while the Europeans are "civilized," and if history evolves through monarchy to democracy—his primary contentions—then how is it that the "savage Iroquois" lived in a free democracy while the "civilized Saxon" lived in a repressive monarchy? Either Western civilization is not evolution's apex after all, or Europe is moving backwards.

This discussion merely looks dated at first blush. Likening the Iroquois to the Greek, then watching savagery evolve up to its God-given goal (civilized America) through the glorious mediation of Saxon genius is a formulation disconcerting to modern Euro-scholars only in its diction. Instead of challenging the egregious racial bias, if not the outright master race fantasy, of such "history," they "fix" the problem by modernizing the language. Thus a self-styled expert on the Iroquois such as James Axtell casually announces to National Public Radio reporter Catherine Stifter, during interviews of October 14–15, that "there's very little intellectual debt to the Indian," and no one asks him for his documentation. It is just as well, for he could not supply any. The primary sources demonstrate precisely the opposite.

Nevertheless, the damage is done. Lay commentators, taking their cue from the flaccid thinking of anti-influence scholars, feel free to present formulations that are shockingly eugenic in their insistence on "purity" of descent. Journalists like Charley Reese can reassure a presumably European "us" that "All institutions of American government are derived from our European culture. None comes from Africa or Asia or American Indians";[8] while conservative political columnists like Linda Bowles can flatly state: "America was conceived and built by religious, white men mostly from Europe. Blacks, women, and others made contributions, but they were secondary."[9]

Again, no one corrects them. In the case of Bowles in particular, the modern political agenda behind the influence debate becomes uncomfortably clear. In the column just quoted, Bowles was calling for an end to affirmative action. She somehow supposes that the tenuous claim that Euro-Christian men dreamed up the Constitution all by their lonesomes justifies ending affirmative action. The only possible connection between these positions is race.

Bowles does not invent party lines; she follows them. Had her social and academic mentors not already created a climate in which she could sneer at multiculturalism with impunity, her editors might have insisted that she support her claim or drop it. Bowles, herself, betrays a guilty awareness that her premise of America's "pure" descent from "white" manhood is shaky, at best, when she nods briefly to African-Americans, women, and some amorphous Others. Notwithstanding, she studiously avoids the true flash-point of the debate on constitutional origins, the Iroquois League. Those faceless "others" who, she grudgingly allows, made unspecified yet surely secondary contributions were, in fact, the originators of a unique and fascinating form of government that caught the attention of the deist—not Christian— Thomas Jefferson and the agnostic—not Christian—Benjamin Franklin. Yet, Bowles does not even mention Native Americans.

The bald-faced eugenics of journalistic arguments like these are possible in modern discourse precisely because the biased illogic behind the nine- teenth-century "stages of history" theory has never been honestly examined or explicitly disavowed by Western scholars.

Morgan's pronouncements are equally rash and skewed on matters of religion. A dedicated Christian whose bias was undisguised, Morgan did not hesitate to characterize Native religions as "inferior spiritualities"[10] whose "blemishes" he put down to their being "shut out from the light of revela- tion."[11] He imposed a Christian framework on Iroquois cosmology, slimming Sky Cycle stories of multiple creators down to the Christian story of a pitched battle between God and Satan, as embodied in the Sky Twins, the "good Sapling" and the "evil Flint." This Euro-forming wrote female creators like Sky Woman and earth animal creators like Turtle and Beaver right out of the picture. At the same time, *orenda* was misrepresented as the omni- science of a monolithic "Great Spirit," constituting the "good" half of Morgan's superimposed dichotomy.[12] These interpolations and excisions are all old missionary ploys; and it is no wonder that Morgan used them, since his purpose in examining Native religion at all was to determine just how much uplifting it would take to bring the benighted savages into the Christian fold.

In one particularly appalling section, Morgan pairs enforced social evolu- tion with his missionary theme. The comments come as his conclusion, in which he frankly discusses what his chapter title announces, the "Future Destiny of the Indian," a common theme of the period. Fancying themselves "Friends of the Indian" (a designation they never bothered to confirm with the Indians), Euro-Christian reformers typically posited the Indians' alternatives as genocide or assimilation, a grimly false choice. Instead of noticing that many other possibilities existed, reformers championed assimilation as the "human- itarian" choice, to be accomplished through "civilization and christianiza- tion," the catch-phrase of the reformers. In Morgan's formulation of this old saw, if the "Indian family" is to be "reclaimed," that is "civilized" as opposed to exterminated,[13] then "There are but two means of rescuing the Indian from his impending destiny; and these are education and Christianity."[14]

Morgan agrees that it will be "a great undertaking to work off the Indian temper of mind," awash as it is in crass superstition and resistance to improvement.[15] Morgan even believes that "education and christianization of the Iroquois is a subject of too much importance, in civil aspect, to be left exclusively to the limited and fluctuating means of religious societies."[16] Instead, he recommends that the state take over these functions, so that they can be accomplished systematically on a captive population. In other words, instead of physical genocide, Morgan, Friend of the Indian, urges cultural genocide.

"Yes, yes," mainstream scholars will agree, distractedly averting their gaze, "Morgan did say those things. But you must realize that modern scholarship is completely free of these biases." This riposte is so familiar as to have evaded scrutiny, yet the most superficial glance at modern scholarship belies the claim.

Official bias did not quite move directly from Christianity to psychology. The interim step between the two was the early twentieth-century notion of "universal" mythology, a concept articulated first and most popularly by J. G. Frazier in *The Golden Bough* (1918). This profoundly influential work ran through several editions over the next sixty years, exciting scholarship on magic, religion, mythology, and superstition. Frazier wrote in the wake of Darwinianism, which had shattered the faith base of Christianity and momentarily opened Europeans to the spiritual insights of other cultures. *The Golden Bough* was really a salvage effort aimed at restoring Europe's right to define "civilized religion," the better to distinguish it from "primitive myth." Frazier's engaging hybrid of dry scholarship and juicy imagination first moved academic discussion of Native religion away from overt Christianization, dragging discussion into the vicinity of the Euro-occult. Before the *Bough* broke, a cottage industry of ethnologists and folklorists had worked up a whole library on the "universals" of "primitive religion." Indeed, the effort survives today in the work of folklorists like Joseph Campbell.

Native American religion was first pulled through Frazier's "universal myths" and within the reach of psychology by Ake Hultkrantz's *The Religions of the American Indians* (1967). Hultkrantz's postulations are all neatly Euro-formed, after the model of Frazier in *The Golden Bough;* that is, they conform perfectly to Western expectations for "primitives." Like Frazier, Hultkrantz synthesized older Christian approaches with newer "scientific" perspectives. Unlike Frazier, who retained the sense of mystery that is essentially religious, Hultkrantz flattened out myth by explaining it in mundane terms, in a way that is essentially psychological. Thus, while Frazier had placed his hybrid closer to Christian religiosity, Hultkrantz pulled his closer to psychology. In neither case did the hybrid genuinely represent Native thinking, but in each case, it had the advantage of sounding exotic enough to pass for Native thought at the same time it felt familiar enough to be grasped by Euro-centrists.

It is easy to see why Hultkrantz's book became a standard. He was among the first scholars to invest Native American religion with the respect "naturally" accorded Western monotheism, but his contribution to the study of Native religion ends with this bit of open-mindedness. *Religions* reads as though someone stole the bones of Native philosophy, then re-clothed them in alien flesh, leaving Native concepts just barely discernible in outline.

Christian cultural values are injected throughout *Religions of the American Indians*. The Euro-notion of "One" frequently guides discussion. For instance, Hultkrantz asserts that the Algonquins venerated a "Supreme Being,"[17] despite the fact that "Manitou" is simply not equivalent to "God." I was never confident that Hultkrantz caught the distinction between God and Manitou for, had he really understood that the Western concept of "one God" was irrelevant for Native Americans, he would not have tried so hard to force discussion into terms of one "Supreme Being."[18] I had the impression that Hultkrantz was attempting to legitimize Manitou in Western eyes by presenting it as one of those supposedly "universal" concepts "transcending" culture that Europeans liked to believe existed.

His Manitou-God equation properly Euro-formed, Hultkrantz goes on to assert that various "cultural heroes" are but incarnations of "Supreme Beings,"[19] thus neatly resurrecting the relationship of the Christian God, Jesus, and the saints in psychological terms, wherein good and evil still exist but as mental, not cosmic, constructs. The trickster, or "transformer"[20]—"Flint" to the Haudenosaunee, "Coyote" in the Southwest—is a healer and a creator, as well as a sacred clown enamored of practical jokes that sometimes get out of hand. He especially enjoys a good "dirty" joke. Flint (Coyote) no more has a Christian equivalent than Manitou does; yet, Hultkrantz Euro-forms so relentlessly that I could almost hear the gears ticking: Flint (Coyote) cannot be "good" because the Euro-model only provides for one "good" Supreme Being, so Hultkrantz presents the trickster as Satanic in his obscenities[21]—a resplendently Western analysis. It is only Europeans who think that humor and religion are mutually exclusive. Moreover, Native thought never grimly equated sexuality with evil, nor was evil, as such, posited at all. Hultkrantz never gets near authentic Native philosophy.

Hultkrantz's free-wheeling cross-references among diverse Native cosmologies—from the Pacific Northwest to the woodlands of the Northeast

—on the basis of shaky metaphorical links is vintage universalizing. For instance, Hultkrantz states that the pillar of Sky World, which he casually promotes to the status of "the cosmic pillar" and likens to Pacific totem poles, is "central to the high-god concept in America."[22] That is something like equating a circumcised penis with a church steeple, then asserting that both are portals to Valhalla, simply because Judaism, Christianity, and Odinism once coexisted on the European continent.

On the other hand, the one Native place where symbolic metaphor really does assert primacy—in kinship terminology like "Mother" Earth and "Father" Sun[23] (or, among the Haudenosaunee, "Brother" Sun)—is the one place Hultkrantz takes concepts at face value.[24] He is so busy interpolating the European concept of anthropomorphic "gods" (as appropriate to "primitive" thinking) that he misses the deeply textured meaning that kinship terms have in a kinship-based society. His norm is, as always, Europe. Because Europe operates on a truly "primitive" notion of kinship as nuclear and blood-literal, Hultkrantz is left unprimed to catch the layered significance of Native thought in figurative kinship relations.

Not content merely to cross-reference unrelated Native cultures, Hultkrantz consistently equates Native concepts with superficially similar concepts in Africa,[25] Iran,[26] Polynesia,[27] subcontinental India,[28] China,[29] Asia,[30] Japan,[31] and Europe[32] on the theory that all "primitive" cultures are alike in their primitiveness—the very soul of the universalization effort.

Hultkrantz moves from universalization to psychology in his analysis of shamanism, relentlessly personalizing what are, in fact, communal acts. Instead of seeing spirituality as a community endeavor, Hultkrantz diagnoses shamanic conjuring as private mental events taking place within individual shamans, somewhere between self-delusion and conscious scams, declaring, "The essential relationship between the guardian spirit and the medicine man is based upon personal inspiration."[33] Community actions, like reenactments of dreams, are dismissed as "dramatic pantomime"[34] while sweat lodges, also a ceremonial group activity, are demoted to "sweat baths" and misdefined as a kind of "sauna."[35] Thus have shamans been transformed into snake oil salesmen; Sky ancestors into Greco-pagan "deities;" sacred sweats into hygienic steam baths; and *orenda* into delusion. In addition to the flagrant insult such descriptions offer Native cultures, there is also the problem of accuracy. Hultkrantz has recast the community focus essential to Native religion as the individual search for personal salvation that religion is for Christians, then described religion as psychological fulfillment.

Euro-forming of Native religion intensified in 1970, when Anthony

Wallace published *The Death and Rebirth of the Seneca,* his psychoanalysis of Handsome Lake's Longhouse Religion. For the Haudenosaunee, this book completed the leap Hultkrantz had begun from universalization of myth to psychologizing of culture. Wallace compounded matters by suggesting that he spoke from the Native point of view despite the fact that, by stubbornly Euro-forming the Longhouse Religion, Wallace had left it virtually unrecognizable to its practitioners.

Wallace's interpretation of Seneca dream lore—just to pull up one point at random—reduces everything to Freudian-style wish fulfillment. He describes dream culture as "the nagging need to define the unconscious wish and satisfy it before some disaster occurs."[36] In other words, he presents dreams as a psychological defense mechanism erected against personal adversity. It is Euro-forming with a vengeance to diagnose the source of dreams as individual fears and to put their community re-enactment down to the nurturing of fragile personalities that need to be satisfied passively.[37]

To Natives, who largely regard Western psychology as empty talk, such interpretations are bizarre, for dream-time deals with spirit, not with mind. "Dream-guessing," the common ethnographic term, misleads by misstating the purpose of dream-telling, presenting it as a child's game of twenty questions, instead of a communal act in which all cooperate to bring forth a new reality. For the traditional Haudenosaunee, reality does not come into focus until everyone is on the same wavelength, receiving and "cooperating with the same vision. *Êthno niiohtôñha'k ne onkwa'nikôñ:ra*—"Now Our Minds Are One," goes the Thanksgiving Address. The communal nature of dream-time is part of Iroquois consensus philosophy. Dreams are communications from the spirit realm containing messages, instructions and/or warnings. Dream workers, traditionally female for the most part, explain meanings (if they are not obvious) and prescribe ways to respond to a message, comply with instructions, and/or deal with warnings. These acknowledgments must involve the community, or at least a portion of it, or they will not be effective.

Thus, dreams are simply not the personalized mental health tips that Wallace would have them to be. Far from coddling infantile male egos, as Wallace argues, dream work embodies the reciprocal responsibilities that community members bear one another. Furthermore, half of all Seneca dreamers—and communities—have always been women, while dream workers have been disproportionately female. These facts do not square with Wallace's discussion, which presents an exclusively male cadre of dreamers, dream workers and dream reenactors. Finally, all dreamers are interacting with outside, self-aware spirits, who operate as their own agents to effect nonhuman agendas. Despite obvious lapses like these, only Euro-scholars were invited to respond to Wallace's thesis, so he got away with it. The bias underlying his theory was invisible to academics because psychoanalysis fit so neatly into their prevailing mindset in 1970.

In his rush to psychoanalyze the Seneca and find them psychologically wanting, Wallace obviated all context. Thus, instead of widening inquiry, Wallace narrowed interpretation of Seneca culture, reducing the Longhouse Religion to a case study in mental illness. Retroactively psychoanalyzing Handsome Lake and his followers superimposes Western values on the Seneca no less than "christianizing" them had done earlier, and incorporates the same level of distortion into the picture.

Euro-forming Native religion did not stop once Freudianism fell out of fashion. William N. Fenton continued Euro-forming *orenda* in *The False Faces of the Iroquois* (1987), just not quite as blatantly as Hultkrantz or Wallace, from the point of view of this generation. ("False Faces" refers to both the wood-carved masks and the society of male maskers who use them during certain sacred, seasonal ceremonies.)

Fenton begins by traveling in the right direction, remarking on the Native pairing of humor and terror.[38] He is quite right to do so. Healing is in Flint's province, as is humor, hence the spirit-infused False Faces stimulate both awe and laughter in the course of their ceremonials. Grasping the "Paradox of Fear and Humor"[39] is a vital first step to understanding Haudenosaunee and many other Native perspectives generally. The juxtaposition, so obvious in sacred clowning, is a consistent thread shooting throughout the culture, an appropriate way to come at matters of importance. Thus, I was pleased to see Fenton pick up on it. I grew increasingly less pleased as he "explained" the paradox: "This example of the frivolity that may pervade an otherwise serious ritual conveys the ambivalent way that the Iroquois regard the False Faces: They are at once both terrifying and amusing."[40] Fenton's periodic use of the word "ambivalence" to "explain" the funny/frightening nature of the Native interface with *orenda*[41] is part and parcel of his insistence on psychologizing the whole of False Face ritual. The notion that laughter-*cum*-fright indicates emotional ambivalence is entirely Western. For Native Americans, laughter and fright go together naturally, like dawn and twilight; like red and black; like Flint and Sapling.

Laughter keeps people on an even keel and maintains their moral bearings. On the purely sociopolitical level, irreverence has a delightfully subversive effect. It deflates pomp, thus keeping diverse camps from polarizing into warring camps. Laughter-*cum*-fright also discourages personality cults by preventing orators from leading with their egos, while encouraging "four-winded" discourse, a conversation including the whole community, in which multiple valid points of view coexist. On the spiritual level, pairing the funny and the frightening opens a window on *orenda* by busting up ordinary consciousness. There is nothing "ambivalent" about any of this. Native Americans simply unite mind and body, as laughter does. If any "separation" exists, it is a breachable one between physical and *orenda* realities.

Fenton does not stop Euro-forming with "ambivalence." A frank admirer of Anthony Wallace's use of psychoanalysis to explain Iroquois dream rites,[42] Fenton flatly asserts that the medicinal effects of False Face healings are merely psychosomatic: "The patient's mind is relieved."[43] In a long section actually entitled "Hysteria,"[44] Fenton puts down all False Face effects to mental trickery. Similarly, when a speaker prophesies, Fenton believes that he only "pretends that the maskers have communicated" with him.[45] Finally, Fenton reduces clairvoyant dreams to "nightmares."[46] We are back to Hultkrantz's snake-oil salesmen, who were themselves direct descendants of Morgan's unchurched savages, shut out from the light of revelation.

Because Euro-forming the spiritual data has not been properly challenged, scholars feel empowered to conflate antique African, Asian, Middle Eastern, and Native American beliefs as equivalently "primitive"; to analyze Native Americans as fragile personalities in search of cosseted, passive satisfaction; to denigrate ceremony as hysteria; in short, to accuse Native spirituality of talking like a fool when, in fact, it is merely working from a non-Western frame of reference.

It is easy, if slightly embarrassing, for modern Western scholars to slide past biased and insulting contents like these, but not, as rumored, because "we" have all moved past such supposedly dated thinking. It is because such thinking really does not bother most Euro-American scholars in the first place—they do not derive from the specimen population. It is fair to ask how detached scholars might remain had they been the objects of Morgan's inquiry. Rather than examine this question forthrightly, most scholars duck it.

Towards the end of *False Faces*, William Fenton at least acknowledges the issue, although his purpose in doing so is to refute Native critics of ethnohistory. While purportedly defending museum collections, he is also covertly tackling the larger criticism, that of ethnohistorians' frequent and cavalier dismissal of Native points of view. This charge has obviously been eating away at Fenton since 1968, when he decried "the fallacy that Indian culture was inherited" in his introduction to *Parker on the Iroquois*.[47] This is how Fenton was characterizing his critics by 1987: "Too often they were bitten by the 'genetic fallacy'—that being of Indian descent gives one especial insight into one's native culture, and they resented persons of other ethnic stock who had studied and written about their people."[48]

In a manner typical of anti-influence critics, this summary misstates the criticism, the better to ridicule and dismiss it.

First, let me state that I adamantly oppose a practice that is distressingly fashionable in academia today: the use of race as a credential. The theory that biology determines intellect is eugenics, not a blow for social equality, and I decided long ago that I would not cooperate with racist imperatives, even when they were cleverly disguised as progressive politics. Race is an accident of birth, not a cosmic place-marker. For my money, intellectual equipment is pretty evenly spread among humanity as a whole. Our primary identities as human beings supersede any secondary divisions of ethnicity —or gender, or health, or sexual orientation, for that matter. Anyone who sincerely wishes to understand anyone else's point of view, can—given the right teachers and an open mind.

Second, let me point out that this is, historically, the Native point of view. That small faction of "government-issue Indians" who argue solely on the basis of their biological identity are, as Ward Churchill once pointed out to me, often paid by the U.S. government to "be" Indians. They represent the backwash of Dawes-inspired quantum counting, not tradition; blood quantums are a Dawesian, not an Indian, idea. The quintessential Native theory of identity, as embodied in the law of adoption in nearly every Native nation, promotes exactly the opposite idea. Clan adoption traditionally creates new citizens out of those born into other cultures, granting them status as absolute equals in their new Native culture. These ancient Native adoption customs are direct evidence that traditional Native thought was inherently nonracial.

Thus, "genetic memory" (which Fenton slightingly calls the "genetic fallacy") is not equivalent to the European fallacy of racism, as Fenton obviously assumes. Whereas racism is about the inheritance of race-based superiority or inferiority, genetic memory is an entirely spiritual concept that concerns access to ancestral memories through the medium of *orenda*, or psychic ability.

Native Americans generally believe that *orenda* talent runs in families, like musical talent. It is, therefore, a psychic talent that is inherited and—if properly nurtured—used to key into other dimensions. Like their ancestors, the original Sky People, the Haudenosaunee (and other Natives) have the refined psychic techniques to tap into what Europeans call "time." Just as talented individuals can see into the future, they can see into the past and access the knowledge of the ancestors. It is easier to talk to your own family lineage than anyone else's for the same reason it is easier to communicate with your own relatives in real time: You are both used to the same terms. It is this psychic pathway to knowledge that constitutes "genetic memory."

Europeans can tap into *orenda* too. Unfortunately, their repertoire of techniques was nearly extinguished by medieval Christianity. Latent talent does still exist among Europeans, however, and was happened upon recently and most famously by Carl Jung, who dubbed his Euro-based spirit guides "archetypes," then made the mistake, in proper colonial style, of calling them "universal."

Under forced assimilation, psychic skill has been forgotten by many Native Americans as well, but, notwithstanding, the ancestors and Sky People continue communicating through the old *orenda* channels. Since the only way for them to be "heard" is psychically, they will necessarily seek out people who possess and exercise *orenda* talents. Their search can alight on talented Euro-Americans because it is talent, not race, that matters. If few Europeans are sought, they have only their own ancestors to thank: After all, Church leaders did spend two centuries burning at the stake anyone who was remotely psychic, even taking care to execute the children of known "witches." Killing all carriers of an inherited ability will stamp it out.

I believe the resentment Fenton has run into is a warranted outgrowth of frustration over long-standing injustice. The objection is not to the race of Euro-scholars, but to the smug arrogance so many of them exhibit. Perhaps the only way for academics to understand Native impatience with Western scholarship is for them to partake of the same level of structural invisibility that Natives typically experience. Simulating the situation is simple enough. For scholars to share the resentment, they need only select an ethnographic passage and alter the "specimen" being studied; that is, instead of Natives under scrutiny, pretend it is Europeans.

What follows is one of those passages in Morgan that is most likely to be recommended by modern scholars as displaying his famous sympathy with his Native objects. This is the sort of passage offered up to Natives as evidence of Morgan's good heart:

> *The Iroquois will soon be lost as a people, in that night of impenetrable darkness in which so many Indian races have been enshrouded. Already their country has been appropriated, their forests cleared, and their trails obliterated. The residue of this profound and gifted race, who still linger around their*

native seats, are destined to fade away, until they become eradicated as an Indian stock. We shall ere long look backward to the Iroquois, as a race blotted from existence; but to remember them as a people whose sachems had no cities, whose religion had no temples, and whose government had no record.[49]

Let's imagine that the situation is reversed so that the dear, and nearly departed, culture is European:

The Europeans will soon be lost as a people, in that night of impenetrable darkness in which so many white races have been enshrouded. Already their country has been appropriated, their cities levelled and their highways obliterated. The residue of this profound and gifted race, who still linger around their suburban homes, are destined to fade away, until they become eradicated as a white stock. We shall ere long look backwards to the Europeans as a race blotted from existence; but to remember them as a people whose businessmen were ignorant of gift-giving, whose religion had no dreams, and whose government had no kinships.

Such a passage would no longer look, nor feel, quite so benign to Euro-Americans. Sections casually knocking their religion, under the guise of describing it, would incite resentment. They would shiver at discussions of how best to stamp out their "savage" culture by kidnapping their children and imprisoning them in "White Schools." Listening helplessly as all-powerful conquerors openly predicted their demise would chill them to the bone.

If the European fixation on abstractions were consistently labeled childish; if their penchant for separating mind and body were reformulated as magical thinking; if their disregard of psychic matters were said to preclude true intellectuality; if they were required to read not just this one passage, but volume upon volume of similar drek, honored as "primary sources," Euro-scholars would start feeling abused. Patronizing "defenses" of their "primitive" intelligence as being but in its infancy would not promote gratitude; it would raise hackles. Euro-Americans would certainly not consider the authors of such passages as "Friends of the Anglo-Saxon."

The lingering legacy of the primary sources is, then, their skew. Since it has never been forthrightly confronted, it continues to guide scholarship by force of trajectory. The sheer right of one group to speak as the authority on another—the basic assumption of anthropology, ethnology, folklore, history, and even botany—has yet to be challenged. Consequently, Euro-forming focuses on dictating the relative positions of the studier and the studied so that, when a new ethnographic work is announced, we all know in advance who the "experts" will not be. No matter how seemingly benign the work, bias may be quickly exposed simply by turning the dominant group into the specimen population.

For those who do not need to speculate on how it feels to belong to a specimen population, because they already do, the lasting impact of such demoralizing works cannot be overstated. For those who must first imagine to understand, imagine this: Finding a multitude of denigrating works on a required reading list from which there is no appeal, then learning that a response to, or a critique of, the biases in those sources is frowned upon as unintelligent and lacking any scholarly merit in an academia that is overwhelmingly Euro-American.

This process of short-circuiting potentially embarrassing discussions by never allowing them to begin is called "silencing," and it is a fairly regular occurrence in academia. Silencing does not require sound objections; insinuations and slurs will do. Opponents need only hint that your Mama wears combat boots for you to be denied access to the forum. Although it is conservative scholars who scream the loudest about "political correctness" —their term for silencing when it is turned against themselves—it is, in fact, conservative scholars who practice silencing most often, especially against any pesky student brave enough to challenge Euro-dogma.

Several times—once giving a paper at a conference, twice in papers for publication, and once in a graduate oral exam—I was expressly forbidden to detail racist skews in the primary sources, or trace through their impact on modern scholarship. Interestingly, my efforts were deemed objectionable, not because they were *groundless,* I was told, but because they were *tasteless.* The exact nature of the "tastelessness" was left dangling but, presumably, Euro-sensibilities are too tender to stand for a moment what Native sensibilities have been standing for five centuries. In short, mentioning Euro-racism is what is construed as impolite, a breach of academic etiquette. The silencing power of such "etiquette" is no trivial thing. While it may be a step up from burning dissenters alive (the preferred Euro-technique until fairly recently), I sometimes get the feeling that, if they thought they could still get away with it, conservative Euro-scholars would start gathering wood.

From the foregoing, it should be becoming clear why so few modern "Others" embark upon scholarly careers. The bias at the base of the humanities tends to drive non-Europeans from the field. The picture is not complete, however, until it is realized that not only is the data relentlessly Euro-formed; the "Other" is, as well. The old missionary agenda of "civilizing and christianizing" has not been foregone; it has just been retooled. The updated version seeks to "standardize and psychologize" outsiders, whose "lack of sophistication" makes them appear "childish." In other words, they are strangers to the Western frame of reference. The onus is entirely on the Other to reform. Westerners are under no obligation to understand them. In academia, the only good Other is a dead quiet Other.

Occasional exotic dashes of food and clothing are tolerated as long as the Other smiles for the camera in the "safe" zone of cultural tokenism. Euro-formed mindsets remain a must, however: Western styles of speech, abstraction, polarization, and presentation are required in a surrealistic replay of forced assimilation. Given the non-negotiable rules, it is hardly surprising that there are almost no role models of Others who have "made it" in academia.

In Native America, one seminal role model who "made it," kind of, is Arthur Caswell Parker, usually presented as a "grand-nephew" through the male line of Ely S. Parker.[50] The Seneca, however, count descent the old way, through the mother. By Seneca count, Parker was not really Haudenosaunee until he was formally adopted into the Bear Clan,[51] after which, by Seneca count, he was 100 percent Indian. Parker clearly understood that adoption had rendered him wholly Seneca to the Iroquois, forming his entrée into traditional circles. "My work immediately became easier," he remarked.[52]

The "white" world, of course, did not need to jump through so many hoops before declaring Parker wholly "Indian." To Euro-Americans operating on the "one drop" theory of racism, any "tainted blood" automatically rendered one Other. To them, Parker was always an Indian, despite the fact that most of his "blood" was "white" (meaning that most of his forebears claimed to be European).

It is noteworthy that Parker's acceptance in academia was in direct proportion to his presumed distance from his Otherness, as defined by Euro-scholars. In his 1968 mini-biography of Parker that acted as the introduction to *Parker on the Iroquois*, William Fenton seemed under the impression that to defend Parker's claims as a scholar, he had first to diminish Parker's identity as an Indian. Fenton thus declared that "Arthur Parker was certainly no more than one-fourth Seneca, and probably nearer one-eighth."[53] The quadroons and octoroons of Parker's heritage seemed to matter greatly to Fenton, who spoke patronizingly of Parker as an Indian "who emerged from behind the buckskin curtain"[54] but who was still "at home on either side of the buckskin curtain."[55] Buckskin curtain, indeed: Would Fenton describe himself as "emerging from behind the Jesus jalousie?"

In a section I think Fenton intended to be humorous, he described Parker's efforts to break free from his debilitating Indianness. Early on, "Parker wrote a typically Indian letter,"[56] purportedly showing him to be more Native than civilized for including such items as colic and green apples, fights and lickings, plus various visits to "old warriors" and "big white chiefs."[57] Unable to cope with "the long academic route"—it was "impractical for him" —Parker moved "laterally" along the ladder of success, not up it.[58] In other words, lacking intellect, Parker made do with biology, depending upon his Indianness to gain him "admission to secret medicine societies."[59] Fenton hints that, because academia never formally certified Parker as smart, he was not a real scholar after all, but a pseudoscholar who took "short cuts."[60]

Fenton thus interprets the gatekeeping Parker encountered in academia as Parker's personal failing. Absent from his discussion of famous turn-of-the-century anthropologists with whom Parker interacted[61] was their habit of confining their students of color to the role of ethnic ringer. An admission ticket into the core of exotic culture was all that anthropologists like Franz Boas were after from ringers like the Native American, George Hunt, and the African-American, Zora Neale Hurston. Hunt and Hurston were delegated to gather raw data that Boas would analyze later in their absence, just as Parker was delegated to do for F. W. Putnam.[62] Hurston, for instance, stood "on a Harlem street corner measuring people's skulls" with a "pair of calipers" for Boas, a task no Euro-student could have accomplished.[63] (Measuring cranial capacities—"craniology"—was basic eugenics research into "comparative" black-white intelligence, as determined from skull size.) If neither Hunt, Hurston, nor Parker made it past the data-gathering stage to their graduate degrees under such mentors, perhaps the reasons lay beyond some fatal flaw in their "colorful" personalities, in a system that would cynically exploit them as ethnic ringers, but not accept them as intellectual equals.

Towards the end of his mini-biography, Fenton tellingly sums up his own bias by analyzing Parker's presumed strengths and weaknesses. Parker's strengths "are in the descriptions of social customs attending the maize cycle and the eating customs of the Seneca in which activities he was himself both participant and observer."[64] In other words, Parker's strength is his racial ticket into the specimen pool. Fenton's discussion of Parker's weaknesses also reveals bias. As "science," he declares, Parker's work cannot stand up to the real thing, more appropriately done by a Lewis Henry Morgan, an F. W. Waugh, or a Franz Boas. Fenton feels that after one consults "Waugh's more scientific study, which has the advantage of having been done in the years after the appearance of Parker's bulletin, one begins to see the deficiencies in Parker."[65]

Conceding that Waugh had the benefit of hindsight only appears to soften Fenton's harsh conclusion: Waugh had the superior intellect. What a coincidence! So did Morgan, Putnam, and Boas. Apparently, real intellect is a function of European descent.

When Fenton finally lists his specific reasons for declaring Parker an inferior scholar, they consist of editorial errors of the typographical and spelling variety.[66] While this seems enough for Fenton to cast him into outer darkness, all it really means is that, like every other scholar, Parker needed a copy editor, except that, unlike every other scholar, Parker was not rich enough or connected enough to acquire one. The system that was perfectly willing to overload him with work was perfectly reluctant to grant him the titles, access, and pay that would have accompanied it, had it been performed by a Euro-scholar.[67]

In opting out of academia, Parker was not showing his lack of intellectual mettle, as Fenton insinuates. Instead, he was rejecting personal Euro-forming, the intense pressure exerted by academia on all non-European students in a concerted drive to purge them of their ethnic frame of reference in favor of Western values and norms. By resisting the resurrected missionary scheme, Parker presented just the sort of face least welcome in scholarship and, therefore, the face most quickly denounced as unscholarly: one that will not disown its identity in order to gain a hearing. Academia consigns all such unreconstructed Others to the silence originally described by Morgan in this kindly reminder: "It cannot be forgotten, that in after-years our Republic must render an account, to the civilized world, for the disposal which it makes of the Indian."[68] Only the "civilized" European world will render judgment because the savage world will politely remain silent as Europe "disposes" of it—a Euro-forming attitude that has remained consistent since May 4, 1493, when Pope Alexander VI casually took it upon himself to divvy the Americas up between Spain and Portugal. One of the more pressing evils of Euro-forming, then, is its exclusionary tendency, not only towards data, but towards people.

The most recent disguise donned by scholarship is ethnic dress. It has become fashionable of late to present oneself as representing a "Native" point of view. The fashion is, however, as superficial as cosmetic surgery. It ultimately fails to interrupt the direct line of descent from Morgan.

"Ethnohistory," William Fenton stated in his 1987 *False Faces of the*

Iroquois, "employs the perspective of the native culture for interpreting the past,"[69] a laudable goal but one so faintly realized in the preceding five hundred pages that it stunned me to think Fenton believed it described what he had been doing. Far from employing "the perspective of native culture," Fenton devoted numerous asides to *refuting* the Native perspective. Thus, I finished *False Faces* boggled by this disconcerting mismatch between stated intention and demonstrable result. It stands as a perfect case study of latter-day Euro-forming.

For example, early on in his introduction, Fenton notes, "the disregard of native theory in ritual practice makes a shambles of overnice formal distinctions,"[70] a solid insight that needs to be kept in mind if the ethnological goal is to work from a Native perspective. Shortly thereafter, in discussing "Use and Type" of False Faces, Fenton reiterates:

> From an Iroquois standpoint, any consideration of mask types is contingent on the uses to which they are put. They are not rigidly definable on the basis of form alone because, to a large extent, use determines type. Role supersedes form, native practice disregards native theory, and the overnice taxonomic distinctions based on form alone fail to find confirmation in Iroquois culture.[71]

Again, this is a vital truth.

Yet, having duly noted this much, Fenton immediately reverts to a Euro-perspective, forcing just those hard-and-fast, categorical distinctions he has warned against. Capping off his discussion is a reworked grid of False Face features, resurrected from one he had created earlier in his career. It remains based on form, not function. The refinement consists of pointing out where categories overlap.[72] It seems to me that if Native perspective were really to be respected, then use, not mouth shape (even one pointed out by a Native "informant") would stand as the determining factor. Indeed, four-square, pigeon-holed grids would be abandoned entirely as contrary to the Native circular/spherical world concept, in which everything in the universe is inextricably interrelated.

Despite the fact that interrelation is the heart of Native thought, Fenton continually seems bewildered whenever he encounters two or more versions of something, clearly assuming that only one version can be "correct," thus neatly embodying the mono-principle of the West. For example, in discussing whether basswood is the "appropriate" wood for making False Faces, Fenton notes that Parker supported carving into a living basswood tree,[73] while numerous later informants/carvers cited in the rest of the chapter favored ironwood, elm, and so on, often in dead blocks. The important point here is that theory is irrelevant to the Native world view. The wood form does not matter. Everyone is "right." Notwithstanding, theoretical categories remain the focus of Fenton's linear effort to straighten things out.

Color codes provide another example of Native practice exploding theory, yet theory continuing to be presented as the defining feature of the study. Sometimes, red and east/black and west are considered naturally united. Other times, red goes south; white, west; black, east; and blue, north. The first schema talks about the apportionment of the day; the second depends on the sacred Four Winds (or cardinal directions) for its content. The plot thickens further when the *orenda* of colors comes into play. Depending on the circumstance, then, nuances are added, and meanings pile up through association and metaphor. Since the same color may mean more than one thing, and may well mean it simultaneously, it is clear that far more attaches to color-coding than what Fenton has considered in *False Faces*. Nevertheless, Fenton force-fits the matter into one dimension, concluding, "Deferring the description of the rite to a later chapter, its importance here is that [this second] orientation of the black and red masks contradicts the usual placement of red (east) and black (west)."[74]

Fenton sees regimentation, not color, as the one, true center of his mono-dimension, forcing a false either/or choice in which one color code "contradicts" another, which is more "usual." Native perspective, on the other hand, knows that multiple versions need not imply that one is correct, and the others, debased or confused. It will consequently nod untroubled assent at any and all schemas, the daily and the directional, the *orenda* and the physical, plus any other associations that may pop up. Traditions differ. There is no sense of contradiction.

Here, then, is a concise example of the mismatch between intention and result. The moment Fenton determines that the point of color-coding is the slavish repetition of one model whenever colors come up, with one color necessarily more correct than any of the others, he has departed from any pretense of a "Native perspective" and forced the discussion along mono-linear lines. Now, if Mr. Fenton wants to think in categorical distinctions, he certainly may. What he may not do, however, is claim that they represent a Native perspective.

A related problem attends the issue of informational gaps. Scholars tend to assume that they are in full possession of all information. Stereotypes of Natives as mental children shore up this conceit. For example, via the pen of Arthur Parker, the chronicles state that Chief Cornplanter was so "careless" that he "lost the papers" of the transcribed Code of Handsome Lake (the founding tradition of the Longhouse Religion), "sheet by sheet" after "he had memorized" them.[75] Scholars have not thought twice about accepting the lame story that Chief Careless Cornplanter lost the Code. The possibility that the loss might have been deliberate, a repudiation of the dead hand of Western literacy on the breathing spirit of Handsome Lake, has not been considered. Left tantalizingly unasked is whether Arthur Parker, himself, as he came to identify more with the Haudenosaunee than with the Europeans, might have aided in keeping certain data from the scholars.

The same possibility is overlooked today. Misleading the experts is an old Indian practical joke that has been going on since first contact: In 1536, the Haudenosaunee, realizing that Jacques Cartier was after precious metal, sent him straight out of Iroquoia with the tall story of gold deposits over yonder, mined by woollen-clad inhabitants in the mysterious Kingdom of Saguenay.[76] In 1819, after living forty-eight years with the Iroquois, the Moravian missionary John Heckewelder recorded the great delight the Haudenosaunee took in pulling the legs of unwary ethnographers, who solemnly took down their straight-faced jokes as gospel truth.[77] And how many in the enthusiastic audience for the G-rated movie, Pocahontas, realize that "Pocahontas" translates roughly as "Penis Girl?"[78] Despite the fact that some modern Native informants openly admit to continuing this practice, full— and accurate—disclosure is still blithely assumed.

The upshot of believing that all modern data is complete and clean, when it may not be, is illustrated by Fenton's mighty struggle with Harriet Maxwell Converse, a turn-of-the-twentieth-century ethnographer, adopted by a clan of the Seneca, and thus privy to "secret" information. In 1968, while acknowledging that Converse "enjoyed a special relationship with the Senecas," Fenton insisted that she "reinterpreted" the "folklore" she "collected" into "romantic poetry,"[79] a format that he uncritically assumes is destructive to the data. By 1987, Fenton no longer tip-toed around his charge of fraud:

> We may conclude, therefore, that Mrs. Converse wrote into the record more than she was told, certainly more than she observed, and the learned world is the unwitting victim of willing informants who politely assented to leading questions.[80]

Fenton's allegation of fabrication rests mainly on the fact that "no field worker among the Iroquois since her day has been able to substantiate" her "poetic titles . . . suggesting fanciful roles" for False Faces.[81] It apparently does not occur to Fenton that it may be he and his colleagues who are the unwitting victims of willing informants who politely assent to their leading questions. I have come across several stray references in the literature which suggest that Mrs. Converse may have been onto something—including a reference in *The Code of Handsome Lake* contained in the 1968 compilation of Parker's writings edited by William N. Fenton.[82] Indeed, the confusion may well have been instigated by Fenton's own insistence on distinguishing among hard-and-fast categories, as opposed to the Native approach that easily unites disparate elements. Perhaps the "problem" is that Mrs. Converse knew something Mr. Fenton does not.

Really approximating a "Native perspective" requires an understanding of four-winded discourse, the conversation of a consensus society that seeks to include all points of view. The circle of community cannot exist without the four reference points of the cardinal directions—the Four Winds—demarcating its perimeter. This perimeter expands as necessary to accommodate everyone within the safe space of community, however far "apart" they might wander, figuratively or literally. The essential point here is that the circle of community cannot exist without the four, widely scattered points to pinion its circumference. The directions only look mutually exclusive to Westerners, who see difference as opposition. To the Western mind, east is the opposite of west, just as north sits opposite south. But, to the Native mind, east is the complement of west, as north reciprocates south. The circle of community needs all four pinions and can only exist as long as the Four Winds stand "apart" in their permanent reciprocity. Take away one of the directions, and the circle caves in, collapsing community. Downsize the circle into a smaller area, and community is squeezed. The ideal community, then, is a large, inclusive one in which multiple, valid points of view work to support each other's existence.

Euro-scholars, operating from the Western, linear frame of reference, do not see community as a circle, but as a line. Opinion is scattered along the line, and the ideal community is one that brings everyone's opinion "into line," preferably centered midway between "the two extremes." The "straight and narrow" is a crowded place, but great distance between ideas is dreaded as a threat to the center. Those ideas farthest away from dead center are considered to be "beyond the pale" of acceptability. In hierarchies—and academia is most emphatically a hierarchy—that line is usually imagined as vertical, with status being a "higher" or "lower" position.

Information is distributed differently in each framework. In the Western, linear mode, information is packaged and stacked in neat categories, with any linkages implied by their proximity to other data. By contrast, in the

Native framework, information scatters naturally, however it happens to fall. Links between data are associational, not forged, resembling a spider web or a fish net. Interlocking ideas may be arrived at via any number of routes through the web, similar to the way information is accessed on the Internet. Thus, at the outset, the two frames of reference are entirely at odds. These two ways of ordering information are really not compatible:

TABLE 1.

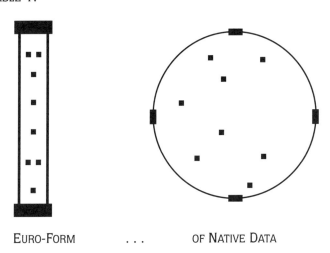

EURO-FORM   . . .   OF NATIVE DATA

This illustrated disparity is more than theoretical. It carries over into meaning. In Native culture, the context is part of the information. Data includes all of the associations, pathways, and metaphorical connections that result from its position on the web. When ethnographers lift tidbits of data out of the web and repackage them in the discrete bundles of Western categories, they seriously distort Native ideas, isolating them from their full meanings.

For example, the Haudenosaunee "direction of the Sky" falls along the east-west axis. This is a fairly common tidbit of ethnographic knowledge. On the face of it, to Westerners the phrase seems quaint, perhaps, but no more. However, in its Native matrix, the "direction of the Sky" is a conceptual node that connects to several other nodes, creating an extensive network of metaphors, each of which modifies all the others. "Sky" is a reference to the First Cycle of Tradition, which recounts the Haudenosaunee's descent from the Sky People. This pathway will eventually lead us into the *orenda* of the

First Cycle twins, Flint, who is associated with the west, and Sapling, who is associated with the east. If we continue to follow these networks out, each direction will lead us into colors (Sapling/east/red and Flint/west/black) relating to spirituality. Then, again, you may want to pick up on the figurative aspect of the east-west node, traveling out along that pathway into social theories of reciprocity.

On the other hand, the idea of "direction" leads us into a discussion of physical, geographical positions. If the direction of the Sky is east and west, then the north-south axis "splits the Sky," another common phrase yielding an equally complex series of associations, each with extended discussions of its own. You can continue cruising the spider web this way forever, just as you can cruise the Internet. This brief discussion hardly exhausts the possibilities inherent in the direction of the Sky, but it should suffice to show that ripping just one node out of the web, then presenting it in isolation as all there is, eliminates most of its meaning. Once more, we can see an enormous difference between Native meaning and the Western way of repackaging it:

TABLE 2.

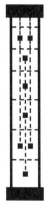
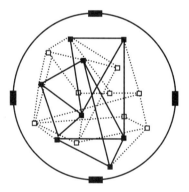

■ Direction of the Sky (East/West)
--- Euro-formed Connections

■ Direction of the Sky (East/West)
□ Split Sky (North/South)
— Primary Network - Native
······ Secondary Network - Native

CONTEXT AS PART OF THE DATA

Ethnographers may genuinely feel that their presentation accurately reflects a Native perspective. They will point to the differences between their work-up and the typical format, insisting that because their arrangement of information looks more random than the tidy arrangement common to Western theory, that their version must be authentically Native. The problem with this argument is that they have only considered Western vantage points; that is, they have Euro-formed the data, leaving out the fact that the two starting points are apples and oranges, entirely at odds.

Perhaps in recognition of and in response to this criticism, the most recent attempt at Native perspective seeks to retrofit the Western world-view with a Native appendage, superimposing a Western line on a Native circle. This partial resuscitation of the Native perspective may feel exhilarating and look authentic to Euro-scholars but, since the retrofit tends to be patronage not revision, they do not really use the tacked-on Native space. It remains mostly empty in their presentations so that Euro-scholars eventually discard it altogether as superfluous. The small amount of data that had been placed in Native space is left dangling, a curious anomaly that cannot be integrated into "known" data.

The only honest solution is to recognize that Euro-forming, itself, is the problem. Euro-scholars must allow data to express itself in its natural context and resist the temptation to gussy it up in terms more familiar to themselves. And, more difficult, they must overcome their latent fear that the Other is an Angel of Destruction, ominously humming, "Fe, fi, fo, fum, I smell the blood of an Englishman." European culture is simply not imperiled by the existence of other cultures. Indeed, the peril has always flowed in precisely the opposite direction.

For Euro-scholars, popping the Western frame of reference into more natural proportions, as but one among many possible perspectives, may seem to diminish its stature, but that is an optical illusion. It will wear off. The truth is that Europe was never as large as its shadow made it seem.

NOTES

1. Natasha Rafi, "Indian Activist Will Speak at UT," *The Blade,* 10 October 1995, Peach Section, 5.

2. Giovanni Verrazano (Jean de Verrazane), *Rapport: Possibilités religieuses,"* quoted in Jacques Haber, *La vie et les voyages de Jean de Verrazane* (Ottawa: Le Cercle du Livre de France, 1964), 149–50.

3. "Eugenics," *Encyclopedia Americana,* vol. 10 (New York and Chicago: Americana Corporation, 1949), 567.

4. "Eugenics," *EA,* 570.

5. Lewis Henry Morgan, *League of the Haudenosaunee or Iroquois*, 1851, new edition in two volumes with additional matter, edited and annotated by Herbert M. Lloyd, vol. 1 (New York: Burt Franklin, 1901, reprinted, 1966), 55.

6. Morgan, *League*, vol. 1, 166.

7. Ibid., 74–98.

8. Charley Reese, "Americans: Knowledge of Past Is Key To Retaining Your Liberty," *Orlando Sentinel*, 1 February 1994, A–8.

9. Linda Bowles, "An Affirmative Slide into a Spoils System," *The Blade*, 4 August 1995, Section 1, 9.

10. Morgan, *League*, vol. 1, 143.

11. Ibid., 142.

12. Ibid., 147–48.

13. Morgan, *League*, vol. 2, 109.

14. Ibid., 111.

15. Ibid., 113.

16. Ibid., 116.

17. Ake Hultkrantz, *The Religions of the American Indians* (Berkeley and Los Angeles: University of California Press, 1967), 23.

18. Ibid., 22–23.

19. Ibid., 36–38.

20. Ibid., 33.

21. Ibid., 35.

22. Ibid., 23.

23. Ibid., 29.

24. Ibid., 50.

25. Ibid., 34, 131.

26. Ibid., 41, 113.

27. Ibid., 31.

28. Ibid., 50.

29. Ibid., 52, 113.

30. Ibid., 131.

31. Ibid., 161.

32. Ibid., 52.

33. Ibid., 99.

34. Ibid., 120.

35. Ibid., 106.

36. Anthony F. C. Wallace, *The Death and Rebirth of the Seneca* (New York: Alfred A. Knopf, 1970), 74.

37. Ibid., 75.

38. William N. Fenton, *The False Faces of the Iroquois* (Norman: University of Oklahoma Press, 1987), 28.

39. Ibid., 451.

40. Ibid., 271.

41. Ibid., 19, 271, 457.

42. Ibid., 159.

43. Ibid., 341.

44. Ibid., 147–58.

45. Ibid., 450.

46. Ibid., 450–51.

47. William N. Fenton, "Introduction," *Parker on the Iroquois* (New York: Syracuse University Press, 1968), 8.

48. Fenton, *False Faces*, 455.

49. Morgan, *League*, vol. 1, 137.

50. Fenton, "Introduction," *Parker*, 1.

51. Ibid., 13.

52. Ibid., 13.

53. Ibid., 5.

54. Ibid., 8.

55. Ibid., 2.

56. Ibid., 6.

57. Ibid., 7.

58. Ibid., 10.

59. Ibid., 10.

60. Ibid., 28.

61. Ibid., 9.

62. Ibid., 9-10.

63. Robert E. Hemenway, *Zora Neale Hurston: A Literary Biography* (Urbana and Chicago: University of Illinois Press, 1977), 63.

64. Fenton, "Introduction," *Parker*, 27.

65. Ibid., 27.

66. Ibid., 28.

67. Ibid., 18. The facts are Fenton's; the interpretation is mine.

68. Morgan, *League*, vol. 2, 123.

69. Fenton, *False Faces*, 501.

70. Ibid., 15.

71. Ibid., 29.

72. Ibid., 51.

73. Ibid., 206.

74. Ibid., 133–34.

75. Arthur C. Parker, *The Code of Handsome Lake*, 1913, in *Parker on the Iroquois*, Reprint (New York: Syracuse University Press, 1968), 8.

76. Ramsay Cook, ed., *The Voyages of Jacques Cartier* (Toronto: University of Toronto Press, 1993), 73.

77. John Heckewelder, *An Account of the History, Manners, and Customs of the Indian Nations Who Once Inhabited Pennsylvania and Neighboring States*, 1819 (New York: The Arno Press and the *New York Times*, 1971), 321–22.

78. Or, more literally, "she plays with penis." J. Leitch Wright, *The Only Land They Knew: The Tragic Story of the American Indians in the Old South* (New York: The Free Press, A Division of Macmillan Publishing Co., Inc., 1981), 72.

79. Fenton, "Introduction," *Parker*, 9.

80. Fenton, *False Faces*, 11.

81. Ibid., 10.

82. Parker, in Fenton, *Parker*, footnote 3, 27–29.

APPENDICES

APPENDIX A

Recent Debate Regarding the Multicultural Roots of Democracy

DONALD A. GRINDE, JR.

Predicting the future is not an exact science. By the late 1990s, as this book was prepared for the press, in certain quarters the debate over Native American precedents for democracy showed no signs of dying away, as Dean Snow had forecast early in the decade. Instead, the debate seemed to sharpen.

Johansen's annotated bibliography of reactions to the "influence" idea reached 900 items by the end of 1997, an increase of 230 for the year. Fervent approval and condemnation rolled in side by side in a rich variety that had not been exceeded since the debate was stoked by the Columbus anniversary in 1992. Vine Deloria, Jr. supported the idea in a book on the evolving relationship between anthropologists and Native Americans, with essays by several different authors, many of whom key their contributions to Deloria's critique of their field of study. The conclusion of the book, "Anthros, Indians, and Planetary Reality," by Deloria himself, includes a detailed description of the controversy over the Iroquois and democracy, in which Deloria writes: "This fight over the Six Nations' influence has been a bitter one, and if it had been submitted to a jury for fair deliberation the anthropological profession would now be paying reparations to the Six Nations, for the evidence and the argument weigh heavily in favor of the Iroquois and their supporters" (Biolsi, 215–217).

The idea was panned rather crudely in *Lingua Franca*, a trade magazine for professors. The headline on the piece ("Tribal Lore") seems to have emerged from a copy desk where Native Americans make "lore," and non-Indians make "history." The piece included a portrait of Cornplanter that is well known to all but the most ignorant students of eighteenth-century American Indian history and captioned it "Iroquois Indian" (Oppenheimer, 9). Oppenheimer ends his piece with a string of quotes discrediting the influence idea from well-known critics of it such as James Axtell, Wilcomb Washburn, and Daniel K. Richter. Surveying his self-selected sample of commentary, Oppenheimer concludes with an air of apparent authority that "the scholarly community is unswayed" (Oppenheimer, 8–9). In a reply to the *Lingua Franca* piece which was not published, Grinde and Johansen found Oppenheimer's piece to be "an absurdly biased appeal to authorities with which he chooses to agree. . . . Instead of engaging our historical arguments, this piece seems to prefer racist innuendo."

William Starna, writing with George Hamell, condemned the idea vehemently in *New York History*. Usually, when scholars' ideas are attacked with such unabashed vigor, journal editors offer rebuttal space, as before, with us, in *Ethnohistory* and the *William and Mary Quarterly*. In this case, Starna and Hamell's piece found its way to us through a chain of friends nearly a year after its publication date, too late for an effective reply.

Starna and Hamell must have spent many hours ransacking our footnotes in *Exemplar of Liberty* and other works. They find a handful of factual errors which they admit are minor. The problem here is that Starna and Hamell are so engaged in debunking details that they do not address any of the ideas that were communicated between the Iroquois and colonial Americans. Instead they debate, with excruciating attention to detail, whether Canassatego had brawny arms, and whether he was known for being unsociably direct after he had had a few drinks. As an elicitation of historical truth, this argument rings rather hollow. The piece is really ideologically driven character assassination masquerading as historical criticism.

In their rush to condemn us, Starna and Hamell fail to extend their gambit beyond the debate over Iroquois influences on the Albany Plan, beginning with the words of Canassatego at the Lancaster Treaty Council of 1744. They ignore most of our case, which takes the influence idea from the early seventeenth century to the end of the nineteenth. They also restrict their inquiry to New York sources, forgetting, perhaps, that representatives from other colonies (notably Pennsylvania) sent representatives to the important events of the time, who left records in their respective archives. Starna and Hamell all but accuse us of fabricating evidence that is available to anyone in the archives of Pennsylvania, Massachusetts, and Virginia.

An anthropologist (Starna) and a museum professional (Hamell) fall victim to some interesting scholarly traps. It is remarkable how slavishly they replicate the arguments of an anthropologist, Elisabeth Tooker, by asserting that "the linchpin of their arguments for Iroquois influence on the design of American government . . . is the 1744 treaty council at Lancaster, Pennsylvania . . ." (Starna, 429). They are relying on a dated argument by an anthropologist (Tooker) who asserts that there is no evidence to support the Iroquois influence thesis after 1775 (Tooker, 312–313). Starna and Hamell take this claim at face value and then proceed with their critique of *Exemplar of Liberty* by claiming that one treaty council in 1744 is central to our argument. Furthermore, they argue that their positivistic interpretation of the 1744 event has some implications for the history of ideas relating to the development of American government. Hence, their argument is not only highly derivative of Tooker's work, but also grounded on the idea that the 1744 treaty council at Lancaster, Pennsylvania is so important that some minor errors of fact and nuance in discussing this event destroys our larger argument.

As historians, we would never argue that one event and statements made in 1744 would have had such an indelible mark on the outcome of the U.S. Constitution more than forty years later. In the history of ideas scholars focus on numerous antecedents and patterns emerging over time to chronicle the evolution of concepts.

Like Tooker's, a hallmark of Starna and Hamell's anti-influence thesis arguments is to deny events and interpretations that take place after 1775. Instead, they shift our gaze to minor errors and assertions of historical truths (which are much more contested by scholars than they admit). Indeed, Starna and Hamell engage in racist stereotyping of "drunken Indians" (Starna, 442–444), in an effort, perhaps, to discredit the idea that Indians have been partially responsible for some of our most important national ideas.

Subliminal appeals to racism which have been central to much of the larger debate go hand-in-hand with an urge to preserve "whiteness" in colonial and early American history. Starna and Hamell ignore over 90 percent of the text and argumentation in *Exemplar of Liberty,* which is our principal work on the subject of the Iroquois influence on democracy. They make no criticisms of John Adams' statements in 1787 about "politicians . . ." attempting "to set up . . . governments of modern Indians" (Grinde, 200). Nor do they address Franklin's statements at the Constitutional Convention, including the comment that the U.S. government had a "Great Council fire" (Grinde, 206). They also fail to deal with James Wilson's use of Covenant Chain imagery and his notations about discussing Indian government in the committee that drew up the first draft of the U.S. Constitution (Grinde, 208). These documented facts are far more integral to our argument about the formation of the Constitution than a single event in 1744. The data we analyze demonstrate an ongoing curiosity about Native American political systems on the part of some of the founders that Starna and Hammel do not even touch. Starna and Hamell seem to find it difficult to address ideas and the transference of those ideas in the revolutionary period. Their systematic neglect of evidence coupled with their racially exclusive arguments makes it hard to imagine that an agenda of preserving the "whiteness" of ideas is not at work.

This controversy reflects an issue that is at the heart of the conflict over return of Haudenosaunee wampum belts. Experts such as William N. Fenton fought the return of the wampum belts from the New York State Museum to the Iroquois chiefs for a generation following initial controversy over the issue during the 1960s. The desire to retain power over the wampum belts displayed by anthropologists at the New York State Museum caused scholars dedicated to the maintenance of white hegemony to denounce traditional Iroquois forms of government and declare that the wampum belts were as "American as apple pie." In the end, however, the wampum belts were returned to the Iroquois and many of the opposing white anthropologists showed up for the returning ceremonies in spite of their long-standing opposition and ad hominem arguments about the contemporary leadership of the Iroquois confederacy.

Unlike Starna and Hamell's critique of the Iroquois influence on the United States Constitution (which completely ignores the evidence surrounding the Constitutional Convention), Lawrence Hauptman's "Speculations on the Constitution" (Hauptman, 27-38) attempts, at least, to examine some of the important arguments relating to the influence debate that relate to the framing of the U.S. Constitution. Initially, Hauptman asserts that in *Exiled in the Land of the Free: Democracy, Indian Nations and the U.S. Constitution,* Professor Grinde argues that "The United States Constitution owes much of its emphasis on unity, federalism, and balance of power to Iroquois concepts" (Hauptman, 27). Hauptman alleges that since 1987 numerous "Native American and non-Indian educators constantly raise this idea" at workshops and speaking engagements that he has conducted and thus he has been forced to address its veracity at this historical moment (Hauptman, 28).

Strangely, Professor Hauptman fails to point out that educators at his workshops might be asking him questions about Iroquois influence because he was, at least until 1992, an integral part of a group which advocated the Iroquois influence thesis. Paradoxically, the first book that Hauptman cites and criticizes in his essay, *Exiled in the Land of the Free,* is a work that he helped to plan and write.

Hauptman states that he will focus on James Wilson in his critique of the Iroquois influence debate because he alleges that:

> *1) he is familiar with James Wilson's published and unpublished writings in the Historical Society of Pennsylvania;*

> 2) he believes Wilson's involvement with Native Americans is not extensive and
> that a brief article is appropriate to draw conclusions about the influence of Native
> Americans on his intellect;
>   3) Wilson is a key person mentioned by those who cite the Iroquois contributions to
> the Constitution. (Hauptman, 28)

After these assertions about the Iroquois influence thesis, Hauptman constructs an argument about Wilson being influenced by the Enlightenment, the Scottish Common Sense School of Thomas Reid, Montesquieu, and Vattel. He asserts that Wilson was interested in dispossessing Native Americans, western land speculation, and exploiting American Indian weakness after the Revolution. According to Hauptman, Wilson's allegedly "white" intellectual and economic activities made him unable to appreciate and appropriate Iroquois political ideals (Hauptman, 30).

The first of Hauptman's three assertions about Wilson is quite interesting because he never cites nor discusses any of Wilson's unpublished papers in the Historical Society of Pennsylvania. Not only does Hauptman fail to discuss Wilson's unpublished sources that he is allegedly familiar with, but he also ignores the unpublished manuscript sources quoted and cited by Grinde and Johansen.[1]

A perusal of Wilson manuscript sources cited in *Exemplar of Liberty* may give an indication of why Hauptman avoids such sources. In discussing the creation of western states during the ratification period, Wilson asserted that government officers were

> chosen by the people to fill the places of greatest trust and importance in the country;
> and by this means, a chain of communication and confidence will be formed
> between the United States and the new settlements [emphasis added]. (Wilson, "...of
> a plan," 2:132)[2]

This statement demonstrates the use of Iroquois Covenant Chain imagery in Wilson's discourse.

Hauptman also refuses to deal at all with Wilson's manuscript notes on drafting the U.S. Constitution. Wilson was on the Committee of Detail which created the first draft of the Constitution in late July and early August of 1787. In discussions on drafting the preamble of the Constitution, Wilson notes that the committee's deliberations focused "on the original authority of the people . . ." Wilson adds that the committee meant to discuss "the different points in question." Among the points the committee intended to discuss was: "the Ind[ian] sense of the States in Common." (Wilson, Propositions . . . 2:61–68). Instead of discussing Wilson's words, Hauptman shifts our gaze to an elaborate discourse on Wilson's western land speculations, which he asserts, prove Wilson's lack of interest in Native American political ideas.

During the ratification period, Iroquois imagery was used in newspapers to describe Wilson's intentions. In describing Wilson's role at the Constitutional

Convention, an essay entitled "The New Roof" in the *Charleston Columbian Herald* styled Wilson as an architect of the constitution and asserted that Wilson's "intention was to make a firm and substantial roof by uniting the strength of the thirteen rafters." This imagery is used by the Iroquois to describe relationships within the Confederacy. It is derived from the structure of the Iroquois longhouse.[3] If Wilson was as European-minded as Hauptman believes, why does he sometimes use Iroquois imagery?

Obviously, the contemporary sources at the time of ratification described Wilson as having been influenced by Iroquois ideas. Hauptman ignores this data completely and refuses to address it in his argument even though he claims to be acquainted with Wilson's ideas and people's perceptions of him. Once again, Hauptman chooses to ignore primary evidence that might compromise his arguments.

Hauptman's second assertion, that Wilson's minimal involvement with Native Americans refutes the influence thesis, does not withstand factual scrutiny. Hauptman simply ignores Wilson's allusions to Iroquois imagery. He seems less interested in a factual analysis of the debate than speculation about Wilson's intellectual motivations that he believes to be exclusively European in their origins.

Hauptman also overemphasizes Wilson's centrality to the Iroquois influence thesis. Wilson's role is only one component of the database which supports the argument about the Native American roots of American government. Charles Pinckney, Benjamin Franklin, Thomas Jefferson, James Madison, and John Rutledge also figure prominently in our evidentiary base in *Exemplar of Liberty*.

Hauptman makes a great deal of James Wilson's land speculations as "proof" that Wilson was not interested in American Indian political theory. In a non-sequitur, Hauptman asserts, without documentation, that "Wilson's highly materialistic side makes it unlikely that he drew inspiration from the Iroquois Longhouse" (Hauptman, 38). This kind of interpretation attempts to psychoanalyze or mind-read a historical figure and then assign motivation where no historical documentation or psychological motivational data exists.

Such argumentation also demonstrates Hauptman's inability to comprehend a multidisciplinary approach to the documentary evidence rooted in intellectual history. In essence, the argument that you must love and respect American Indians in order to adopt their political theories is specious. This is a feeble attempt to ascribe racial categories to ideas. If we were to apply this reading to the origins of the U.S. Constitution then it would not have any English roots because many Americans disliked the British and their traditions immensely after the American Revolution. Indeed, Wilson asserted during the Constitutional Convention that:

The British Government cannot be our model. We have no materials for a similar one.
Our manners, our laws, the abolition of entails and primogeniture, the whole genius of
the people, are opposed to it. (Wilson in Koch, 85)

Essentially, Hauptman ignores much of the evidence in *Exemplar of Liberty* which associates Wilson with Iroquois ideas. Just as he ignores his own involvement with Iroquois influence publications, Hauptman seeks to hide Wilson's involvement with Native American political theories. He accuses Grinde of drawing grand conclusions ". . . from the notes made by the Founding Fathers at the Constitutional Convention, even though much of the note-taking was incomplete or cryptic" (Hauptman, 29) but he fails to address *any* evidence at all.

Starna's and Hauptman's tracts are trenchant, but scholarly in tone. Those who are ready for some real academic mudwrestling may wish to consult Alvin J. Schmidt's *The Menace of Multiculturalism*. As his title indicates, Schmidt, a professor of sociology at Illinois College, Jacksonville, is a take-no-prisoners opponent of multiculturalism. At the beginning of a chapter titled "The Facts Be Damned," Schmidt lists a number of "facts" that he says multiculturalists have "invented." One of these is that "the Constitution of the United States was shaped by the Iroquois Indians" (Schmidt, 43–44). He also denies the idea that Crispus Attucks, the first casualty of the Boston Massacre, was black (Attucks' father was black; his mother was Native American). Since he has never heard of any of the many books and articles documenting it, Schmidt says that the influence idea is "undocumented." Schmidt would rather history stress the cruel and violent aspects of Native American cultures, which he says squishy-soft multiculturalists downplay. Schmidt is barely getting warmed up. Later in the book, he argues that American Indian cultures were environmentally destructive and that women in native societies lived "in virtual slavery." Returning to the Iroquois influence issue, Schmidt calls it a "fabrication," as well as "historical fiction" (Schmidt,53–54).

Mary Lefkowitz, a professor of classics at Wellesley College, began a March 24, 1997 *Wall Street Journal* review of *The Menace of Multiculturalism*:

Does the U.S. Constitution owe more to the 18th-century Iroquois than it does
to the ancient Greeks? No, but many younger people may answer yes, because it
is what they have learned in school. The history that children learn is not neces-
sarily a record of what actually happened in the past; rather, it is often an account
of what parents and teachers believe they ought to know. (Lefkowitz, A–16)

Later in her review, Lefkowitz writes, "however impressive the governmental organization of the Iroquois nation, the inspiration behind the Constitution may once again be credited to the European Enlightenment, and the ancient Greeks . . . "

(Lefkowitz, A–16). Lefkowitz, the author of *Not Out of Africa*, a widely quoted critique of Afrocentric education, is much more practiced at protecting the Greeks from purported African influences than shielding the United States' founders from Iroquois ones. Replying to Lefkowitz in the *Wall Street Journal*'s letters column April 10, 1997, Johansen said that giving credit to the Iroquois does not demean classical Greek or English precedents for United States basic law, but "simply add[s] an Iroquois role to the picture. He concluded: "We can have our Greeks, and our Iroquois, too" (Johansen, A–15).

A week after his letter was published, Johansen found a message in his e-mail inbox from Professor Lefkowitz, who acknowledged his main point: that we can study the Iroquois system and its impact on subsequent history without packing up the Greek and the Magna Carta and sending them, along with the rest of Europe's classical history, back across the ocean. She also thanked Johansen for sources on the debate, and said that she had modified *Not Out of Africa* in paperback to take account of criticism. "I never doubted that the Iroquois and other Native Americans gave ideas to the European settlers," she wrote. "All I was questioning was the proportion."

During these e-mail exchanges, Johansen and Lefkowitz seemed to be approaching a middle ground where a consensus of our history may settle, with regard to Native American influences, once the debates have been had and the feathers have flown, at the beginning of a new millennium on the Christian calendar. The middle ground that we seemed to be seeking also has been explored tentatively by Peter D. Salins in his book *Assimilation, American Style* (1997). Salins writes:

> As Americans were differentiating themselves from their nominal or actual English ancestors in the realm of ideas, attitudes, and values, whatever remained of English cultural influences was also being progressively diluted by their contact with an ever-expanding array of non-English peoples. First, the European settlers were changed by contact with the real "native" Americans . . . who introduced them to new foods, new arts and crafts, new modes of shelter, new strategies for survival in the wilderness, and perhaps even some important civic principles. (Salins, 90)

The cacophony of debate over the issue of the Iroquois' impact on democracy's development on a world-wide scale was being developed, as we closed for the press on *Debating Democracy*, by Max Skidmore, a professor of political science at the University of Missouri—Kansas City. Skidmore's examination of how American political ideas have affected world political systems, "Legacy to the World: A Study of America's Political Ideas," includes extensive treatment of Iroquois political institutions and the ways in which the founders of the United States used them, citing from various works by Grinde and Johansen, especially *Exemplar of Liberty*

(Skidmore, ms. 60–65). After examining the debate over the issue, Skidmore writes (ms. 65) that their argument "seems to be a reasoned, and reasonable, conclusion" (Skidmore, ms. 65).

Skidmore's analysis brings us full circle, in a temporal sense, to similar observations by ethnologist William M. Beauchamp, early in the century. While discussing the federal structure of the Iroquois Confederacy, Beauchamp wrote in 1907 that "Local affairs were left to national councils, as in our general and state governments" (Beauchamp, 342). Beauchamp later returned to the idea of Iroquois similarity to the United States political system, writing that ". . . the chiefs do not seem to have worn any distinctive badge. . . . This is one of the curious resemblances in our national political system and that of the Iroquois." (Beauchamp, 437).

We trust the observations of Beauchamp, who was accepted into the Iroquois councils of his time, much more than those of present-day "Iroquois experts" who somehow have built their scholarly reputations in estrangement from living Iroquois people and their present-day realities. The influence idea never died in the Iroquois' oral history; throughout the written records, its lineage stretches from Franklin and Jefferson to Lewis Henry Morgan, Beauchamp, Julian Boyd, Felix Cohen, Ray Fadden, and many others to our own time, when the debate has been enhanced by contemporary debates over other issues. One of these is the growing influence of Native Americans (among other people of color) in American scholarship, with concurrent conservative reactions against notions of multiculturalism in education. The changing demographic nature of Turtle Island in our time will have an impact on the history that is studied by future generations of students. Much of the reaction against multiculturalism, like resistance to the idea that the Iroquois helped shape democracy, is a fear-reflex by guardians of past assumptions in defense of established privilege.

NOTES

1. See Hauptman's footnotes for his essay (Hauptman, 129-133). In his critique of the Iroquois influence debate, Hauptman never cites any manuscript sources from the Historical Society of Pennsylvania or anywhere else, for that matter.

2. Wilson, James. ". . . of a Plan concerning the new states," James Wilson Papers, 2:132, Manuscript Division, Historical Society of Pennsylvania; and see also "Notes from Mr. Wilson's Lectures by Joseph Hopkinson, 1791," Joseph Hopkinson Papers, Historical Society of Pennsylvania. Wilson's statement about western lands and settlements is quoted on page 208 of *Exemplar of Liberty*.

3. See quotation from *Charleston Columbian Herald*, 24 and 28 April 1788. See also Paul A. W. Wallace, *White Roots of Peace*. Santa Fe: Clear light Publishers, 1994, 79, and Michael K. Foster, ed., *Extending the Rafters*. Albany: State University of New York Press, 1984, xiv, for discussions of Iroquois Great Law usage of "rafters" imagery.

REFERENCES

Axtell, James. "Paddling Their Own Canoes." [Book review, Calloway, *New Worlds for All*] *London Times Literary Supplement*, June 6, 1997.

Beauchamp, William M. "Civil, Religious, and Mourning Councils and Ceremonies of Adoption of the New York Indians." New York State Museum Bulletin no. 113. Albany, N.Y.: New York State Education Department, June, 1907.

Biolsi, Thomas, and Larry J. Zimmerman, eds. *Indians and Anthropologists: Vine Deloria, Jr., and the Critique of Anthropology.* Tucson: University of Arizona Press, 1997.

Force, Peter, ed. American Archives. Washington, D.C.: M. St. Clair and Peter Force, 1837-1846, Fourth Series.

Ford, Worthington C., ed. *Journals of the Continental Congress.* Washington, DC: Government Printing Office, 1906.

Grinde, Donald A., Jr., and Bruce E. Johansen. *Exemplar of Liberty: Native America and the Evolution of Democracy.* Los Angeles: UCLA American Indian Studies Center, 1991.

Hauptman, Laurence M. "Congress, Plenary Power and the American Indian, 1870 –1992" in Oren Lyons, et al., *Exiled in the Land of the Free*, 317–336. Professor Donald A. Grinde's essay "Iroquois Political Theory and the Roots of American Democracy" is in the same volume, 227–280.

_____. "Speculations on the Constitution," in *Tribes and Tribulations: Misconceptions about American Indians and Their Histories.* Albuquerque: University of New Mexico Press, 1995.

Johansen, Bruce E. "The Iroquois: Present at the Birth." *Wall Street Journal* [Letter to the editor], April 10, 1997, A–15.

Lefkowitz, Mary. "Out of Many, More Than One." *Wall Street Journal*, March 24, 1997, A–16.

Lyons, Oren, John Mohawk, Vine Deloria, Jr., Laurence Hauptman, Howard Berman, Donald A. Grinde, Jr., Curtis Berkey, and Robert Venables, *Exiled in the Land of the Free: Democracy, Indian Nations, and the U.S.Constitution.* Santa Fe: Clear Light Publishers, 1992, 2.

Oppenheimer, Mark. "Tribal Lore," *Lingua Franca: The Review of Academic Life*, March, 1997, 8–9.

Salins, Peter D. *Assimilation, American Style.* San Francisco: New Republic/Harper Collins, 1997.

Schmidt, Alvin J. *The Menace of Multiculturalism.* Westport, Conn.: Praeger, 1997.

Skidmore, Max. "Legacy to the World: A Study of America's Political Ideas." New York: Peter Lang Publishing, proj. 1998. Page references are from the author's manuscript.

Starna, William A., and George R. Hamell. "History and the Burden of Proof: The Case of the Iroquois Influence on the U.S. Constitution," *New York History*, October, 1996, 427-452.

Tooker, Elisabeth. "The United States Constitution and the Iroquois League." *Ethnohistory* 35, 4 (Fall, 1988): 305–336.

Wilson, James (June 7, 1787). In Adrienne Koch, ed., *Notes of Debates in the Federal Convention of 1787 Reported by James Madison* (Athens: Ohio University Press), 1966.

_____. "Propositions, Objections [etc.] in Debates on Adoption of the Constitution," in James Wilson Papers, 2:61-68. These words by Wilson are quoted in *Exemplar of Liberty*, 208.

APPENDIX B

Treatments of Native American Democracy in Legal Journals

Alschuler, Albert W. "A Brief History of the Criminal Jury in the United States." *University of Chicago Law Review* 61 (Summer, 1994): 867. As an aside in his study of the jury system, Alschuler writes that "A few Native American governments may have been more democratic in some respects, particularly in the extent to which they permitted women to participate in governmental affairs." Alschuler is Wilson-Dickinson professor at the University of Chicago Law School.

Ball, Milnar S. "Legal Storytelling: Stories of Origin and Constitutional Possibilities." *Michigan Law Review* 87 (August, 1989): 2280. Ball, Caldwell Professor of Constitutional Law at the University of Georgia School of Law, writes in footnote #85 that American Indian tribes existed as legal entities "long before the state and federal governments were formed." He notes "persuasive evidence that American democracy began between 350 and 500 years before the American Revolution with the Iroquois Law of the Great Peace." Ball uses this fact to support his assertion that " . . . Tribes, unlike local governments, have inherent authority to govern; they need not rely on outside legislative power to give them authority to act."

Bennoune, Karima. "As-Salumu Alaykum: Humanitarian Law in Islamic Jurisprudence." *Michigan Journal of International Law* 15 (Winter, 1994), 605. Bennoune describes Islamic contributions to international law, and decries attempts to trace world-wide standards for justice to any single (especially European) culture or geographic area. The author writes, in footnote 217, that "Such recognition of the multicultural roots of legal principles is occurring elsewhere in historical and legal studies. One such debate is that over the Native American, and most particularly Iroquois, roots of the U.S. Constitution."

Clinton, Robert N. "Symposium Rules of the Game: Sovereignty and the Native American Nation: the Dormant Indian Commerce Clause." *Connecticut Law Review 27* (Summer, 1995): 1055. Clinton, who is Wiley B. Rutledge Professor of Law at the University of Iowa College of Law (as well as associate justice of the Cheyenne River Sioux Tribal Court), surveys the Iroquois role in British and French colonial history. This 47,000-word article contains a detailed treatment of the Albany Congress of 1754, which contains a footnote (#68) about the debate over Franklin's debt to the Iroquois.

Cohen, Felix. *Handbook of Federal Indian Law.* Albuquerque: University of New Mexico Press, 1942. On page 128, Cohen writes, regarding American Indians' ability to govern themselves: "Indeed, it may be said that the constitutional history of the Indian tribes covers a longer period and a wider range of variation than the constitutional history of the colonies, the states, and the United States. It was some time before the immigrant Columbus reached these shores, according to eminent historians, that the first federal Constitution on the American Continent was drafted, the Gayaneshagowa, or the Great Binding Law of the Five (later six) Nations (Iroquois). It was in this constitution that Americans first established the democratic principles of initiative, recall, referendum, and equal suffrage. In this constitution, also, were set forth the ideal[s] of the responsibility of governmental officials to the electorate, and the obligation of the present generation to future generations . . . "

Crawford, J. D. "Looking Again at Tribal Jurisdiction: 'Unwarranted Intrusions on Their Personal Liberty.'" *Marquette Law Review* 76 (Winter, 1993): 401. Crawford notes with some irony that while the U. S. House of Representatives Subcommittee on Constitutional Rights in 1967 held that tribal judges lacked experience, training, and familiarity with "the traditions and forms of the American legal system" history indicates that "the organization of the of the Iroquois Confederation influenced the Articles of Confederation."

Crawford, Neta C. "A Security Regime Among Democracies: Co-operation Among the Iroquois Nations." *International Organization*, 48, no. 3 (Summer, 1994): 345–385. This article, published by the *Journal of the World Peace Foundation*, Massachusetts Institute of Technology, outlines the formation and operation of the Iroquois Confederacy. Crawford compares the Iroquois League to the Concert of Europe, and says that it is an example of Immanuel Kant's idea of a system of "perpetual peace." The article conveys an erroneous impression that the Iroquois Confederacy ceased to exist in 1777, during the American Revolution.

Delgado, Richard. "Review Essay: Derrick Bell and the Ideology of Racial Reform: Will We Ever Be Saved . . . " *Yale Law Journal* 97 (1988): 923. Most of this review essay is concerned with the intractable nature of racial tension in American society. Delgado finds that civil-rights law usually acts only as a corrective for minorities when it runs congruent with established interests. Delgado says that the books of Derrick Bell, a professor of law at Harvard, bears this out. As an aside, Delgado writes that "Although books praising the Constitution and tracing the origins of its miraculous ideas generally neglect to mention this fact, some of the ideas in our form of government came from the Iroquois. Before Columbus 'discovered' America, the Five Nations of the Iroquois had formed a constitutional confederation based on a document called the Great Law of Peace . . . ." Delgado then lists a summary of similarities.

_____. "Rodrigo's Chronicle." *Yale Law Journal* 101 (Spring, 1992): 1357. In this review of Dinesh D'Souza's *Illiberal Education: the Politics of Race and Sex on Campus* [1991], Delgado, a law professor at the University of Colorado, lists a number of books on various multicultural themes that serve to refute D'Souza's arguments. He has a section on "Essays and books on the influence of American Indian ideas on the U.S. Constitution" which includes Felix Cohen's essay "Americanizing the White Man," [1952], Johansen, *Forgotten Founders* [1982, 1987], and Weatherford, *Indian Givers* [1988].

Delgado, Richard, and Jean Stefancic. "Norms and Narratives: Can Judges Avoid Serious Moral Error?" *Texas Law Review* 69 (June, 1991): 1929. Delgado and Stefancic write that "Many colonial leaders, including Benjamin Franklin, championed the Indians' cause," as they describe "the 'constitutional' system of the Iroquois, a system the influence of which on Benjamin Franklin was freely acknowledged by him." Delgado is Charles Inglis professor of law at the University of Colorado; Stefancic is a legal librarian at the San Francisco University School of Law.

Hoeveler, J. David, Jr. "Original Intent and the Politics of Republicanism." *Marquette Law Review* 75 (Summer, 1992): 863. Hoeveler, chair of the history department at the University of Wisconsin, Milwaukee, is discussing liberal and conservative interpretations of the doctrine of original intent. In this context, he discusses Arthur Schlesinger, Jr.'s arguments in *Disuniting of America* [1992]. In a footnote, Hoeveler mentions the New York State "Curriculum of Inclusion," asserting that "the curriculum guide for American history demanded that that the 'Haudensaunee' [sic] (Iroquois) political system be acknowledged as influencing the development of the American Constitution."

Jacobs, Renee. "The Iroquois Great Law of Peace and the U.S. Constitution: How the Founding Fathers Ignored the Clan Mothers." *American Indian Law Review* 16

(1991): 497–531. While the founders adapted some aspects of Iroquois law, Jacobs makes a strong case that they were nearly totally blind to the equity of the sexes that was woven into Haudenosaunee fundamental law and political life.

Kickingbird, Kirke. "What's Past Is Prologue: The Status and Contemporary Relevance of American Indian Treaties." *St. Thomas Law Review* 7 (Summer, 1995): 603. Kickingbird is director of the Native American Legal Resource Center and assistant professor at the Oklahoma City University School of Law. He is also a Kiowa. He surveys the role of Indian treaties in United States law, writing that "The concept of an Indian confederation of governments was well-known to the colonial governments along the Atlantic Coast. The most powerful example was the Iroquois Confederacy which Benjamin Franklin suggested as a model for colonial alliance at the Albany Conference in 1754." Kickingbird then quotes Canassatego at Lancaster in 1744 advising colonial representatives to form a union on an Iroquois model.

Macklem, Patrick. "Distributing Sovereignty: Indian Nations and Equality of Peoples." *Stanford Law Review* 45 (May, 1993): 1311. Macklem is discussing ways in which Native American notions of liberty and sovereignty mesh with non-Indian traditions and beliefs. He notes that " . . . Many features of the American federal system were influenced by the structure of North American Indian confederacies." Macklem is an assistant professor of law at Toronto University.

Malloy, Robin Paul. "Letters from the Longhouse: Law, Economics, and Native American Values." *Wisconsin Law Review* (September/October, 1992): 1569. These are personal reflections of Malloy, who is a Kahnawake Mohawk and Professor of Law and Economics at the Syracuse University School of Law. Malloy notes that the United States Senate and House of Representatives have passed resolutions recognizing Iroquois contributions to United States fundamental law. This piece outlines the origins and procedures of the Iroquois Confederacy. Malloy writes that " . . . Upon the shores of Onondaga Lake . . . democracy in its purist form flourished among the Haudenosaunee a thousand years . . . these first citizens of liberty enjoyed the freedom of religion, expression, conscience, speech, movement, and all the other freedoms that we all take for granted." Malloy makes an unattributed statement that "one third of the United States Constitution can be traced back to the five Iroquois nations' form of government."

McSloy, Steven Paul. "Back to the Future: Native American Sovereignty in the 21st Century." *Review of Law & Social Change* 20 (1993): 218–300. In a footnote (p. 221), McSloy mentions the debate over the influence issue as evidence that Native Americans had complex governments before contact with European law. He quotes from Franklin's 1751 letter to James Parker arguing for emulation of the Iroquois Confederacy in a colonial federation.

Morocco, Maria. "Rediscovering the Roots of American Democracy." *Human Rights* 17, no. 3 (Fall, 1990): 38-39. Morocco covered the panel on the Iroquois and democracy at the American Bar Association 1990 convention for the event's daily newspaper (below). In this article, she develops material from the panel at greater length in *Human Rights*, citing Grinde, Kickingbird, and Johansen from the ABA panel. *Human Rights* is published by the American Bar Association in Chicago, where Morocco was a copy editor in 1990.

Newman, Frank C. "The Randolph W. Thrower Symposium: Comparative Constitutionalism. . . . " *Emory Law Journal* 40 (Summer, 1991): 731. This is the printed text of remarks by Newman during a symposium at Emory University, in which he discusses the U.S. Bill of Rights and other, similar concepts. He notes that " . . . Colonial leaders learned about the Iroquois government at treaty councils. . . . They returned with a taste for natural rights—life, liberty, and happiness—that they saw operating on the other side of the frontier." Newman, now retired, was Jackson H. Ralston Professor of International Law at the University of California, Berkeley and a justice of the California Supreme Court. He cites Maria Morocco's piece in the American Bar Association publication *Human Rights* [1990].

Resnik, Judith. "Dependent Sovereigns: Indian Tribes, States, and the Federal Courts." *University of Chicago Law Review* 56 (Spring, 1989): 671. Resnik, a professor of law at the University of Southern California, argues Indians' right and ability to govern themselves, observing that "Indian tribes, such as the Iroquois Confederacy, had a structure of government that predated and may have influenced the drafting of the United States Constitution."

Weintraub, David. "Iroquois Influence in the Founding of the American Nation." *Court Review* 29 (Winter, 1992): 17–32. This is a very detailed summary of the Iroquois League and ways in which it helped to shape American concepts of democracy. Weintraub, a third-year law student at Touro College Jacob D. Fuchsberg Law Center, used this piece to win first prize in the American Judges Association/ American Judges Foundation 1992 Law Student Essay Contest.

Williams, Robert A., Jr. "The Algebra of Federal Indian Law: The Hard Trail of Decolonizing and Americanizing the White Man's Indian Jurisprudence." *Wisconsin Law Review* (March, 1986): 219. Williams supports his case for Native American self-governance by describing the Iroquois Confederacy and its historic influence on the formation of the United States. He cites Canassatego's advice to colonial representatives in 1744, and Benjamin Franklin's 1751 letter to his printing partner James Parker, as well as Thomas Jefferson on Indian governance. He also cites Felix Cohen's 1952 essay in *The American Scholar*. Williams, a member of the Lumbee tribe, was a visiting professor of law at the University of Arizona when this article was published.

_____. "Gendered Checks and Balances: Understanding the Legacy of White Patriarchy in an American Indian Cultural Context." *Georgia Law Review* 24 (1990): 1019. The main emphasis of this article is ways in which women's legal and political roles differ in Iroquois and some other indigenous societies *vis-à-vis* mainstream American culture. Williams mentions the influence issue as an aside.

_____. "Linking Arms Together: Multicultural Constitutionalism in a North American Indigenous Vision of Law and Peace." *California Law Review* 82 (July, 1994): 981. Williams describes in detail the origin and procedures of the Iroquois Confederacy and its Great Law of Peace, arguing, as his title indicates, that the Iroquois have an effective model for a multicultural society. He strives to "avoid overt engagement in the needlessly acrimonious debate about the degree of influence of Iroquois political ideas on the 'Founders' of the United States and their drafting of this nation's Constitution." Williams, a professor of law at the University of Colorado, does mention the debate and lists sources on both sides.

Index